IVORY'S GHOSTS

Also by John Frederick Walker

A Certain Curve of Horn: The Hundred-Year Quest for the Giant Sable Antelope of Angola

IVORY'S GHOSTS

THE WHITE GOLD OF HISTORY AND
THE FATE OF ELEPHANTS

JOHN FREDERICK WALKER

ATLANTIC MONTHLY PRESS
NEW YORK

Published simultaneously in Canada
Printed in the United States of America

FIRST EDITION

ISBN-10: 0-87113-995-2
ISBN-13: 978-0-87113-995-5

Atlantic Monthly Press
an imprint of Grove/Atlantic, Inc.
841 Broadway
New York, NY 10003

Distributed by Publishers Group West
www.groveatlantic.com

09 10 11 12   10 9 8 7 6 5 4 3 2 1

for Elin

CONTENTS

PROLOGUE: 1898

An African slave belonging to Shundi, the Kavirondo ivory trader and dealer in human chattel, killed the ancient elephant on the slopes of Mount Kilimanjaro. That much is certain.

Shundi's slave was a Chagga tracker, and when he came across the elephant's trail he knew the impressive footprints—each two hand spans across in the soft earth—had been left by a large bull. The crumbled dung piles of half-digested forage spoke of the worn molars of a *m'zay*, an old one, weary and slow-moving, the kind that often carried good ivory. Shundi would want to know if that was so. The Chagga slipped quietly through the sparse bush and kept the wind in his face.

Not long after he found dung mounds still warm to a probing finger, he spotted the bull's gray bulk, humped like the shadow of a hill in the growing dusk. From bush to tree to bush and back again the Chagga drew close and saw how wizened with age the elephant was, his back sloping like a hyena's to his hindquarters, the withered hide sagging over his knees, his temples deep, dark hollows. In this shrunken state his thick tusks, which swept all the way to the ground, looked enormous. The old one swung his trunk listlessly at the grass and ripped up a clump, then paused as if trying to remember something before raising it slowly to his mouth.

As the sinking sun gilded Kilimanjaro's snowcap, the tracker took the one chance he had left in the dying light. Fumbling with his muzzleloader, he clicked back the hammer and pointed the shaking barrel at the bull's turning head just as its ears flared to fix the sound. At the shattering blast, dust spurted in a jet off his forehead, monkeys and birds shrieking as he turned rigid, trunk flung up in a questioning curl. The Chagga dropped his smoking weapon and ran in a lather of terror, feet racing over the grass, daring to slow only when no trumpeting scream rang out to signal doom about to overtake him.

No one really knows how the elephant fell. Had he been shot in the chest he might have stumbled for a mile or more before crashing to earth in a final exhalation, legs bent as if trying to swim sideways. If the thumb-sized lump of lead had punched through the skull he might simply have collapsed where he stood. Then the old one would have sunk back on his hindquarters as his head dropped, burying the tusk points in the earth and assuming the posture of a sphinx; the heavy brow would have been propped high by the ivory posts, trunk flopped lifelessly between.

The slave, heaving for breath and slick with sweat, surely must have been sick with fear for leaving behind a firearm doubtless more valuable to his master than his own miserable self before reaching camp and flinging himself at the feet of Shundi to gasp his tale. We know that the next morning he led Shundi and his men back to the slopes of the mountain where the ancient elephant lay, watched by vultures waiting in the branches of nearby trees for other scavengers to breach the tough hide. Over the next several hours the men chopped at the head with hand axes to free the two tusks, supreme examples of the great natural treasure that had been sought since ancient times. Shundi had the thick white crescents carried to the coast by slaves staggering under their weight and transported by dhow to the ivory market of Zanzibar.

The year was 1898. Photography had come to Africa by then, and a formal portrait was taken of the immense pair of tusks, posed together in a tall ornately carved doorway in Zanzibar City's old quarter. Two Africans in fezzes and white tunics steady the upright curving columns of ivory that tower over them, their tips turned outward in an enticing splay implying the continent's extravagant and seemingly inexhaustible riches. They would come to be known as the Kilimanjaro tusks and remain to this day the largest pair ever recorded. Their size makes it difficult to think of them as elephant teeth but that is what they were. The bigger one weighed 236 pounds; the other 228. Each was more than ten feet long and as thick as a man's thigh.

From their tips, worn smooth from ripping tree bark and gouging water holes, to the thin, chipped edges of the deeply hollowed bases that once held each tusk's nerve pulp, a palimpsest of stains, nicks, and fissures told of a long life in the bush. All this long-burnished, mysterious braille would have felt cool to the hand, even in the African climate, for ivory absorbs sweat.

The carved doorway where the tusks were photographed was the entrance to Nyumba Pembi—"Ivory House"—a high-walled American compound that housed in its courtyard a giant scale for the weighing of elephant teeth. Over the years, many who shaped Africa's colonial history walked through those doors: explorers and adventurers, including Richard Burton, John Speke, and Henry Morton Stanley, the infamous slaver Tippu Tip, Arab traders, Indian merchants, and a succession of American consuls who helped secure the lucrative trade. There, the agent for Arnold Cheney and Company, the powerful New York ivory importing firm, purchased the Kilimanjaro tusks for £1,000 sterling—almost $5,000—then the highest sum ever paid for a pair of tusks.

This photograph is worth study. It sums up not just a moment at the end of the nineteenth century but a cusp in the time line of this seductive substance that is apparent to us only now. The proud door of Ivory House was the gateway for much of the global trade in elephant tusks at the time; Zanzibar was the central market and Americans dominated the business. Millennia of commerce in "white gold" had come and gone before these tusks made their appearance, and prior to the twentieth century there was little talk of dwindling elephant herds affecting the supply of ivory.

We now know that the photograph was taken just before the apex of the long and troubled history of the worldwide desire for this uniquely sensuous material, a desire fanned by its availability. The ivory trade—despite the human cruelty and animal slaughter required to satisfy it—made that possible. In 1898 none foresaw that less than a century later the appetite of uncontrolled commerce would threaten to consume the bulk of the remaining sub-Saharan herds that supplied it; back then, elephants in the yet to be exhausted interior were said to be as thick as flies.

THE STORY OF ivory is nearly as old as the human story. Universally coveted for its beauty, color, scarcity, and ability to be finely carved, ivory has always been imbued with symbolic importance. Though ivory has been a single thread in a far greater pattern, its creamy-white gleam is woven through the fabric of human history, and helped to shape it. The presence of and passion for ivory have been remarkably ever present, openly garish in some cultures, subtle and subterranean in others. Each age, each culture, from prehistoric times to ancient Rome, India, China, medieval Europe, and the Muslim world to nineteenth-century America and Victorian Britain to modern Japan, has found its own uses—artistic, religious, decorative, functional, extravagant, frivolous—for the remarkable treasure that comes from the teeth of elephants and a few other mammals.

The power of this organic substance resides in its sensuousness, its ability to awaken material desire. Long before gold and gemstones held allure, humans were drawn to ivory for crafting amulets, beads, spear points, and figurines. By the beginning of recorded history mammoth ivory and later the similar ivory of elephants had long been a key item of trade, often supplemented by so-called lesser ivories—walrus, hippo, and boar teeth.

Ivory became a synonym for both preciousness and luxury, privilege and perfection. Solomon, Ivan the Terrible, and a succession of Danish kings reigned from ivory thrones. Egyptian and Chinese carvers, Greek sculptors, Byzantine and baroque craftsmen, and Japanese netsuke masters found ivory unmatched as a carving medium for small figurines. For Europeans and Asians, ivory's resemblance to pale skin tone remains an irresistible comparison, repeated in literature from the Old Testament to Shakespeare and the Pre-Raphaelite poets.

The desire to find new sources of ivory spurred the exploration and exploitation of Africa by Arab and European traders who sought it along with gold and slaves, and the ivory trade became linked to the slave trade. Each tusk, some said, cost the life of an African man, woman, or child, so brutal were the months-long marches of chained captives used to transport ivory from the interior to the trading coasts. Ivory's connection to slavery was accepted by Arab and Indian traders, ignored by most European powers, and denied by the staunchly abolitionist nineteenth-century

American manufacturers whose growing fortunes depended on an endless supply of elephant tusks.

By then the appetite for this precious substance was insatiable. The development of the lathes required to carve fantastically intricate ivory sculptures from the sixteenth to the eighteenth centuries contributed to the technological advances that were critical in the industrial revolution in the nineteenth, which itself was partly spurred by American and British efforts to find ways to mass-produce ivory items. This vast commerce in ivory became one of the early successes of the industrial age, and the material itself became virtually the plastic of its time, used for everything from buttons to scientific instruments to billiard balls to geegaws. Along with ivory combs and letter openers, drawer pulls and pistol grips, New England firms supplied ivory keys for piano makers such as Chickering, Steinway, and dozens of others, who made the United States the largest piano manufacturer in the world, with production reaching 350,000 instruments a year by 1910.

With the abolition of slavery, attention finally fell on ivory's other dark cost. Before World War I ivory had become a global business that required the annual demise of some forty-four thousand elephants. By the end of the 1970s the once-routine slaughter of elephants the trade depended on came to threaten the very existence of these extraordinary creatures. Poaching, funded by African and Asian smugglers who hired impoverished rural people and equipped them with military weaponry left over from local conflicts and civil wars, operated openly under corrupt governments. By the end of the 1980s the killings reached record levels in East Africa, provoking a global outcry that led to listing the African elephant as endangered and to a worldwide ban on international trade in ivory.

As a result, many today think of ivory as a tainted substance, faintly stained with blood no matter how carefully polished. But unless we allow ourselves to appreciate its nearly universal allure and the regard in which it has always been held, we will neverly understand why there will always be a powerful attraction to it, one that will be answered by either open trade or the black market. In any case, by now we could not rid ourselves of the global cache of ivory, even if we tried. There is simply too much great art that has been made from it, and too many beautiful things that have made use of it, and most of them are objects we rightly treasure.

The story of ivory is far from a closed book. As long as there are elephants, more ivory is added to the world's store each year, raising the question of what should be done with it now that global trade is banned. Little wonder that the role of ivory in elephant management is one of the most bitter issues in contemporary conservation. Beleaguered as some elephant populations are, there are others whose burgeoning herds threaten to denude their habitat and turn overcrowded African parks into treeless wastes. Fearing for the creatures' survival, and yet all too aware of elephants' inability to coexist easily with agriculture and human settlement, conservationists argue while stockpiles of ivory grow.

How did it come to this? And what will follow from it? This book is a response to these questions. Part 1, "Shapes in Tusks," spans prehistory through the eighteenth century, from the discovery of the luster and touch of the material to its global spread and the creation of countless ivory art objects. Part 2, "Ivory Under the Saw," looks at ivory's industrialization during the nineteenth century and through the mid-twentieth century and what that transformation cost in human and animal life. Part 3, "The Elephant Dilemma," begins several decades ago, when the elephant had finally become more important than the treasure it supplies and stepped out of the shadow of its own tusks to face an uncertain future.

It all started long ago, in the ice age.

PART 1

SHAPES IN TUSKS

1

MAMMOTH TEETH

In 1956 the 28,000-year-old Paleolithic site Sungir was discovered on the outskirts of Vladimir, east of Moscow. It is one of the oldest sites in which ornaments have been found on human skeletons. At least three of the site's inhabitants were buried there, including a sixty-year-old man, a girl of about eight, and a boy of thirteen. Interred in shallow graves dug into the permafrost, they were laid on their backs, hands folded at the hips; the children rested head to head.

Workers who unearthed the three were stunned to find that they were buried with thousands of intricately crafted ivory beads, crisscrossed in strands that might have been sewn to long since disintegrated clothing. The bones of the man's arms were hooped with twenty-five polished mammoth-ivory bracelets. At the boy's throat was an ivory pin that may have once held a cloak; under his shoulder was an ivory sculpture of a mammoth. A massive eight-foot-long ivory lance made from a straightened mammoth tusk lay at his and the girl's side.

The sight of these skeletons showered in tiny bits of ivory must have been startling enough, but the amount of labor necessary to produce the adornment is simply staggering to contemplate, and clear evidence of the deceased's high status. According to paleoanthropologist Randall White, the beads were produced in a methodical, step-by-step fashion; they were, in effect, standardized. There was more.

> They were scored across each face so that when strung they would fall into
> an interlocking, criss-cross pattern. Careful analysis shows that the scoring
> was done on each blank bead before the hole was drilled, indicating that

the creator had the desired aesthetic effect in mind at even the earliest
stages of production.

White's experiments later showed that it would have taken more
than an hour to make each bead. The old man's beadwork, then, would
have taken more than three thousand hours of labor, and each child's
more than five thousand hours.

All the themes that run through the history of human fascination
with ivory are present, in embryonic form, in this prehistoric site: the lure
of the material; its artistic employment, symbolic power, and value; its use
as a means of conferring status; the desire and trade required to obtain it;
efforts at mass production; consciousness of its source; its embrace in
adornment even to the grave—they are all destined to be replayed through
millennia to come.

IT'S IMPOSSIBLE TO know the circumstances in which ivory's properties
were first revealed. We can imagine a firelit corner of a cave, the bank of a
thawing river at midday, or a hundred other scenes, crowded or solitary.
We can picture the thin creamy streaks left by scraping a flint very hard
across a flake of mammoth tusk, or the shallow holes that could be made
by twisting the sharp point of a stone tool into the surface. But we can
only speculate about the first attempts to work ivory, how early humans
unlocked the allure of this unique organic substance and stirred the urge
to use, keep, and treasure it.

We know that humans began carving skillfully in ivory in prehistoric
times. Ivory figures dating back roughly 25,000 years have been known
for some time, but in 2007 archaeologists from the University of Tübingen, Germany, announced the oldest ivory find yet. It is a tiny exquisite
rendering of the very animal from which the carving material itself came:
a woolly mammoth. Less than an inch and a half long, the softly rounded
form is complete with massive trunk, stumplike legs, pointed tail, and
strange details—a half dozen incisions on the head, cross-hatching on the
soles of its feet. Radiocarbon analyses push its origins back some 35,000

years. It's one of more than a dozen figurines made from mammoth ivory unearthed at the Vogelherd cave in southwest Germany, a dazzling discovery that joins a clutch of similar small carved ivories discovered four years previously at another Swabian cave, the Hohle Fels, and thought to date to perhaps 33,000 years ago. These groups of powerful and puzzling ivory carvings may constitute the oldest body of figurative art in the world, an array that includes a horse's head raked with lines, a lovely wing-tucked diving duck, and an enigmatic high-shouldered half human–half cat torso. Their mottled surfaces, burnished smooth and sometimes pierced for suspension, suggest they were amulets, kept close; their precise meanings and purposes are not entirely clear but their animal and human themes are familiar from all subsequent prehistoric art. Indeed, these were created at roughly the same time the first great cave paintings began appearing in Europe.

The profusion of ivory carvings that followed emerged in a period that saw an explosion of plastic expression. Those early uses are not merely the first instances; they are the formative ones, and tell us what to look for as we trace ivory's luster through history.

IT'S NOW COMMONLY accepted that modern man—*Homo sapiens*— arose roughly 150,000 years ago in Africa and eventually set out to colonize the world; 100,000 years later they were supplanting earlier hominids (such as *H. erectus* and *H. neanderthalensis*) who began to migrate out of Africa over a million years before. After *H. sapiens* moved into Europe, Neanderthals, who certainly looked the part of cavemen— their powerful, heavy build was well adapted to the harsh waxing and waning ice age conditions that prevailed throughout this period— disappeared, perhaps in as little as a thousand years in southern France, although they may have overlapped for much longer in northern Europe. Neanderthals had stone tools and possibly a concept of decoration (pierced fox teeth have been found in the Neanderthal site of Grotte du Renne in France), but though that's a sign of more intellectual capability than they are often given credit for, it pales next to the arresting evidence of human consciousness on display on the walls of more than two hundred caves in southwest France and northeast Spain decorated in Paleolithic times.

The art of these anatomically modern humans, still referred to as Cro-Magnons, says more than anything else that those who created it were not so different from us. We sense, intuitively, that it taps into shared imagery. Although the art refers to a world of experience far removed from ours, full of long-gone megafauna—cave bears, huge bison, saber-toothed cats—and shows the pentimenti of various forgotten symbolisms (spots, dots, tridents, handprints), it has a freshness and power that speak directly. Even looking at photographs of the powerfully rendered aurochs painted on the white calcite walls of the Hall of the Bulls in Lascaux, France's most famous prehistoric cave, we feel that our reaction cannot be completely different from that of those who first created them. We see that those painters saw what we would have seen. They traced the bow of a horse's neck, the scooping curve of a tusk, or the spear of a horn the very way we would, using outlines that cut out the animal from its background along the boundary between what it was and what it wasn't: they used drawing, as we do, as an act of definition.

Those little figurines from Germany and all the later ice age carvings that have come down to us are, admittedly, just as shorn of context as cave paintings when seen in reproduction. But by their nature they were designed to carry their meanings with them. Studied directly— even if one has to view them behind protective glass, propped on little pedestals in museum displays, far from where they were created—they still evoke a sense of what it must have been like to hold and carry them, which in turn gives us a glimpse into what it must have been like to make them. As stand-alone, portable, hand-sized pieces worked from chunks and slabs of rock, lumps of clay, and pieces of bone and ivory, they were meant to be handled, caressed, stroked, and pondered by flickering fires, clutched under furs and skins, worn around the neck. The touch of these pieces was surely as important as their appearance, for what can be detected under the ball of the thumb or probing fingertips is apparent even in the dark. What was felt in them surely had to be part of their nimbus of meaning. So many of them were made of ivory.

WHAT WAS IT about ivory that made it a desirable material to early man? There were others at his disposal, from antler and amber to shells and stone. And ivory in substantial quantities—from mammoths or, possibly, in some regions, mastodons—may not have been widely available, although some 15,000 years ago entire shelters on the east European plain were made of mammoth skeletons either scavenged from dead animals or gathered from humans' own kill sites of these creatures. Bones from the huge, impressively furred creatures were used like lumber. Over a foundation of skulls, nearly a hundred mandibles might be arranged around a yurtlike hide tent that used femurs and tusks as tent ribs. As building posts, tusks had certain disadvantages: they could crack, warp, and be chewed by rodents.

Yet surely chunks and flakes from broken mammoth tusks first fell to hand after the hunt, and it would require no elaborate testing to discover what the material had to offer. Ivory's density was obvious from its weight, but its surface was not implacably granitic. Ivory wasn't easy to work, but it didn't split like bone or wood, which made it useful for spear points, needles, and other small tools.

Its primary creative use in Paleolithic times, however, appears to modern eyes to have been artistic. Any flake of ivory was potentially a plaque on which an exquisitely detailed drawing might be laboriously scratched—often images of mammoths, as evocative examples that have been unearthed demonstrate. A chunk of ivory slowly yields to determined gouging, scoring, and chipping with a sharp tool and can be rounded and smoothed by rubbing with fine abrasive substances known to early man, such as red ocher (hematite), which, as White points out, is no different from the jeweler's rouge in use today. It is the last stage of polishing, of course, that unlocks ivory's tactile appeal; something is brought out in the silken surface that makes those who touch it want to touch it

again. That was all it would take. The magic of ivory had wormed its way
into the human psyche.

NOT ONLY IS ivory a perfect vehicle for plastic expression, but in the
right conditions it can last indefinitely. That is why we still have small
ice age carvings whose iconography covers not only the range of then
extant fauna—ibex and aurochs, hook-jawed salmon and migratory
birds in flight, horses and cave lions, mammoths, reindeer and woolly
rhinoceroses, all the bountiful and terrifying life that surrounded early
man—but also forms used to mirror humans back to themselves. Unlike
animal carvings, which are often carefully observed and delicately crafted,
many (though not all) of these latter figures are highly abstract. Some are
little more than simple forks or wishbone shapes, elongated trunks and
pairs of splayed legs with vulva-like notches that seem to mark them
female.

Other woman forms are contrastingly bulbous. These so-called Venus
figures often feature faceless checkered knobs for heads, tiny feet and
swelling torsos, all breasts, belly, buttocks, hips, and thighs, now and then
showing carefully detailed navels and genitals. Their adipose, steatopygous
shapes were first thought a racial characteristic and, later, evidence of their
use as fertility figures, although their precise symbolism is now an open
question. Among various possibilities, they may have been created as objects of veneration, as obstetrical models, or simply to stimulate arousal.
While the most famous, the Venus (or Woman) of Willendorf, is limestone,
many others—including the Venus of Brassempouy or La Poire ("the
Pear"), a headless, bulging female torso from the Grotte du Pape in Périg-
ord; and the highly abstracted, wonderfully geometric, almost ballooning
Venus of Lespugne, found in the Haut-Garonne—are both carved from
mammoth tusks.

That many of these little statuettes were made from ivory suggests
something about the meanings that began to accrue to the material. If
they were objects of reverence or simple teaching tools, ivory, with its
perfect workability, would have been an obvious choice for careful sculp-

tural expression; if they were Paleolithic sex toys, as some have suggested, then too there would be no better material than ivory, with its slip and warmth, to fondle in recalling the pawing and stroking of sex.

Whatever their intended purpose, the considerable effort required to carve an ivory figurine with flint tools would have imbued the resulting object with importance and value. In fact, it's something of a puzzle as to how early man, lacking anything like a saw, managed to reduce mammoth tusks (which could be up to sixteen feet long) into portable pieces. Tusks don't fracture easily, and splitting and wedging techniques—the kind used to split logs—won't work with ivory that isn't already thoroughly desiccated. Whacking a fresh tusk with a stone tool accomplishes little. But segments of mammoth tusk evidently intended for later carving have been unearthed and show that more careful methods, albeit enormously time-consuming, were devised. A flaked hammer stone was used to stipple a guideline around a section of tusk, which was then laboriously widened into a channel. A stone knife would be drawn around and around to deepen the groove, and finally the section was broken free by blows of one hammer stone on another held against the remaining core.

IVORY IS DENTIN, an essential component of teeth.

Teeth are not bones; the two substances are different in their biology, though both are composed of collagen and minerals. Teeth, which lack the blood vessel system of bones, are denser and although connected to the skeleton are exposed, poking through the skin in some fashion. A tooth consists of a root (or roots) and a crown. The roots, which are covered by cementum, an acellular material, are fixed in the bony sockets of the jaws. All teeth feature a pulp cavity in the root, a chamber filled (in the living tooth) with soft, pulpy tissue well supplied with blood vessels. The crown, which is distinguished by its covering of hard enamel, is what's on display in the mouth of most animals.

There are further details but we needn't linger over them; we're after the main mass inside the tooth, underneath the crown's surface: dentin. This "very tough and resilient tissue," as one scientist puts it, is "familiar as the precious material ivory." In nature there is no shortage of teeth, but there are only a few significant sources of this "precious material."

A mere half dozen animals have teeth big enough to yield a significant mass of carvable ivory: the hippopotamus, the walrus, the narwhal, various pigs, a few whales, and, most important of all, the elephant and its ancestors, notably the mammoth.

An elephant or mammoth tusk is an enlarged upper incisor. It's all dentin except for a thin layer of cementum on the surface (called "bark") and a tiny crown of enamel at the tip or distal end; as a result, virtually the entirety of its bulk can be utilized. A large tusk can be more than six inches in diameter and nearly three yards in length. The "lesser ivories" not only are far smaller in comparison but have various drawbacks, including heavy enamel cladding, different layers of dentin density, and uneven coloring. Each of these examples has had an historic role—hippo teeth were carved in ancient Egypt, pig teeth have been used since ancient Greece, walrus and narwhal ivory were important in medieval Europe and still are in Inuit culture, and whale teeth remain Oceania's sole native source of ivory—yet all pale in significance next to "true ivory," which comes from ancient or modern elephants and needs no qualifier.

The exceedingly compact, uniform structure of ivory derives from the network of minute tubules, each about one-fifteen-thousandth of an inch in diameter, that radiate in clusters outward from the pulp cavity. These tiny dentinal structures are surrounded by a meshwork of collagen, whose gelatinous quality contributes to its carvability and polish. It may be difficult to imagine tusks, as solid and weighty as they are, growing, but that's exactly what they do, from the root out. Throughout a creature's life span, specialized mineralizing cells called odontoblasts line up on the growing surface of the dentin that outlines the funnel-shaped pulp cavity, forming tubules that inexorably deposit layer upon layer of calcified tissue, like adding to a stack of cones from the bottom. An elephant's immense incisors grow some seven inches a year.

"HERE, HOLD THIS. Be careful, it's heavier than it looks," Christopher Norris said as he handed me a two-foot-long tip of a stained and mottled mammoth tusk, one of a trove of similar specimens from excavations at Fairbanks Creek in Alaska in the 1950s.

It was surprisingly heavy and hard, a deep mahogany color, and streaked with fissures toward the broken end. It wasn't at all like a mammoth tusk that a cave artist would have used. That would have been fresh, or nearly so. This one was tens of thousands of years old, rough and rocklike.

Norris and I were standing in the Childs Frick building at the American Museum of Natural History in New York, whose seven floors house the largest mammal fossil collection in the world, some 400,000 specimens. On this, the fourth (or "bison") floor, Norris, who is the director of collections and archives in the museum's Division of Paleontology, had laid out some ancient tusks on a table flanked by aisles of metal shelving. They were filled with boxes and crates of specimens, notably eight hundred skulls of the extinct steppe bison.

"I wanted to bring you down here. It's kind of like a little shrine in this corner to the mass extinction of Pleistocene megafauna." Norris is short, with thinning close-cropped black hair, and was dressed in jeans. As he sorted through the specimen boxes and trays, he spoke in rapid-fire paragraphs, weaving an overview of fossil collection issues, but let me steer the conversation toward the subject of ivory.

"Most of what you have on this floor are fossils. It may have once been bone but it's gone through a process of petrification, so that what was once organic material in the bone has been replaced chemically by inorganic components. What you have looks like a bone, may even have the texture of a bone, and you might even be able to slice into it and see the bone structure, but what it is, essentially, is rock."

Was it the same process for fossil ivory?

"It might take longer, because ivory's denser than bone, but over the kind of time scales we are talking about"—he shrugged—"it wouldn't be significant."

The mammoth tusk in my hands was actually a subfossil, in which the organic material hadn't been totally transformed; it was mostly weathered. The ivory had lost some fats and oils but most of the dentin was intact.

Norris poked in a tray of small tusk ends. "The problem with these guys is that they've been soaked in water, frozen, buried. The major problem with a subfossil is that when it's dug up it gets dried out far too quickly. Any salts dissolved in the water crystallize," he explained. Ivory will crack and delaminate if dried out too rapidly. Previously, when tusks would begin to crack, "people used to slather on shellac to try and cope with the fact that most of the crucial damage had been done in the first few days after digging them up."

True fossils don't change much, however. Norris offered me another specimen.

"This is a piece of tusk from *Gomphotherium* from the Snake River in Nebraska, ten to twelve million years old." It felt like stone. *Gomphotherium*, which had both upper and lower tusks, was one of roughly three hundred species in the order *Proboscidea* (named after their obvious *proboscis*, or trunk), which consists of elephants and their relatives. Most of the earlier evolutionary experiments, like the fearsome-looking *Deinotherium* ("terrible beast"), which had tusks that hung out of the lower jaw like a giant two-pronged hoe, fell by the wayside. But a million years ago there were still eleven or so species of giant *proboscideans* roaming the earth's continents on their pillarlike legs, including stegadons and mastadons. The latter went extinct only about 10,000 years ago, as did their widespread relatives the mammoths, of which the best-known species, the woolly mammoth (*Mammuthus primigenius*), lasted somewhat longer. All have disappeared, leaving only three species of *Elephantidae*: the Asian elephant (*Elephas maximus*) and two African elephants (current thinking recognizes two distinct species on the continent, the savanna or bush elephant, *Loxodonta africana*, and the forest elephant, *Loxodonta cyclotis*).

I put the *Gomphotherium* tusk fragment back in the tray. "Most fossils we never see," Norris said as he repacked the box, "they just get eroded away."

Meaning?

"Most of the mammoths found have a tusk or bone or two removed, and the rest stays in the ground and gets eroded and washed down a river and added back into the environment. The natural life cycle of these objects does not include being arrested in time so they can sit on shelves and be studied. Despite the fact that we call this a natural history museum, what we basically do to this stuff is actually very unnatural. We try to stop this process, arrest it by treating it with various things, padding it to prevent mechanical damage, et cetera, so that at the end of the day we can stretch out the process for our purposes.

"The material," he sighed, "always wants badly to degrade."

AFTER MY MEETING I stopped in the fossil halls to look for the mounted skeleton of *Mammuthus jeffersonii*, a non-woolly type dug up on an Indiana farm. Its huge dark tusks looked almost circular from below and crossed over each other at the tips. Norris had told me to take a careful look and, sure enough, they had been wrapped in loops of thin wire in a vain effort to keep them from cracking.

My eyes were also drawn to the mural on the wall behind the skeleton, an ice age scene by Charles R. Knight, the early-twentieth-century illustrator. Knight's evocative re-creations of prehistory have been reproduced so frequently that his iconic images have seeped into our collective consciousness. This panorama features a line of mammoths, their long tusks held out like curled pikes, roaming over the frozen wastes of the open tundra and ice-age bogs. Reindeer resting behind trees give way to the approaching herd.

Mammoths must have been primarily walking mountains of meat to early humans, only secondarily sources of ivory. We know they hunted them successfully; we have the evidence of spear points embedded in their bones. It's difficult enough to bring down far smaller prey consistently, as the practices of any number of hunting cultures demonstrate. It can't have been easy to knock off such towering creatures with clubs and wooden spears or even the advanced bow-and-arrow weaponry later used that made possible slaying from a safer distance.

I couldn't help picturing what Knight implies lies just outside the edges of his mural: hunters hidden in the forest, squinting through face-stinging sleet at shaggy beasts plowing closer and closer through the scattered white drifts. I imagined them watching as the herd crosses below them, narrowing into a single, shuffling file between the slopes and the half-frozen river below, trunks unfurling and testing the wind, the young struggling to stay close to their mothers. They see the animals' steaming breath, the snow clinging to the fringes of their fur. Hearts pounding, gripping their stone-tipped spears and their fur cloaks tighter, the hunters remain motionless in the forest above save for their silent shaking in the deep cold. They tense as the marching line pulls away from a floundering young cow, her small eyes glittering with fear beneath a snow-matted topknot. The silence is rent by screams as the spear-shaking hunters burst out from behind firs and boulders and hurtle down the slope like the crumbling edge of an avalanche . . .

In reality, we don't know if our human ancestors were daring, spear-chucking predators, clever herders who harried their prey over cliffs and finished them off below, or opportunistic carrion feeders, hacking off what chunks of flesh they could before the arrival of saber-toothed cats, dire wolves, short-faced bears, and other assorted rivals forced them to beat a hasty retreat from a tasty carcass. It's likely all these strategies, and others, were put to use in the struggle to survive.

Still, they were successful enough. In fact, many researchers believe that early hunters were so skillful they can be blamed, at least in part, for the extinction of the mammoth and other megafauna across Eurasia, the Americas, and Australia. Others say that's preposterous, for a number of reasons. To pick one: the shift in climate after the last ice age is thought to have had a negative impact on vegetation, the herbivores that fed on it, and the carnivores that fed on them. A creature like the mammoth, so well adapted to cold, might have followed the retreating glaciers northward, then become trapped on the alternately thawing and snow-covered, ever-shrinking tundra left between growing forests and the thick ice sheets. But what appears to be a connection between the rapid disappearance of a number of species from the fossil record and the appearance of the first modern humans makes many theorists think that the drying up of their food supply alone can't account for such a sudden collapse of species.

Early man, it is hypothesized, had the means (lethal, pointy weapons and a brain large enough to plot deadly teamwork) and the motive (hunger) to be considered the prime suspect. It's a major point of contention among scientists, quite a few of whom line up on the side of the "overkill" or "blitzkrieg" hypothesis, while others join the doubters who find overkill too problematic to be plausible.

Did early humans expand in population so rapidly that they permeated every pocket of entire continents? Were they remorseless enough to run every last beast to ground? Even if mammoths and other megafauna were primary sources of nutrition in the harsh conditions of the ice age, it's hard to imagine that there would have been any point to killing more than what was needed. It would have been a waste of time and energy and unnecessarily risky. Whole herds, it seems safe to assume, weren't being slaughtered for their livers—or, for that matter, their tusks. A valuable by-product of the hunt, like bone, skin, and hair, mammoth teeth would be something to carve and use and even trade. For early humans, it seems unlikely that ivory could ever have been the sole motivation behind a hunt. That would happen later, although soon enough in history.

ROSS MACPHEE, a curator in the American Museum of Natural History's Division of Vertebrate Zoology, has his office far from the fossil halls, at the other end of the two-block-long building. But the fossil record is much on his mind. MacPhee studies the causes and consequences of the massive late Pleistocene extinctions in the Americas and northern Asia. We talked in his high-ceilinged, comfortably cluttered office, with its dark wooden cabinets stuffed with books and papers, a huge old globe, and a yellow MAMMOTH CROSSING traffic sign, complete with a silhouette of the long-gone ice-age giant.

Born in Scotland and raised in Canada, MacPhee taught at Duke before joining the museum. His curly gray hair and beard are a lot trimmer than they appear in the AMNH Web site photographs of him on location in Siberia, peering out of a fur-trimmed parka.

I asked MacPhee if he thought early humans had a role in wiping out the mammoth. "I'm comfortable with the idea of early peoples hunting them. I just don't see how they could have concentrated themselves in such as way that it could have had such an impact on populations."

Mammoths, he pointed out, were distributed all across northern landmasses in the Pleistocene. "It's just inconceivable to me that people with their kind of tool kit could have made any kind of difference whatsoever." He paused. "With respect to extinction, we still don't understand even the most rudimentary facts about how losses of this kind occur."

I thought about one sizable denizen of the ice age that's still with us: the musk ox. How did it manage to survive climate change and possible hunting pressure?

"The salient facts are that musk oxen originated in Asia, crossed the Bering Strait, and were quite successful." But they "have reduced genetic variability—obviously went through a bottleneck. Something bad happened, at least that's what appears. Musk oxen pulled through; mammoths didn't."

Why not?

"The usual: bad luck or bad genes. Sometimes species go down for what look like random reasons. Others persist. Rhinos survive in subtropical regions, but the woolly rhino goes down. We had bison surviving in North America and Asia but mammoths went down."

The twilight of the mammoths apparently took place on the bleak, windswept tundra of Wrangel Island north of the Arctic Circle between the Chukchi and East Siberian seas. In the 1990s, scientific expeditions there found mammoth tusks and molars in remarkable states of preservation resting in small rivers running to the Arctic Sea. On a 1998 expedition MacPhee himself stumbled across the only mammoth ulna (forelimb bone) ever recovered on Wrangel. The bone oozed grease, as if it had come from a freshly killed animal. The remnant population of these shaggy survivors managed to defy time, clinging to existence until just 3,700 years ago; the arrival of humans on the island a few centuries before may have sealed their fate. Their tusks would be unearthed in many regions, by accident and design, for millennia after their demise.

AFTER TALKING WITH MacPhee, I got to thinking that there was something else about the overkill hypothesis that made it hard for many to resist, despite its explanatory shortcomings. Killer cavemen on an unstoppable "blitzkrieg" is an image that taps into contemporary feelings of collective guilt that we've been mucking up the environment since we dropped from trees. One doesn't have to subscribe to the notion of "man the destroyer" to be dismayed by how humans have begun polluting their earthly nest, for themselves as well as for other creatures that share the globe. But MacPhee is surely right that, from a planetary point of view, species extinction is a natural process, not just something that's exclusively caused by what people do or set in motion. Humans haven't been around for most of the earth's biological history. Before we came on the scene, all manner of large and small creatures that once roamed the land and swam in the seas had already become fossilized echoes of former life.

Still, that doesn't get us off the hook now, not when we are conscious of our various effects on other species—not just our own predation but the introduction of species alien to specific environments, habitat destruction, and even climate change. The mere possibility that Pleistocene overkill might have happened as some say it did lingers in the conscience as a cautionary tale warning of our capacity for snuffing out entire species, as many in the 1980s had said could happen with the African elephant.

STUDIED CLOSELY, A polished cross section of a mammoth or elephant tusk reveals a complex and unique pattern. In the center of the disc there's always a hole, a large one if the tusk has been sectioned across the pulp cavity, a tiny one if sawn across the central or tip portion where only the nerve channel remains. Surrounding the hole are concentric circles, like tree rings. Less than half an inch apart, these rings are layers of dentin formation, each representing six to eight years of tusk growth. (If the tusk had been cut lengthwise, these rings would have appeared as faint waves, like the moiré patterns on the endpapers of fine old books.) Look again at the surface of the ivory, this time closer to the outer edge of the disc, and you can see a more complex pattern, a characteristic weave of intersecting lines reminiscent of fussy banknote engraving. To scientists of a century ago, these alternating arcs were reminiscent of the delicate scalloped, engine-turned whorls on the cases of pocket watches of the period.

This delicate cross-hatching is known as the Schreger pattern, named after the odontologist Bernhard Schreger, who first described it in 1800. The nineteenth-century biologist Sir Richard Owen regarded it as a defining characteristic: "The name ivory is now restricted . . . to that modification of dentine or tooth substance which in transverse sections or fractures shews lines of different colours or *straie* proceeding in the arc of a circle, and forming by their decussations minute curvilinear lozenge-shaped spaces."

The Schreger pattern is a visual reflection of ivory's structure of microscopic dentinal tubules—microcanals that radiate in rows from the center of the tusk. The tusks of pigs, hippopotami, walruses, and narwhals show no such pattern, which means its presence can be used to distinguish *proboscidean* (mammoth and elephant) ivory from other ivories, and, in fact, it can even be used to distinguish between mammoth and elephant ivory. If you look at the easily seen lines closest to the outside of a mammoth tusk, they create crosshatched sprays of tiny diamond shapes, like stacked chevrons or a sharp herringbone pattern. In elephant ivory, the lines toward the outer edge of the tusk section appear loosely woven, more open, like stretched netting or soft circumflexes.

At first I saw the crisscrossed matrix of this organic material's internal structure as an intriguing oddity, nothing more. Much later I came to think of the tightly interlocked design as curiously emblematic of ivory's story, with its far larger, endlessly repeating historical pattern binding together art and passion, commerce and greed, humans and elephants, down through the ages.

2

Tribute and Treasure

By the time the last of the mammoths were sinking into Siberia's sedimentary strata, half a world away ancient Egypt's great pyramids had already been built. Long familiar with ivory in the form of hippopotamus teeth and elephant tusks, Egyptian artisans had been using it since before the Dynastic era.

Ivory was now treasure. This expansion of its meaning had begun in prehistory, when the material was first used for adornment and sculpture. In the settled, stratified societies around the Mediterranean ivory also functioned much the way gold did: possessing it signaled status and expressed social differences.

Consider the exquisitely carved ivory neck rest buried long ago with Tutankhamen to help ease the boy king's journey to the afterworld. It is a telling example of both the artistry of the period (ca. 1325 BCE) and the importance ivory had attained. The rounded crescent, proffered by a crouching figure flanked by resting lions, is one of thousands of ivory objects that decorated the royal tombs of Egypt. These included game discs, perfume flasks, seals, combs, knife handles, inlaid tomb furniture, and so-called concubine figures, which varied from crude dolls to graceful sloe-eyed sylphs. (It's thought that these slim, hourglass-shaped ivory statuettes were intended to magically assist in providing sexual solace for the departed king in the afterlife, but their interment in female burials as well rather complicates this idea.)

For Egyptians the ivory that first came to hand was probably from the hippopotamus, which lived along the wetlands of the Nile. Eleven feet long, five feet high at the shoulder, and weighing seven thousand pounds, hippos are the heaviest land animal after the elephant.

Hippopotamus amphibius, the "river horse," is immense and piglike, hairless, amphibious, and dangerous when cornered, an impressive creature to Egyptians. It was regarded as a symbol of rebirth and was often pictured in Egyptian art. Its substantial teeth, both upper and lower incisors and canines—especially the strongly curved foot-long lower canines so evident in the hugely gaping jaws territorial bulls threaten one another with—were important sources of ivory. Each type of tooth is distinctive in cross section, triangular or round, with faint, tightly packed concentric lines and its own characteristic central interstitial zone where developing dentin converges.

The heavy armorlike enamel cladding of hippo teeth made carving difficult, particularly with the simple tools then available. Hippo ivory is also relatively small and, although opaque, the innermost layer of dentin is mottled in appearance. As early as the fourth millennium BCE, Egyptians were turning to elephant ivory, a much superior medium with no enamel to speak of, a uniform color, and an even grain. What's more, elephant ivory was large enough to be used for small statuary and other sculpture in the round, and provide flat panels up to five inches or more across and a foot or two in length for bas-reliefs or small boxes.

Local sources of elephant ivory were limited and dwindling, however. Elephants once ranged unimpeded all over the continent, including the Sahara before it became desert, as Neolithic rock paintings there show. Some 5,000 years ago the drying up of the Sahara forced early peoples and elephants to its edges—the Mediterranean in the north, the *sahel*, or "shore," in the south. Evidence suggests that this north African population was the smaller forest elephant (*Loxodonta cyclotis*) rather than the savannah or bush elephant (*L. africana*), but in any case they persisted for some time in Egypt, where they were hunted, even tamed; as early as the First Dynasty (ca. 3000 BCE), different hieroglyphs were used to distinguish between wild and trained elephants. The arid climate and lack of trees and water eventually forced the elephant population farther south, deep into Nubia (today's southern Egypt and northern Sudan).

As historian Edward A. Alpers puts it,

> The Egyptian evidence makes it quite clear that ivory was a major product of the central and eastern Sudanic regions from very remote times.

We cannot know how deeply this demand needed to penetrate into the heart of the continent, nor what impact the Egyptian demand may have had on the elephant population of those regions that supplied successive dynasties. We do know, however, that elephants disappeared from the eastern Sahara after 2750 B.C. and around 2000 B.C. in the central Sahara.

Here, another historical pattern emerges: the relative scarcity of ivory was now adding preciousness to the appeal inherent in the material itself, making this luxury item a status symbol fit for high officials and pharaohs. It became part of the natural wealth of Africa that successive Egyptian dynasties sought to control and acquire.

Increased demand inspired direct action. As far back as the Sixth Dynasty (2420–2258 BCE) in the Old Kingdom, during the reign of Pharaoh Merenre, Harkhuf, the governor of Elephantine, the island trading post (and probable ivory depot) at the first cataract of the Nile, sent ivory-gathering expeditions beyond Nubia's borders.

Ivory in the form of tribute would also make its way from the interior down the Nile to Memphis and Thebes. The Tomb of Rekhmire (ca. 1450 BCE), one of the largest in the necropolis at Thebes, features a tribute scene in which ivory figures prominently. Rekhmire was the vizier of Thutmose III, charged with ensuring the proper payment of taxes in the form of goods from vassal states. The fading wall painting depicts a procession of foreign delegations from Nubia, Syria, Punt (modern-day coastal Sudan or Eritrea), and others bearing incense trees, skins, gold, baboons, an elephant—and shouldering ivory, in the form of pale crescent tusks.

For the Eighteenth Dynasty (c.1570 to 1293 BCE), however, these offerings were clearly insufficient. Both Thutmose I and Thutmose III extended the Egyptian empire by invading Syria. One benefit of the newly expanded borders was a supply of ivory from the population of Asian elephants in the region. While on a military campaign there, Thutmose III took time out to conduct a hunt, slaying over a hundred elephants. His stepmother, Queen Hatshepsut, had five ships, each seventy feet long and accommodating some two hundred men and rowers, built on the Nile and transported across the desert from Thebes to the Red Sea, where they sailed as a fleet to the "land of Punt" for ivory, incense, and other riches. An obelisk erected by Hatshepsut at Karnak bears an inscription attesting to their having brought seven hundred elephant tusks, panther skins, and other goods from Tjehenu (eastern Libya, western Egypt), additional evidence of the wide and significant trade in this material.

IVORY, LIKE OTHER luxury materials, now commonly passed through many hands after it left its source. The structure, mechanisms, and volume of the trade in ivory in the eastern Mediterranean in the Bronze Age, when the use of metals first began (roughly 3000–1000 BCE), is not all that well known, but the outlines of its beginning are clear by the Late Bronze Age (ca. 1600–1000 BCE).

It operated something like this. Ruling elites such as the pharaohs and the kings of minor city-states desired both raw tusks and worked ivory objects for themselves and to use as diplomatic gift exchanges with other powers to show their loyalty, pay tribute, or open trade. This stimulated the expansion of the nascent market in ivory as both bulk material and luxury product by merchants who often functioned as foreign envoys. There were complex trade circuits, and layered interests, which meant ivory was stored here, carved there, delivered somewhere else. Archaeological findings of tusks, blanks, roughouts, pegs and dowels, and waste—bits left over from inlay work, flakes and chips from carving in the round or in high relief—as well as unfinished and finished ivory pieces are the evidence we have of ivory workshops (typically associated with palaces and sanctuaries) in the Aegean, on Cyprus, in Syria, Palestine, Anatolia, and elsewhere.

With no one society dominating trade in the Mediterranean, the Late Bronze Age became increasingly international and cosmopolitan. Specialists—physicians, scribes, sculptors—were exchanged among royal courts and major trading centers. A complex web of political and economic interactions motivated the extraction of ivory as a natural resource from herds of pachyderms and encouraged the culture of craft specialists who exploited the possibilities of the material and adapted it to a wide range of art forms created in variety of styles.

All this makes it difficult (and often misleading) to puzzle out distinct traditions in ivory carvings of the period. We know craftsmen used styles almost like patterns for various clients, often appropriating foreign motifs and iconography without regard to the meanings they originally carried. What's been called the "Egyptianizing" style of much ivory carving in the eastern Mediterranean region may more properly reflect a kind of agglomeration of styles emanating from various carving centers. A common symbolic language began to emerge. A good example of this is the duck-shaped ivory (or partly ivory) container, featuring either a forward- or a backward-pointing head and a winged or oval lid, found in numerous Mediterranean and Middle Eastern sites. Fashionable and popular, it became almost standardized.

One could linger long over ivories from the many minor kingdoms and greater empires that waxed and waned in this region. Syria alone was ruled by Egyptians, Babylonians, Hittites, Chaldeans, Persians . . . but it's enough to look at a few instances of ivory use in the Late Bronze Age, some of which are based on written evidence, to flesh out the archaeological picture.

The Phoenicians, with their city-states along the coast of what is now Lebanon and modern-day Syria, their vast maritime trading network, and their skilled craftsmen, supplied King Solomon with the ivory, precious metals, and experience needed to build and decorate the temple at Jerusalem (ca. 1000 BCE). Solomon entered into a commercial treaty with King Hiram of Tyre. "For the King had at sea a navy of Tharshish with the navy of Hiram: once in three years came the navy of Tharshish, bringing gold, and silver, ivory, and apes, and peacocks. So King Solomon exceeded all the kings of the earth for riches and for wisdom," according to the Book of Kings. He sat on "a great throne made of ivory," with six steps and fourteen lions, and the whole overlaid with gold.

Now firmly entrenched in the pantheon of precious materials, ivory began to gain metaphorical power. In the Song of Solomon, ivory is invoked for flesh ("his belly is as bright ivory"; "thy neck is as a tower of ivory"). Ahab, a later king, added an air of decadence to the substance. He is portrayed in the Old Testament as a sinful ruler—among his various failings, he married the wicked Jezebel, the king of Sidon's daughter, who persuaded him to worship the false idol Baal. Ahab also built an entire palace lavishly decorated with ivory in Samaria, his capital, which doubtless helped link ivory with the idea of sensual extravagance. Certainly the connection was apparent to the Hebrew prophet Amos. "Woe to them . . . that lie upon beds of ivory," he warned. "The houses of ivory shall perish."

SYRIAN ELEPHANTS WERE the prime source of ivory in the Middle East, supplying Assyrian, Babylonian, Egyptian, and Phoenician craftsmen. Ivory was a revered material during the roughly three centuries of Assyrian supremacy. Ashurnasirpal II (883–859 BCE) made Nimrud, on the east bank of the River Tigris, the capital of the Assyrian empire, which eventually spanned the Mediterranean to western Iraq. (All that is visible today of the once great city is a series of earthen mounds south of present-day Mosul in northern Iraq.)

Ivory in the form of elaborately carved objects and wooden furniture inlaid with intricate ivory panels had adorned the lavish royal apartments at Nimrud, and not surprisingly ivory carvings and fragments were found scattered throughout the palaces, temples, and private dwellings excavated by Austen Henry Layard starting in 1845. His great find was the Northwest Palace of Ashurnasirpal II. British archaeologist Max Mallowan reopened the dig in 1949, and over the next thirteen years he subsequently uncovered thousands of ivory carvings along with bronzes, seals, and stone sculpture.

Mallowan's wife, mystery writer Agatha Christie, accompanied him on all his digs. She photographed and worked on the wealth of ivory carvings found at the bottom of wells in the southern wing of the Northwest Palace, thrown there during the sack of Nimrud in 614 BCE. (The empire itself was overthrown two years later by the Medes and Babylonians, who burned and destroyed nearly all Assyrian palaces and public buildings.) In his memoirs Mallowan described the triumphant discovery at the bottom of a "beautifully built brick-lined well—over three hundred courses in depth, with a corkscrew bend in the middle of it." Nearly eighty feet down, his team found "a king's ransom in the sludge under water."

What was safely recovered was remarkable. Apparently, the Mede and Babylonian soldiers had stripped off the gold leaf that covered many of the ivory carvings and then simply tossed the ivory into wells. Christie worked on their restoration. Ivory is hydroscopic; it absorbs water. It swells and shrinks as moisture moves into and out of the material; thus a change of relative humidity—and temperature—can warp an object, or even cause it to split. Christie devised a method of slowly drying out the ivories to prevent cracking. "I had my own favorite tools," she wrote in her auto-biography: "an orange stick, possibly a very fine knitting needle . . . and a jar of cosmetic face cream." This proved useful "for gently coaxing the dirt out of the crevices without harming the friable ivory."

The carvings, many the color of brown silk, proved an interesting mix, evidence of how widespread ivory carving was across the region. Some, created in Assyrian workshops, featured warfare, snarling lions, processions, and other familiar motifs on incised panels or in low relief. Others clearly had been brought to Nimrud as tribute from vassal states with ivory-carving traditions. The Phoenician-style ivories, primarily busily detailed furniture panels with delicate openwork carved on both sides, showed a strong Egyptian influence. The restored Syrian-style ivories revealed bug-eyed, large-nosed figures; wavy-stemmed plants; and nude female figures with curling tresses.

Mallowan reflected on what lay behind the ivories.

> It would be impossible to summarize the variety and range of these carv-ings, but among the most beautiful are the animals, open work, in the round, of oryx, gazelle and other horned beasts. It is surprising that no rendering of the elephant was ever found, the source of the expensive luxuries with which the Assyrian Court was so well endowed. Up till now it has been generally believed that the majority of the ivories came from the tusks of Syrian elephants.

The decimation of elephant populations, which began early in the Mediterranean world with Egyptian demand for ivory, had reached Syria, which would harbor the last herds of elephants in the Middle East. They would all be gone by 500 BCE. Mallowan blamed Assyrian zeal for orga-nizing grand *battues*. A stele of ca. 879 BCE boasts that Ashurnasirpal II himself slew thirty elephants, along with more than four hundred lions and two hundred ostriches.

THE IMPACT OF evolving ivory traditions on elephant numbers was more complicated in the Aegean. Among the ivory-bearing foreigners pictured in the Tomb of Rekhmire are a delegation from Keftiu (Crete), which had no native ivory (a dwarf species of elephant had died out on the island before the arrival of Neolithic man). That a Cretan is shown with a tusk, however, is a clear sign that ivory was an item of exchange and, probably, significant trade.

The Tomb of Rekhmire dates from the end of the Minoan civilization on Crete in the middle of the second millennium BCE. Minoan society was structured around the palaces and courts of priest-kings, of which the one at Knossos is the most famous. There are a number of Minoan ivory carvings, including crocodiles and snake goddess figures with ruffled skirts, exposed breasts, and serpents entwined on their arms. The wonderfully free-form ivory acrobat from Knossos, crafted in a pose similar to that shown in Minoan bronzes of young men vaulting over charging bulls, is far looser in style than the comparatively stiff Egyptian figures of the period.

The seafaring and trading people of Crete were probably crippled by the volcanic eruption of Thera (ca. 1630–1550 BCE), but in any case their island culture was brought to an abrupt close shortly thereafter by conquering Mycenaeans, the Greek-speaking people of the Late Bronze Age.

The Mycenaean period is the historical backdrop for the *Iliad* and the *Odyssey*, which mention ivory in a number of contexts. These epics are literary works, but there is enough verisimilitude in the details to make us feel that what's said about a precious material corresponds to the meaning it bore in the Aegean. Ivory, Homer tells us, ranks with riches such as bronze, silver, gold, and amber; it's used for a horse's cheek pieces (stained) and as "enrichment" for its reins, as well as for scabbards, furniture inlays, and key handles. One charming passage in Book XVIII of the *Odyssey* has the goddess Athena shedding grace and beauty over the sleeping Penelope, making her more statuesque and "washing her face" with the ambrosial loveliness of a dancing Aphrodite; finally, she gives her a complexion whiter than "sawn ivory." All of this is complementary to the set of meanings (luxury, preciousness, skin tone, etc.) that similarly accrued to ivory in the Middle East.

And what were the kinds and sources of ivory in the Aegean? The hippopotamus that once flourished in the prehistoric Mediterranean (pigmy hippos long persisted on Cyprus) was now confined to watered areas of Egypt and Syria, and declining there, but its tusks were important in the brisk Late Bronze Age trade in the eastern Mediterranean, which swept in all manner of goods, including ostrich eggs, copper ingots, stone lamps, swords, daggers, and scarabs. Elephant ivory from the same regions (and almost certainly from North Africa as well) was equally important. The ivory trade probably piggybacked on the metals trade as complementary cargo on larger ships. Both hippo ivory and elephant ivory were utilized in the Aegean for seals, inlays, combs, and the like, sometimes side by side in the same craft environment.

But there was another ivory source, widespread throughout ancient Greece: wild boar, *Sus scrofa scrofa*, the ancestor of domestic pigs, originally found all over North Africa and Eurasia. Males of this tough-skinned, bristle-maned, solid-as-a-barrel species can reach four hundred pounds in weight and are quick and formidable when cornered, armed as they are with upper and lower curling tushes sharpened against each other. These are carried at the perfect height to rip into the groins of hunters who get too close; that is why boar hunting was long a test of Greek bravery.

The modest size of boar ivories—on the average, perhaps six-inch-long crescents—limited their artistic employment. But they had other uses. In the *Iliad*, Homer describes the military value of pig ivory: young warriors wear plain hide helmets, sans plume or crest, reinforced with leather thongs and armored with "wild boars' white teeth," placed "strategically and well." Surviving Mycenaean examples show that lower tusks were split into curved, gleaming plates with holes drilled in the corners.

IT'S IMPOSSIBLE TO think of Athens in the fifth century BCE without conjuring up an image of the Doric-columned Parthenon, still glorious today in its ruined state atop the city's acropolis. The temple, dedicated to the goddess Athena, was the site of one of the most extraordinary uses of ivory in history, the great forty-foot-tall cult statue of Athena Parthenos (or "virgin") that formerly stood within. It was a masterwork designed by the sculptor Pheidias, who also supervised both the building of the temple and its sculptural decoration; he began work on it around 447 BCE.

Athens was at the height of its power, and under the leadership of Pericles its citizens raised the funds for the lavish building project, which took over five years. Its purpose was to reflect religious devotion to the goddess who represented wisdom, including the arts of war and weaving, and, more important, to demonstrate the city-state's might to its rivals. The Greek geographer Pausanias wrote that the helmeted deity was depicted in a full-length tunic, holding a spear in one hand and a statue of Nike (itself the size of an actual person) in the other; at her feet lay a shield and a serpent. The gigantic figure's clothing and armor were formed of sheets of gold. The smooth skin of Athena's face, neck, bare shoulders, and arms, however, was made entirely of *ivory*.

This towering artistic achievement is long gone and we are left wondering how it could have been made. Greek artisans of the period were using sophisticated techniques to maximize the size of pieces that could be cut from the most substantial tusks available—elephant teeth—but the sheer size of the statue would have presented enormous challenges. Could Pheidias have somehow glued together a vast quantity of ivory chunks before sculpting, or affixed thousands of small ivory tiles on a wooden form? No matter how carefully the pieces were joined and matched in color, surely either method would have created a distracting mosaic effect, which would have defeated the very raison d'être for the use of ivory: the subtlety and translucence that make it a more nuanced, more sensual medium than the finest marble—just the thing to represent the flesh of a goddess.

This wasn't the first chryselephantine sculpture—i.e., one that combined ivory and gold. Such pieces have a long history going back to Egypt. Prior to Pheidias, a number of Greek artists and craftsmen had incorporated carefully sectioned pieces of elephant (and hippo) tusks into their gilded wooden sculptures to create the faces and limbs of figures. For Greeks who wanted to create nearly life-size statuary, a number of ivory pieces had to be assembled, like the parts of a mannequin—a section of tusk for an arm, one with greater girth for the head, others for the hands and feet, and so on. To avoid spoiling the overall effect, the joins where sections met were hidden by bracelets and necklaces, under drapery, and at hairlines.

Clearly, Pheidias had to go much further to adapt chryselephantine techniques to the unprecedented scale of a colossal cult statue. He may have accomplished this feat by employing furniture-makers' methods of softening large sheets of ivory and molding them to the required shapes. Techniques for the production of ivory veneers for furniture as thin as an eighth of an inch—a few millimeters—had been in use for centuries.

Art historian Kenneth Lapatin claims that the ancients may have known how to split ivory thinly, like "unrolling a papyrus," by some now forgotten method of peeling a tusk. Certainly they had a number of recipes to soften and shape ivory by steaming or boiling or soaking it in various liquids, including oil, beer, and especially vinegar. Once a thin sheet of ivory was softened, it might have been trimmed and draped over the form of the Athena Parthenos and doweled or glued into place.

A daunting task, certainly, but for Pheidias there would have been no shortage of resources to help him bend ivory to his creative will. He had teams of woodworkers, bronzecasters, and goldsmiths and other specialists. Price was no object—an estimated 40 talents (perhaps a quarter ton) of gold was used in making the cult statue, a staggering treasury in itself. The ivory used may have been nearly as costly.

The statue was built around an armature, which Lucian, Pheidias's nephew and briefly his apprentice, described as "a tangle of bars and struts and dowels driven right through, and beams and wedges and pitch and clay, and a quantity of such ugly stuff housing within, not to mention legions of mice and rats that sometimes conduct their civic business there." No matter; it was the exterior that counted. It may sound as if all that ivory and gold would have been garish in effect. But those who saw the cult figure in the play of torchlight, its visual impact redoubled in the reflecting pool in front of the statue's base, found it wondrous and spiritually moving. More than three hundred ancient replicas of the statue were made, and the image appeared on coins as far away as Turkey. Over the centuries, despite the extra moisture given off by the reflecting pool,

Athena's ivory visage began to crack. In the fifth century CE the statue was looted and taken to Constantinople, where it was later destroyed, perhaps during the Fourth Crusade.

After Pheidias, there would be much great art made of ivory but never again on such a stupendous scale.

EARLY GREEKS KNEW very little about the creature from which large ivory came; the word *elephas* was first used solely as the name for ivory. Only after they encountered elephants in the vastly expanded Greek world opened up by Alexander the Great's conquests was the name extended to the animal. The iconic image of this astounding figure and his brutal, meteoric rise is captured perfectly for us in the young warrior portrayed in the "Alexander mosaic" from Pompeii. His thick hair flying, beardless jaw firmly set, and dark eyes fixed on the prize, he rides his wild-eyed steed, Bucephalos, into the spear-cluttered clash of forces at the battle of Issus. There, in 333 BCE, his army crushed that of Darius III, the Persian king.

Across a vast area long raked by empires, Alexander created one more. The son of Philip II of Macedon, he was leading troops as a teenager. Following his father's assassination in 336 BCE, he transformed the Greek world, welding it together and taking his armies eastward to the Indus valley, north nearly to Russia and south to Egypt. He died at the age of thirty-two in Babylon in 323 after a drinking bout, although some think he may have succumbed, more prosaically, to malaria. Too vast to be sustained, his sprawling new empire broke into quarreling kingdoms run by his generals. But his short-lived dream served to spread Greek ideas and art, establish cultural links with various Eastern states, and, through new military tactics that were developed as well as trade links that were established, facilitate the flow of elephants and their ivory across several continents.

Alexander's military brilliance met a singular challenge during his invasion of India: the full-scale use of elephants in battle. Porus, the king of Pauravas, refused to surrender to the advancing "god-king" and confronted the Macedonian army on the east bank of the Hydaspes (today's

Jhelum river) in the Punjab with a unit of two hundred armored elephants, spaced some thirty yards apart like towers on a garrison wall. All were draped in protective armor and ridden by their handlers and may have carried miniature bunkers of additional warriors on their backs as well. A tamed elephant was more than a powerful beast of burden; it could be turned into a living tank. Much ingenuity went into devising elephants' armor, which often utilized fire-hardened leather and chain-mail drapery. Swords were attached to their trunks, poison-dipped points to their tusks. Elaborate training was required to control an elephant and direct its power against masses of armed men and horses, such as teaching it to sweep up an enemy soldier in its trunk and hand him up to the warriors riding it for quick dispatch. To opposing troops who had never seen them before, the sight of these striding behemoths in full battle regalia was terrifying.

Had he not previously confronted some in Darius's forces five years before, Alexander might not have been prepared to deal with elephants on the battlefield. Impressed, he had taken trained ones as war booty from his Persian campaigns, but never used them directly in battle. Instead, he devised deadly countertactics to deal with war elephants. When Porus left his right flank exposed, Alexander sent more cavalry behind the elephant line and then directed his archers to kill the elephants' mahouts and target the animals' eyes and trunks in a hail of arrows. "So a blood bath then ensued," wrote the military historian Arrian in a later account. The terrified elephants "attacked indiscriminately both friend and foe, trying to beat a path for themselves by any means and trampling and killing everything." His army crushed, Porus surrendered at last.

After the carnage of the battle of Hydaspes, Alexander's exhausted men refused to advance farther east. As his army marched south and eventually back through Mesopotamia, however, Alexander continued to incorporate trained Asian elephants, eventually two hundred of them, into his military machine. When he died in Babylon, his mourning pavilion featured an honor guard of elephants.

Alexander recognized that, as weapons of war, elephants were a two-edged sword. Their appearance alone could unnerve enemy forces, but once wounded they were uncontrollable and could be equally damaging to their own troops. Alexander's successors, however, were enamored of

them. Elephants represented the latest in war weaponry, a means of tip-
ping the balance during the bitter power struggles over control of the god-
king's empire. The ancient world's arms race was on.

Ptolemy, one of Alexander's generals, ended up ruling Egypt from
his base in Alexandria and fought for control of southern Syria against Se-
leucus, who held all of Mesopotamia and Persia. Both relied heavily on
war elephants. The Seleucids bordered India and thus were able to add to
their corps of fighting pachyderms. Ptolemy's Indian elephant corps
could not be replenished; overland routes were not in his control and
ships that could transport elephants on long ocean voyages had not been
invented. His son, Ptolemy II, turned to a local source: Africa. He had
previously set up hunting outposts along the Red Sea coast to exploit the
elephant herds in Ethiopia where, the Greek historian Polybius reported,
elephants' tusks were so common they were used as doorposts in houses.
Although Ethiopian hunters relied on stealth and venom-tipped arrows
shot from powerful bows to ambush elephants, such opportunistic hunting practices could not have had the impact on the herds that relentless
pursuit by organized hunting parties of encircling lancers, archers, and
cavalry must have made. A volley of arrows, a few well-placed spears, or a
hit-and-run hamstringing with an ax and the beast would be down, gur-
gling and gasping its last.

But the pressing need to replenish the dwindling stable of the
Ptolemies' war elephants suddenly gave the Ethiopian herds value over
and above the ivory they carried and the mounds of meat they could provide. For the first time, elephants were now worth something alive.

Ptolemy II founded a new elephant-hunting station, Ptolemais
Theron ("Ptolemais of the Hunts"), some two-thirds the way down the
Red Sea coast, to begin capturing wild elephants, an enterprise that the
Ethiopians, with their hunting traditions, disdained. The complexity of
this undertaking was enormous. It may have required up to a thousand
men to locate, surround, and drive wild elephants toward an enormous
walled corral over the course of weeks or months. In this vast enclosure,
trained elephants (presumably bred in captivity from the original Ptolemaic herd) and expert handlers recruited in India and lured to make the
voyage by promise of high pay would calm the animals. With great difficulty, these animals were then transported on ships from the Red Sea

coast, which required engineers and crews to rebuild port structures and docks to handle animals that weighed four or five tons. In addition, naval architects had to design an entirely new vessel, a sailing ship that could carry elephants for a voyage of at least a week and perhaps as long as a month, with stops at the hunting stations along the way to take on new fodder for the always hungry animals. "Obviously beasts fresh from the wild could hardly be coaxed up a gangplank onto a ship, much less be kept restrained once aboard," one scholar wrote. "They needed a certain amount of preliminary training first, and bases had to be equipped to provide this." Next to all this, the final step of the journey, marching them all across the Eastern Desert to the Nile and eventually to Memphis, where elephant stables had been established, seems almost a cakewalk.

Was this gigantic effort worth it? The Ptolemies used African elephants successfully in battle during the mid-third century BCE, but they fared less well against the Asian elephants deployed by the Seleucids during the Battle of Raphia in Palestine in 217 BCE. The African elephants in that clash were forest elephants, *L. cyclotis*, smaller in stature than the Asian species, and in any case outnumbered. "Unable to stand the smell and the trumpeting of Indian elephants, and terrified, I suppose, by their great size and strength," wrote Polybius, "they immediately run away." The Ptolemies finally soured on using elephants in warfare. But elsewhere in Africa elephants were still considered the key to conquest.

The belief in the advantages of war elephants had spread from Egypt to Carthage, the powerful city-state founded by Phoenicians in what is now Tunisia. The Carthaginians captured forest elephants then found in the coastal plains along the Mediterranean and the foothills of the Atlas mountains. Modeling their elephant corps after the Ptolemaic model, and using Indian trainers possibly obtained from Ptolemy II, they built up a powerful force, best remembered for its use in the Punic Wars against Rome, especially Hannibal's daring invasion of Italy in 218 BCE, in which he brought thirty-seven elephants through Spain and France and across frozen passes in the Alps to the Po Valley without losing a single one— although nearly half his men, some twenty thousand infantry and horsemen, perished. Once in Italy the elephants began succumbing to disease, starvation, and the many battles of Hannibal's fifteen-year campaign, which brought him to the gates of Rome. But Roman troops figured out how to harass and maim the elephants and by 204 BCE were taking the offensive to Carthage itself. At the battle of Zama near the city of Carthage two years later, Hannibal deployed a phalanx of eighty war elephants but was outmaneuvered by the legions of Scipio, the Roman general. Hannibal was defeated and, as part of the peace struck with Rome, all of Carthage's elephant corps had to be surrendered.

The enormous demand for African elephants as a substitute on the battlefield for those from Asia was waning fast in the Mediterranean world, but its impact lingered far, far longer. In the effort to obtain elephants, new avenues for accessing ivory had been opened in the African continent. A steady trade in tusks obtained from existing herds continued long after the time when the animal itself was deemed of military interest. After Alexander, African ivory would come to rival that from Indian sources, and would soon overtake it in importance.

THE PEOPLES IN and around the Indus Valley in the western Indian subcontinent were probably the first to domesticate the elephant. They had developed an exceedingly complex relationship with *Elephas maximus* from very early times; for example, there is a carved steatite seal from Mohenjo-Daro from the third millennium BCE showing an elephant wearing a saddle blanket. An elephant's intelligence and great strength make it possible for it to be trained to undertake a wide array of heavy tasks, from pulling trees and hauling timber to towing huge carts and lifting heavy loads. But elephants may have first been used symbolically—there could hardly be a more impressive mount for a ruler to sit on than a tamed elephant—and as a fearsome weapon of war; early Sanskrit texts extol elephants primarily for their military value. Elephants can be made to do gory jobs—directed to execute prisoners by squashing them or pitted against other elephants in fights to the finish—so it's not surprising that by the first millennium BCE they were being used in battle to smash through infantry and push down wooden fortifications, all the while operating as mobile platforms for archers. Indian potentates kept the tradition of war elephants alive many centuries after it had been abandoned elsewhere, primarily for prestige, the way mounted cavalry units are maintained in modern armies and trotted out for parades.

The elephant functioned as a symbol of power and other noble attributes in many cultures. In India the creature would go beyond that to became the focus of religious devotion, even worship. By the second millennium BCE there was a deeply entrenched Indian elephant culture, regarding not only the animals' capture and training and use in warfare but their role in religion. Elephants are everywhere in Hinduism: they serve as the pillars of the world, carrying the earth on their heads; thunder-bolt-hurling Indra rides on the back of Airavata, the mighty elephant born of the primordial sea of milk; corpulent Ganesha, the one-tusked elephant-headed demigod, is the beloved Lord of Beginnings, invoked at the commencement of all undertakings. Buddhist lore, too, is full of elephant legends and imagery; the Buddha's reincarnation as the historical Prince Gautama took place when the chaste Queen Maya was impregnated by being touched on her side with a white lotus held in the trunk of a divine white elephant.

It is far too simple to say that from the beginning of history "Asia preferred its elephants alive and Africa, dead," as one writer put it, but it seems clear that the value elephants had been given in India through domestication and the regard in which they were largely held were incompatible with the kind of wholesale eradication of herds that was taking place in Syria and North Africa. In fact, elephant protection in India was first articulated in the *Arthasastra*, a treatise on statecraft from the third century BCE. It proposed the setting up of elephant sanctuaries, and even suggested the death penalty for anyone killing an elephant within their borders. In any case, the hunting that went on would have had a negligible effect, because in the ancient world India's forests were teeming with elephants.

And those elephants supplied substantial quantities of ivory. The long tradition of ivory carving in India goes back to the third century BCE in the Indus Valley, where an ivory workshop and pieces of ivory used for small items such as combs and boxes have been excavated at Lothal ("mound of the dead") in the state of Gujarat. One ivory object of great interest is a 5-inch-long scale, marked with tiny divisions, the smallest known in Bronze Age civilization: 27 graduations over 1.8 inches, each marking a mere 1.7 mm. The object illustrates that ivory's ability to take tiny uniform markings was recognized early on, foreshadowing its later ubiquitous use as dials on European scientific instruments.

Archaeological excavations at Begram in Afghanistan have brought to light a number of objects indicating that within a few centuries there was a brisk trade in Indian ivory carvings. Begram, northwest of Kabul, was an important stop on one of the routes of the Silk Road, the vital trade route that wound across central Asia from China to the Mediterranean and played a key role in Eurasian cultural exchange from the first century BCE on. The ivory (and bone pieces) found at Begram include animal, human, and mythological subjects in an eclectic range of styles and techniques: high and low relief, open work, double faced. They may have entered the trade route at various points from China to India but also from the opposite direction, the Greco-Roman West. Some of these ivories may have been produced locally in Begram's cross-cultural environment by itinerant Indian artisans. In any case the Indian ivory carving tradition would be impressively far-flung; one Indian ivory statuette was even discovered in the ruins at Pompeii.

ASIAN ELEPHANTS, ALSO native to China, were its first source of ivory. Among that civilization's oldest examples of worked ivory is a carved plaque with sun and bird imagery excavated in Zhejiang Province and dating from the sixth millennium BCE. By the Shang Dynasty (ca. 1600–ca. 1046 BCE) a highly developed ivory carving tradition had taken hold. One impressive bit of evidence for this is a nine-and-a-half-inch-long intricately carved ivory handle in the British Museum with much the same hooked and spiraling motifs found on the great bronzes of the period.

Ivory was prized in China but elephants were not. Still, they were first tamed during the Shang Dynasty and used for work and for war. They are represented with some realism in that dynasty's art. By the next dynasty, the elephant is depicted more fancifully (in one case, like a long-nosed piggy bank), evidence that it was becoming more and more unfamiliar. China's growing human population diminished the herds through habitat loss. Hunting, not simply for meat but for ivory, thinned out the rest. The *Zuo Zhuan*, a historical narrative of events between 722 and 468 BCE, speaks of the elephant's tusks as the reason for the creature's demise. As a revered material second only to jade in the Chinese imagination, ivory was suitable tribute and its use signaled luxury. Hairpins, chopsticks, bow tips, and inlays in furniture and on chariots were made of ivory, as was an entire bed presented to the prince of Chu in the third century BCE. Dwindling numbers of elephants lingered longest in southwest China, but it was always possible to meet the demand for ivory from southeast Asia, where an elephant culture analogous to India's had developed, and of course from India itself. In fact, ivory appears to have been a familiar, if scarce, luxury commodity across the whole of Eurasia, flowing in several directions at once, from land and sea, from source to artisan to end user.

By the Han Dynasty (206 BCE–220 CE) China was engaged in world trade. Small carved ivory objects were included in caravans sent out along the Silk Road, along with the lighter-weight luxury export items in which China specialized, such as lacquer as well as silk, which it effectively monopolized. Under the emperor Wu (141–87 BCE), the western limit of the Han empire reached the Ferghana Valley (modern Uzbekistan), but the final destination of the silks that changed hands farther west in Parthia (modern Iran) long remained a mystery; it was, of course, the Roman empire. Eventually, envoys from both east and west made direct contact in the first and second centuries CE. The *Hou Hanshu* ("History of the Later Han") records that in 166 CE, a Roman embassy to Emperor Huan arrived by sea from southeast Asia bearing gifts of rhinoceros horn, tortoiseshell, and ivory.

MOST ROMANS THOUGHT silk grew on trees, like a kind of arboreal fleece. Along with other luxury products of Asia it found its way on the caravan and sea routes to centers and ports such as Antioch and Tyre, and finally to Rome, becoming costlier with each mile. Silk was an extravagance, scandalously used. Seneca the Younger (ca. 4 BCE–65 CE), Roman statesman, playwright, and adviser to Nero, was disgusted by the sheerness of silk clothing then fashionable—"If materials that do not hide the body, nor even one's decency, can be called clothes," he sniffed. Seneca clearly had a selective view of decadence; he looked askance at diaphanous garments yet felt no compunction about owning five hundred ivory-legged tables. But then, by Seneca's time, lavish display was the order of the day among the ruling elite, and ivory, like precious metals, was an ideal material to flaunt: scarce, sensual, and unmistakable.

Ivory had been important to the Romans from early on; an ivory scepter and an ivory chair were part of the insignia of power of the early Etruscan kings. Later it was a fixture in triumphs granted to military commanders who had been victorious in foreign campaigns. Scipio Asiaticus paraded 1,231 ivory tusks along with assorted prisoners, gold, and silver in his procession in 188 BCE; Julius Caesar's triumph in 46 BCE included ivory models of captured towns. In imperial Rome, ivory was not only a traditional signifier of high office and the booty of conquest but, increasingly, the agent nonpareil of extravagant display. The wealthy and powerful vied with one another to find ever more conspicuous uses for it and could not seem to get enough of its waxy, cool feel and its aura of luxury. The emperor Caligula's favorite horse, Incitatus, ate from an ivory manger; the vaulted ceilings of Nero's Golden Palace were covered in ivory. Chariots, couches, chairs, beds, birdcages, back scratchers, doors, dolls, dice, statues, stools, shoe buckles, writing tablets, and toilet articles, including *discernicula* (rods for applying hair pomade) and the useful *strigil* (exfoliating scraper), were made from it or decorated with it.

Even Roman poets and writers utilized ivory—for its metaphorical suggestiveness. In Ovid's telling of the story of Pygmalion, in which the sculptor carves an ivory statue of a beautiful girl and then falls in love with his own creation, it is the material's fleshlike surface that encourages Pygmalion's delusion.

> *The flesh, or what so seems, he touches oft,*
> *Which feels so smooth, that he believes it soft.*

Interestingly, Ovid, Catullus, Horace, and Martial often referred to ivory as *dentibus Indis*, or Indian teeth (i.e., tusks), a term that points to the Middle East and Asia as Rome's principal source of the material. Still, poets are not geographers. Historian Anthony Cutler suggests that the "choice of place names seems to have been largely determined by a concern for meter." He argues that by the second century CE Africa "offered the richest lode of ivory to the Mediterranean world." Rome gained control of the ivory trade throughout the Mediterranean after the destruction of Carthage in the third Punic War in 146 BCE as well as unhindered access to the remaining North African elephant herds in the Atlas Mountains. With the conquest of Egypt in 30 BCE, Rome was able to extract ivory directly from Ethiopia, much of it shipped from Adulis, the Red Sea port for the kingdom of Aksum. Finally, when the empire wrested Syria from the Parthians in 64 BCE, it enjoyed an unfettered flow of ivory from the East to supplement African sources.

The rivers of moving tusks became entangled. In the first century CE ivory was shipped from the Horn of Africa eastward to India and westward from north of Mumbai as well as the Bay of Bengal. The specifics of trade were complex, full of middlemen, craftspeople, and sophisticated arrangements; a century later there is an account of Proclus of Naucratis, an Egyptian Greek sophist and merchant of luxury goods who lived in the Nile Delta southeast of Alexandria, doing a brisk business exporting ivory and myrrh to dealers in Athens catering to the wealthy.

Ivory was so efficiently extracted from its sources during the fourth to the sixth century that it became far more available, and though it was never cheap its price, relative to other precious materials, fell markedly. Diocletian (ca. 245–ca. 312 CE), the emperor who initiated the idea of splitting the empire into eastern and western halves, sought to curb inflation with his Edict of Maximum Prices in 301 CE. It fixed ivory at one-fortieth the price per weight of silver (pure silk was twenty-four times pricier). No longer a rarity, the prized material began to be used not only for religious or imperial purposes but for various baubles, even toys for the children of the wealthy.

MOST OF THE visitors wandering through Gallery 46 between the grand Cast Courts of London's Victoria and Albert Museum seemed to be on their way to more eye-catching exhibits the day I was there. In a cavernous building full of treasures, it's easy to walk by a quiet monochromatic piece, even one that repays the attention given to it, as the foot-tall yellowed ivory panel I studied then certainly did.

The famous Symmachi panel, a Roman relief from the beginning of the fifth century CE, depicts a priestess in profile under an oak tree before an altar. She is dressed in a long tunic, part of which is gathered and thrown over her shoulder, and bends her head, intent on the moment, the delicate fingers of one hand poised over the bowl (of incense, perhaps?) that she holds in the other. In the background a small child brings a vase and possibly fruit. The figures are graceful in form and rendered in masterful low relief and are bordered by a repeating lotus-and-palmette frieze that has broken off here and there. The top is inscribed "Symmachorum," a reference to the Symmachi, a prominent Roman family.

Originally the panel was joined to a similar but, alas, much more damaged one now at the Musée National du Moyen-Âge in Paris, the Nicomachorum, referring to the Nicomachi family. The diptych these two leaves formed is thought to celebrate the marriage of two important families; in both, priestesses offer sacrifices to Dionysus. As the museum's literature puts it, the panel provides "material evidence of the dying gasp of paganism in aristocratic Late Antique Roman society." This small souvenir of a fallen empire is a special postcard from the past in more ways than one. It resonates with all the inherited iconography of the Greco-Roman world—the folds in the priestess's garment alone are a visual treat—and the material itself echoed the loss of all those elephant herds that once ringed half the Mediterranean in the ancient world.

Consider this: it is nearly five inches wide, which means that each of the panels for the original diptych had to be cut from the central girth of a very large elephant tusk. Diptychs of this size were among the largest single slabs of ivory ever carved. The form itself became one of the most popular uses for ivory in the latter stages of the empire, in part because it was the tradition for Roman consuls, on elevation to office, to present carved ivory diptychs to highly placed friends in order to mark their ascension to this dignified plane. In effect, they were ostentatious announcements of political power. Because these diptychs functioned as emblems of office, laws had to be passed to forbid lesser officials who were not consuls from adopting the practice and issuing their own. Consuls in both eastern and western parts of the empire issued a hundred or more of these yearly; over two centuries, the number might have reached a hundred thousand. The late-fourth-century poet Claudian described "huge ivory tusks, which carved with iron into plaques" and engraved with the consul's name, circulated among "lords and commons. All India stood in speechless amaze to see many an elephant go shorn of the glory of his tusks."

The amount of ivory used was enormous, for the stupendous tusks that were necessary to produce the most imposing diptychs could have made up only a small fraction of the total ivory collected; the average tusk was far too small. Eventually, there were signs that this natural resource was being overexploited: there were fewer large tusks available as the total supply shrank.

I took a last look at the Symmachi panel before leaving. Now I saw something more in the scene—the tiny frown the priestess wears, perhaps a moment of reflection in the midst of her rites. Her world was passing. The chipped panel of old ivory had the finality of a gravestone.

NOT ALL ROMANS were oblivious of the connection between the extravagant use of ivory and the dwindling numbers of elephants. Pliny the Elder contemplated the eradication of African elephants as early as 77 CE, and by the fourth century Themistius of Constantinople was voicing alarm about the North African herds. By the late sixth century CE not a single elephant could be found in Africa north of the Sahara.

The lust for ivory was certainly a factor in their demise, but there was another Roman taste at work that sped up the process. The Roman military had never been very impressed with elephants as weapons of war, and although its armies used them against their enemies who employed them, their use was abandoned when the empire's strategic posture became largely a defensive one. The Roman's interest in live elephants devolved into incorporating them into performances—doing tricks in amphitheaters, and, far less happily, as part of gladiatorial combat. Pliny the Elder reports that the spectacle of slaying elephants could backfire, and he described the reaction to one such event sponsored by Pompey in 55 BCE.

> When, however, the elephants in the exhibition given by Pompey had lost all hopes of escaping, they implored the compassion of the multitude by attitudes which surpass all description, and with a kind of lamentation bewailed their unhappy fate. So greatly were the people affected by the scene, that, forgetting the general altogether, and the munificence which had been at such pains to do them honor, the whole assembly rose up in tears, and showered curses on Pompey.

Given the context, the outcry reflects a surprising identification with elephants. Most of the time sensation-seeking crowds not only would be unmoved but would fully expect to be thrilled by human-animal bloodbaths. Most of the time, of course, they were. These "entertainments" were so popular, in fact, that they may well have had a greater impact on elephant populations than that caused by the long-standing addiction to ivory. "It is likely that the use of elephants in the amphitheaters of the late Roman and early Byzantine world," Cutler soberly concludes, "contributed more to their extinction than did the exploitation of their tusks."

3

THE MASTER CARVERS' MEDIUM

On the colorful, elaborate chart of the East African coast published in Frederick de Wit's *Zee Atlas* of 1675, ships with billowing sails ply the waters of the Arabian Sea between the Horn of Africa and India's Malabar coast. They had been doing so for a millennium or more, drawn by what the map's decorative cartouche, with its cornucopia of animal and vegetable life and sumptuously garbed figures, symbolizes: the fabled riches of Africa, especially its seemingly endless supply of ivory.

In the story of ivory's global spread, common themes in its use and trade emerge again and again. But none is more constant than the ongoing impact of that trade on Africa and its once numberless herds of elephants.

FROM ANCIENT TIMES coastal commerce around the Indian Ocean had linked the East African coast to Arabia and the Persian Gulf and beyond. Arab traders in search of ivory and other goods took advantage of the seasonally alternating monsoon winds to sail to the coast south of the Horn of Africa. Arriving in ports in their lateen-sailed dhows, they bartered trinkets for tusks with the "people of Zanj" (the local inhabitants) and traded for slaves. The ivory supply, however, was limited to what local hunters could obtain from elephant herds near the coast. In the tenth century, the Arab geographer al-Masudi wrote:

> It is from this [Zanj] country that come tusks weighing fifty pounds and more. They usually go to Oman, and from there are sent to China and

India. This is the chief trade route, and if it were not so, ivory would be common in Muslim lands.

Why would African ivory find a market in countries that had their own indigenous supply? India's sources of ivory were limited. Both male and female African elephants carry tusks, but only male Asian elephants normally have them, and these are usually smaller than those of their African cousins. And in Africa, elephants were hunted, but the peoples of India chose to domesticate many of theirs. As a result, elephants and their ivory were controlled largely by the wealthy and powerful for their own princely purposes. Yet there was a steady demand for tusks to provide the usual dagger and sword hilts, boxes, and handicrafts, and also to make the traditional and indispensable ivory marriage bangles worn by virtually all Hindu women. "In the days of *sati*," writes Abdul Sheriff, "the widow followed her dead husband into the funeral pyre bedecked with her bridal ornaments. After the abolition of *sati*, the bangles were nevertheless broken as a demonstration of her grief. If the wife happened to predecease her husband, she was of course cremated together with her bridal ornaments." This created an enduring market for imported African ivory, which was larger in diameter and provided more bangles per tusk and was often less brittle to work than Indian ivory.

In China, al-Masudi assured his readers, "the kings and their military officers use carrying-chairs of ivory; no official or person of rank would dare visit the king in an iron chair, and ivory alone is used for this purpose." Such uses were nothing new. There is evidence that Chinese officials in the Tang Dynasty (618–907) used ivory tablets as emblems of their office. By al-Masudi's time China's ever-shrinking elephant population had long since been inadequate to supply the empire's need for this status-symbolizing substance. But far-flung trade routes made African ivory available.

After the Prophet Muhammad's death in 632, the new religion of Islam spread rapidly east and west from Arabia. Propelled by the hereditary caliphates and later by religious reform, Islamic states stretched from what is now Pakistan to the Atlantic, taking in the Middle East, all of North Africa, Sicily, and much of Spain by 850. Muslim Arab conquests across

North Africa established powerful kingdoms and trade routes across the Sahara in search of gold and ivory. Camel caravans linked Marrakesh and Fez with Timbuktu and other entrepôts where Africans exchanged elephant tusks for salt and swords and pots and pans. These new sources of ivory helped take up the slack in supply caused by the Roman extirpation of North African herds, although tusks were still being shipped east and west from the Horn of Africa. In 991 a Berber prince was able to send the caliph of Córdoba "eight thousand pounds of the most pure ivory."

Islamic Spain, like every other major court in the medieval Mediterranean region, commissioned ivory objects. Córdoba, the capital of the Umayyad caliphate, became the most sophisticated city of Europe and a center for the production of luxury goods, including ivory vases, chess sets, and caskets to hold perfumes. Fussily detailed, deeply carved reliefs of humans, animals, and birds, looping knots, and elaborate borders typically fill the ivory panels of these portable expressions of power. Many carry informative inscriptions; from these, scholars know that the ivories were largely commissioned by members of the ruling family. A pyxis (cylindrical container) made for Ziyad ibn Aflah, the caliph's prefect of police, is replete with images of authority. It shows a seated figure (probably Ziyad himself) riding on an elephant among a riot of other animals and attendants. But such objects were put to poetic as well as propagandistic purposes. The shape of a pyxis topped with a domed cover lent itself to use in Arab poetry as a metaphor for a beloved's breast. One such lovely rounded ivory pyxis covered in vegetal designs from the workshops of Madinat al-Zahra carries its own interpretation in an inscription on the lid.

> The sight I offer is the fairest, the firm breast of a delicate girl.
> Beauty has invested me with splendid raiment,
> which makes a display of jewels.
> I am a receptacle for musk, camphor, and ambergris.

When elephant ivory was scarce, thin panels were used to maximize the material; they were decorated with painted scrolling arabesques in lieu of carving. When ivory was abundant, it could be used to create "oliphants," elaborately carved hunting horns made from elephants' tusks; their sheer weight makes it unlikely these were ever used for anything other than ostentatious display.

SHIPMENTS OF IVORY to Byzantium were disrupted by its war with Persia in 540. Thirty years later, after the Persian conquest of southern Arabia closed off Red Sea trade routes to Constantinople for ivory from both Africa and India, they largely halted. Ivory carving in Byzantium didn't resume on a large scale until the late ninth century, about the same time as the first extant ivories from Islamic Spain. Ivory was then coming to Constantinople on Arab vessels, as it was to Spain. But the material would never be as abundant in Byzantium as it once was, and its scarcity increased its preciousness.

Ivory became a vehicle for Christian religious art, which turned to new styles of expression. Classicism, with its fidelity to nature, fluidity of form, and delicacy of expression, lingered on in the secular art of luxury objects for centuries after the adoption of Christianity as the official religion of the Roman empire. In religious art a derived naturalism was still being used—there's the splendid sixth-century carving representing the Archangel Michael in the British Museum—but even that style would fade, spurned as if inappropriate for the sacred subject matter. Figuration became less gracile and began to wear its symbolism heavily, as if artists were uncomfortable depicting the body. Doubtless it had something to do with the eighth- and ninth-century doctrinal struggles with iconoclasm—the rejection of religious image making—that preoccupied the empire and finally ended in a cultural stance that rejected the religious images of others as idols but regarded Christian images as icons worthy of veneration.

Yet despite the shifting depictions, the ivory carver's exacting, time-consuming craft remained the same. How best to utilize the structure of the tusk had been known even in prehistory. There was no way to predict what subtle interior grain patterns might show up in the final piece, but they were more prominent toward the exterior of the tusk and almost unnoticeable in the milkier center surrounding the nerve canal. Small plaques could be cut with their backs to the pulp cavity, but large slabs had to be cut vertically from the thick section of tusk above that. To ensure matching color and similar grain pattern, slabs for diptychs had to be cut from the same tusk.

None of this was easy before the ancient world added metal tools—saws, burins, scrapers, chisels—to the carver's kit, which made it possible to extract the largest-size slab from a tusk, cut pyxides, and execute precise patterns and minute details.

Some carving was surely done freehand, but elaborate pieces were planned with care, the design for reliefs drawn on and then lightly scored. A groove was carefully incised around a face or the bordering frame as a precaution when undercutting the surrounding ivory with an inshave. Although it was possible to disguise a minor scratch or draw the eye away from an imperfectly proportioned foot, slicing through the ear of an emperor or nicking the halo of a saint with a slip of a sharp tool would ruin months of work. The carver's guidelines were always smoothed away with a bit of abrasive fishskin before polishing with emery, but these are sometimes still noticeable as ghostly marks in angled sunlight.

I picture these artisans at their benches, working with infinite patience over their commissions in a demanding craft whose traditions and skills were centuries old. As time went on, however, fewer got to practice it. Although ivory remained available (in ever-smaller quantities) in the workshops of Constantinople through the eleventh century, as Cutler notes, "it all but disappeared thereafter." The only known ivory pyxis from the later Byzantine empire is a diminutive version created for the imperial court, a mere inch and half in diameter.

After the fall of Rome in 476, elephant ivory was scarce in Europe for centuries, and even the detailed knowledge of the animal that the ancient world possessed was largely lost. Instead, many objects were carved from the poor man's ivory: bone. Bone is always available, wherever animals are slaughtered, and although it can be worked with some effectiveness its variable, sometimes spongy structure, flecked through with minute telltale channels that once held nerves and blood, make it of interest primarily as a cheap carving material. To be fair, the compact outer area (as opposed to the inner, cancellous part) of, say, the leg bones of cattle or horses is hard, dense, smooth, and workable and was widely utilized from the fourth century on for utilitarian items such as knife handles, buttons, spoons, pins, and boxes. The carvable part of bone is thinner and more brittle than ivory, but as it can be polished and waxed to give it a shine it was often used in combination with ivory—for example, to provide passable inlays and minor marquetry when there wasn't enough costlier ivory available to completely cover a small casket.

However, there was another dentin available in Europe: walrus tusk. The walrus ("whale horse"), also called "morse," did for the medieval world what the hippopotamus had done for the early eastern Mediterranean—provide an alternative source of ivory. The ponderous Atlantic walrus, *Odobenus rosmarus rosmarus*, moves its substantial one-ton bulk clumsily on land but gracefully in the water, diving to depths of three hundred feet in search of mussels, snails, crabs, and fish on the sea bottom. Native to the polar north from the Canadian to the Russian Arctic, it inhabits coastal pack ice, migrating with the seasons and heaving its wrinkled, bulbous body onto land in herds that can number in the thousands. Its most striking feature is great spikelike tusks, which both bulls and cows have. These large canines are bigger in the bulls, reaching two feet or more in length and up to twelve pounds in weight.

Viking traders were probably the first to introduce walrus ivory into Europe. Following settlement by Iceland in the late tenth century, Norse society in Greenland traded polar bear skins, gyrfalcons, and walrus ivory for iron, wood, silk, and silver. The king of Norway, who later received walrus ivory in tax payment, distributed it as gifts to other rulers. Volga Bulgars even brought walrus ivory to central Asia, where it reached the Muslim world as "fish-teeth" and was prized for the crafting of sword hilts and dagger handles. The availability of the material was helped by the fact that walruses ranged much farther south during the Middle Ages than they do now, reaching Scotland and the North Sea. In fact, walrus tusks provided the material for nearly all the ivory carving done in northern Europe in the eleventh and twelfth centuries and remained an important source. Not surprisingly, walruses were ruthlessly hunted to meet the demand, and their numbers declined drastically as a result.

The primary limitation of walrus ivory, like that of hippo ivory, is its relatively small size, which restricts its use to plaques that fit in the palm of the hand and modest sculpture in the round. In addition, the tusks are oval in cross section with a cementum covering over an outer layer of primary dentin (which shows virtually no grain) and a secondary or inner dentin, marbled in appearance, which can sometimes be noticed on the backs of relief carvings. But these material restraints were hardly drawbacks for northern European artisans of the period. This was the age when monastic foundations were principal centers of artistic production, and where scribes, hunched over copies of the Gospels in their *scriptoria* (workshops), created jewel-like worlds within the confines of a capital letter. The effort it took for a monk to wheedle and worry a recalcitrant bit of dentin into a lustrous relief that glowed with religious feeling was inseparable from his vocation and devotion. The arts of manuscript illumination and ivory carving were closely allied, and the fact that many small ivories share imagery with these manuscripts—and were often painted similarly—makes it likely that they were produced side by side in workshops.

Ivory sculpture, especially reliefs of sacred book covers and diptychs, which functioned as small shrines, achieved great importance in Europe in the ninth and tenth centuries. The pair of tenth- or eleventh-century carved ivory plaques of David dictating Psalms and the Judgment of Solomon now in the Louvre are indicative of the genre. Each is crowded with figures—the latter squeezes in King Solomon with four soldiers, two pleading women, and another pair of soldiers about to cleave in half the disputed baby, held upside down by his feet—and still makes room for borders of acanthus leaves, all on plaques little bigger than index cards. The inward-looking and spiritually intense vision here is squirming for room in these reliefs; the exactitude of medieval art is all about the exquisite delineation of meanings for which the visual is often simply a shorthand of significations.

It is true that most ivory carvings of the period—altar crosses, bishops' croziers, reliquaries, book covers—were religious in nature but secular impulses were also expressed in dentin. In the lower Rhine, walrus ivory gaming pieces were being made and exported across Europe. The Lewis chessmen, a group of small twelfth-century walrus ivory carvings that form parts of several chess sets and were probably made in Norway, were found on the Isle of Lewis in the Outer Hebrides in 1831. Stolid, simple, and blocky, the figures feature lidless stares and a monumentality all out of proportion to their size.

Many of these early ivories have disappeared. Over time, most fell victim to fires and pillage, Viking raids, later revolutions and robberies, or sheer neglect—the usual winnowing of history. What we have left, however, is of great interest and makes up for the paucity of monumental sculpture that remains from 500 to 1050. "By turning to the art of the ivory carver," writes historian Paul Williamson, "it is possible to reconstruct, almost without a break, the stylistic and iconographic changes that occurred in the Middle Ages."

THE CRUSADES REINTRODUCED elephant ivory to Europe. Christian forces conquered Jerusalem on the First Crusade in 1095, and remained in the Middle East until 1291. Soldiers, pilgrims, and merchants came into contact with a refined Eastern culture and its luxury goods: silks, inlaid metalwork, painted glassware, ceramics, and ivory. European interest in elephant ivory stimulated shipments of tusks from East Africa along the Red Sea to Alexandria and from trans-Saharan routes to Tunis and other ports and then on across the Mediterranean to Venice, Genoa, and Marseille. After being largely unobtainable in northern Europe for several hundred years, by the middle of the thirteenth century elephant ivory was supplying a massive, religiously based carving industry in Paris.

"In liturgical prayers ivory was a synonym for the chastity of the Virgin," as one researcher observes, "and the luminous quality of its surface, particularly desirable from the latter half of the thirteenth century, naturally affected viewers' perceptions of space and mood." Ivory's qualities no longer embodied the kind of luxurious decadence the Romans exulted in—its voluptuousness had been appropriated to worship, prayerful reflection, and praise of the divine, and not necessarily in the context of a church. Williamson notes:

> It is significant that when ivory was used again in vast quantities, patronage had changed. In the late thirteenth century the ivory carving industry in the Ile-de-France was totally geared towards producing large numbers of object for private devotion, such as small diptychs and triptychs with scenes from the Passion of Christ, and ivory statuettes of the Virgin and Child. The richer the patron, the grander the object.

Some ivory sculptures pushed the limits of the size and shape of the tusk. The Sainte Chapelle Virgin (ca. 1250), now in the Louvre, is more than sixteen inches tall; a demure Mary puts her weight on one leg while supporting the Christ child on the same hip, a very natural stance and one that takes advantage of the typical curve of the tusk. These leaning Virgin and Child poses adopt a kind of Gothic *contrapposto* that was originally ivory-driven but proved so popular they were replicated in materials that didn't require it, such as wood and stone, and even show up in manuscript illumination of the thirteenth and fourteenth centuries.

Yet Gothic ivory carving was never entirely in thrall to the church. Commerce and courtly love were among the increasingly secular concerns incorporated into ivory products in the 1300s. Medieval merchants used small hand scales to confirm the weight of coins, a sensible precaution in an age that commonly clipped them. These balances and weights were kept in boxes. Fancy ones were made of ivory, with fitted compartments and religious subjects on their covers, perhaps as a way for traders to increase customers' confidence by means of a modest display of piety during their worldly transactions.

Luxury materials like ivory were appreciated openly, albeit often in the context of religiosity. An ivory casket decorated with carved panels addressing the biblical tale of the prodigal son allowed the artist to dwell on the subtheme of lust by remaining ostensibly within the moralizing narrative framework of the traditional parable. This visual cat-and-mouse game also allowed the imagination and eye of the casket's owner to linger on the earthly aspects of the story and the sublimated sensuality of the softly

carved figures, confident the tale closed with a moral lesson as neatly as
the lid on the box itself.

IN MEDIEVAL TIMES any number of fanciful ideas were taken as gospel.
One of them was belief in the existence of the unicorn. Today it's pictured
as a white horse with a pointed spiral horn sprouting from its forehead,
but the mythic creature of the Middle Ages was smaller, shown with a
goatlike beard, a lion's tail, and cloven hooves. It was also swathed in lore;
it was immortal, only the pure heart of a virgin could tame it, and so forth.
No matter—the important thing for credulous kings was that the unicorn
had protective powers: its horn could counteract poison. The availability
of a trickle of narwhal teeth through Arctic trade created an opportunity
for middlemen to sell these hitherto unsuspected, scarce tusks for far
more than their weight in gold, not just as evidence of the unicorn's existence but as magical objects in their own right.

The narwhal (*Monodon monoceros*) is an fifteen-foot-long cetacean
that looks like a mottled blubbery torpedo tipped with a long straight, spiraling spear. Related to the beluga whale, it inhabits icy channels of the
Arctic in large pods, pursuing cod, squid, shrimp, and similar prey and
disporting itself at the surface, often waving its single tusk in the air.
Males (and occasionally females) grow one of these spectacular teeth
from the left side of the upper jaw. Six to nine feet long, and tightly
twisted counterclockwise (if viewed from the proximal end), the tusk is a
great curiosity of nature. Narwhal ivory is as hard as that of the hippo and
in cross section it exhibits concentric, wavy bands. On the other hand, its
long pulp cavity renders much of it hollow and offers small working space
for the carver. Cut into pieces, it looks barely suitable to make napkin
rings, gaming pieces, or saltshakers, but short sections made handsome
sword hilts and longer ones impressive scepters for likes of the doges of
Venice and the Hapsburg emperors.

The twelfth to the sixteenth centuries in Europe were the heyday
of this vast collaborative fiction. It was possible, of course, only because

the narwhal was virtually unknown in Europe. Informed Scandinavian merchants wisely kept any details of the animal's tusk a trade secret. They understood perfectly that the narwhal was insignificant as a source of ivory, but its extremely limited supply was nicely in step with what was coveted and known to be rare: unicorn horns. They found a way to supply them. Such "horns" found ready acceptance in ecclesiastical contexts. Their spiraling forms were associated with divine potency and became magnets for sacred attributes. What more impressive processional staff could there be than that made from a unicorn's singular spike?

But it was emperors and kings, those who feared poisoning and could afford this wildly expensive antidote, who most craved unicorn horns and had them made into cups to foil assassins and ward off illness. The last reigning duke of Burgundy, Charles the Bold (1433–77), had a number of them and was careful to use a piece of one to test the dishes he was served. When the wealthy Renaissance art patron and collector Isabella d'Este died in 1539, an inventory of her possessions listed a "unicorn horn" and a "fish's tooth 'three palms long'"—clearly narwhal and walrus tusks. By Elizabeth I's time a narwhal tusk that had been presented to her was added to the crown jewels as the Horn of Windsor and valued at £10,000—the cost of a castle.

In 1646 Sir Thomas Browne wrote, "Great account and much profit is made of *Unicorns horn*, at least of that which beareth the name thereof; wherein notwithstanding, many I perceive suspect an Imposture." Actually, a Danish naturalist, Ole Wurm, had unmasked these myth-enshrouded "horns" as narwhal teeth eight years before, but belief in their medicinal powers lingered for over a century more.

UNBURDENED BY ANY precise knowledge of the elephant, the medieval world was free to imagine rather strange things about the creature. In any case, the artists of the bestiaries of the period were more concerned with depicting the supposed character of the beast, which presumed traits of restrained strength, constancy, and levelheadedness. It took several more centuries before exposure to accurate accounts or direct experience of the animal began to influence the artistic imagination.

Here and there, live elephants showed up in Europe, mostly as diplomatic gifts. The caliph of Baghdad gave one to Charlemagne in 802. It created a sensation whenever the Frankish king brought it with him on his travels. In 1254, Louis IX, king of France, sent to Henry III, king of England, an African elephant, which he kept in his royal menagerie at the Tower of London and allowed to slurp wine. Matthew Paris, a Benedictine monk and historian, made a naively charming but well-observed pen-and-wash illustration of it. But even in the 1500s illustrations of elephants in books could be highly creative. Conrad Gesner's *Historia animalium*, published in Zurich in the mid-sixteenth century, shows a pachyderm with puddling pylons for legs, a segmented trunk like a vacuum hose, and ears that unfolded like a lady's fan.

These notions about the elephant evolved in tandem with the development of science and changing European views toward the animal world. But something else was afoot. Attitudes toward the elephant were developing separately from how ivory was regarded; it was as if the animal product and its source species occupied different worlds.

In many ways they did. Ivory was being removed, transported, and reshaped far from its "original ecological context," allowing the elephant to become conceptually distanced, even uncoupled, from its own teeth. Ivory's increasing availability did not bring familiarity with the elephant along with it. As a rare material obtained from distant lands, ivory lacked the kind of immediate association with its origins that was made, say, between fine wood and forests. To Europeans the elephant was an exotic creature that inhabited faraway realms. Before it was ever seen, it was as fabled as a unicorn and just as unknown, and even after it made an appearance it still seemed a walking marvel. How ivory was obtained for trade remained mysterious and largely stayed that way, far into the future. By then the elephant would be clothed in a whole new set of meanings, valued in ways that in effect gave it a new identity. Eventually, when the connection between ivory and where it came from was made inescapable, this altered regard for the elephant would change everything about ivory—or perhaps just painfully sharpen the issue.

THE SECULAR USE of ivory in Europe proliferated after 1400. It was not only employed for the expected—inlays and panels in furniture, mirror backs and buttons, hilts and handles, knobs and nit combs—but, increasingly, incorporated into new forms of weaponry and musical and scientific instruments. Given ivory's long history of use in the decoration of spears, bows, knives, and swords, it would inevitably be worked into newer weaponry, such as the lavishly produced matchlocks and similar newly invented firearms for rulers such as the emperor Charles V (1500–58), who doted on them. Years of collaborative effort on the part of metalsmiths, engravers, and carvers might be needed to join ivory, rare woods, steel, and gold to make the sets of pistols and bird guns used by monarchs of the day, who had a taste for eye-catching scrollwork and nymph-laden inlays of hunting scenes drawn from classical mythology.

Ivory was used in flutes, lutes, guitars, and harpsichords. In the hands of a seventeenth-century master craftsman such as Matteo Sellas, the back of a guitar could be enveloped in a dizzying geometric pattern of ebony and ivory zigzags. Ivory would be used for complicated folding compasses, rulers, and sundials not simply because of the decorative possibilities it afforded, but because its surface could be scored precisely, leaving tiny markings that could be filled with ink to create a compass rose, detailed graduations for measurement, or indeed any kind of dial desired for the scientific instruments then being invented. Sundials were widely used to set the unreliable timekeeping devices of the period. Nuremberg in particular became famous between 1500 and 1700 for its ivory sundials—pocket-sized, folding diptychs, some of which could be used in different latitudes. Other uses for ivory aided personal hygiene. Ornate ivory flea traps became an aristocratic fashion accessory in the eighteenth century; these hollow, perforated cylinders, baited inside with blood or honey, were worn around the neck as a pendant.

By contrast, the artistic use of ivory became less inspired after 1400 and more standardized in spite of growing refinement. The production of small sculpture and reliefs that reworked a small set of familiar subjects gradually ceased, although workshops continued to turn out derivative altarpieces and formulaic marriage caskets. It's curious that Renaissance artists showed comparatively little interest in ivory, although any number of factors might have been at play. Perhaps it was that ivory carving seemed by then a minor art more suited to the hermetic expression of religious feeling than the expansive ideas of the new humanism. For some, the material might have been too restrictive in size, but the kind of monumentality in miniature in which Benvenuto Cellini, using gold, so brilliantly excelled would surely have been possible in the right hands. In the end, the lack of interest might have been largely a matter of fashion. But by then the idea of ivory had embedded itself in the European imagination, along with its inevitable associations. Ginevra de' Benci, the famous young beauty whose portrait was painted by Leonardo da Vinci in the 1470s, was described by her contemporaries as having "fingers white as ivory." It was only a matter of time before ivory would make its artistic comeback.

IN OCTOBER OF 1582, an expeditionary band of well-armed Cossacks led by the Volga River pirate Yermak Timofeyevich defeated the army of the Tartar khanate in western Siberia after a three-day battle. Yermak had been hired by the Stroganovs, a powerful merchant family, to protect their trade in the Urals against attacks by the Tartars. The khanate's forces revolted three years later, wounding Yermak, who tried to escape by swimming a river but, dragged under by the weight of his chain mail, drowned. But the counterattack was ineffectual; Siberia was retaken, colonized, and eventually annexed into the Russian empire. One bit of lore attached to Yermak is the claim that he saw a large hairy creature while exploring the wind-swept taiga. Later speculation had it that he had seen a mammoth. This is pure legend; that mammoth ivory began to be shipped to Moscow after the time of his conquest is not. It even reached London by 1616.

Cossacks, hunters, explorers, soldiers of fortune had set out to explore the vastness of Siberia after the Russian conquest, and when the fur trade waned they discovered yet more riches in the shape of tusks.

Mammoth ivory—*mamontova kost* in Russian—had been unearthed in Siberia since ancient times. Indigenous peoples there would come across tusks emerging from the banks of rivers during spring thaws and would pull them out and barter them in village outposts. But they feared digging further, unsure as to what kinds of creatures the great bones and parts of frozen carcasses belonged to and the forces that might be disturbed. The Yakuts thought they might be the remains of giant rodents that made the earth shake as they tunneled underground with their immense horns; other peoples imagined the beasts were aquatic. Still, Siberians had made use of this fossil ivory, carving pendants and other figurines, and they knew others found the tusks valuable. Since the ninth century, Arab and Asian merchants had sought it.

The tusks had also made their way to China, where they provided an additional source of ivory to supplement what could be obtained locally and by land and sea from Africa. Emperor Kangxi, who was fond of expounding his learning, addressed his ministers in the last year of his reign, 1722, on the subject of the "great animal of the rat kind" found "in the northern regions, under the ice layers." He reminded his audience that the Russians who had recently presented themselves at court had confirmed the presence of year-round ice, and went on:

> Now, in Russia, near the shores of the Northern Ocean, there is a *shu* [rat or rodent] resembling the elephant, which makes its way under ground, and which dies the moment it is exposed to light or air. Its bones resemble ivory, and they are used by the natives in manufacturing cups, platters, combs, and pins. These we have ourselves seen, and we have been led thereby to believe in the truth of the story.

The idea that the tusks were the fossilized remains of a long-extinct ancestor of the elephant is a modern one. At first, many Europeans thought that the various fossils that had been dug up by then were "figured stones" or "sports of nature" or, of course, evidence of unicorns. The Dutch traveler Nicolaas Witsen used the word "mammoth" for the first time in Europe in his *North and East Tartary* (1692); he heard the term spoken by Russian settlers in Siberia, who used it to describe the kind of giant bones and teeth he was shown.

Its puzzling origins did nothing to discourage Europeans from making serious use of mammoth ivory by the early eighteenth century, although it was typically more brittle and yellowed than that of elephants. In the mid-nineteenth century one naturalist estimated that two hundred tons of it had been sold during the previous two centuries; this amount would have required that the tusks of a hundred mammoths be recovered annually. That would not have been difficult, considering that Siberians, sparked by greed for the tusks, had long had centers specializing in the trade in tusks from the tundra.

The mammoth had reentered history—preceded by its ivory.

AS THE APPETITE for ivory spread across the whole of Eurasia, merchants from Europe to the Far East turned to Africa to obtain more tusks through trade. Whenever that proved insufficient to meet the demand, elephant-rich regions were often simply plundered, typically as part of a larger scheme of colonization.

Both coasts of Africa were affected. India and China had been the major markets for the East African trade since the tenth century and remained so into the nineteenth. For the Africans, it was an economy based on the exchange of their raw materials—ivory—for manufactured goods and luxuries: bolts of cloth, brass wire, bright beads. By the fifteenth century elephants were disappearing from the Indian Ocean coast and had to be sought hundreds of miles inland. There is abundant evidence of ivory trading and ivory-working centers deep in the interior, such as those on the north bank of the Zambezi (in today's Zambia) and in the Limpopo Valley (modern South Africa). A similar push inland occurred in Abyssinia (Ethiopia), bringing new ivory-producing lands into existing trade networks. The Indian Ocean ivory trade became increasingly international, taking ivory to Europe as well to as the East.

The ivory riches on the other side of the continent were sought as well. The trade vastly increased following Portugal's pioneering voyages of exploration in the mid-fifteenth century. The Portuguese were not seeking ivory when they traveled down Africa's Atlantic coast, but they were quick to recognize its value, along with gold, peppercorns, and slaves. Dutch, English, Spanish, French, Swedish, Danish, and German traders soon followed, naming chunks of the coastline after the products they found: the Grain Coast (modern Liberia), the Gold Coast (Ghana), the Slave Coast (Togo, Benin, and western Nigeria), and the Ivory Coast. (Curiously, the last is the only one of the names that has stuck, an impressive geographic reminder of ivory's potency in the history of world trade.)

These riches—gold, ivory, and slaves—traded places in importance. The slave trade grew in the sixteenth century as the Portuguese and Spanish developed overseas plantations. It came to dominate the transatlantic trade after the Dutch elbowed the Portuguese aside in the seventeenth century and, along with the British and the French, developed slave plantations in the Caribbean and, later, America. In general, the ivory trade as a whole never approached the value of the slave trade and was less important than gold from the Gold Coast. But in areas such as the Ivory Coast, where the slave trade was not as developed, the export of tusks was the key to obtaining prized European imports. Among the desirable goods were firearms; in the mid-eighteenth century, the city of Birmingham in England was producing a hundred thousand muskets annually for the West African trade. What did the Europeans get? From the evidence in Dutch and English shipping records, at least 2,500 tons of ivory—over a quarter of a million tusks—left West Africa in just the twenty-six-year period between 1699 and 1725.

The European-driven ivory trade piggybacked on the modest trade in elephants' teeth that local rulers had controlled. As the system of exports cranked up, traders dealing through African middlemen were able to exploit herds close to the coast. The trade in tusks was so heavy, and the competition so keen between the English and the Dutch along the Upper Guinea coast, that in 1663 a Portuguese missionary was astonished to see an English ship loaded with what looked like thousands of tusks, some weighing as much as four *arrobas* (128 pounds). "Every year, a ship comes to take a similar cargo," wrote André de Faro, adding,

This does not take account of the ivory that is purchased in the other rivers of Guinea, where there are similar factories, which dispatch other ships; and the Dutch are also buyers in the ports of these rivers. There are, therefore, more elephants in Guinea than there are cattle in the whole of Europe.

At first the supply of ivory seemed to be endless. The elephant-hunting Vili people of the coastal kingdom of Loango above the mouth of the Congo River had been trading ivory with the Europeans as far back as the 1570s. In 1608 they were selling twenty-three tons a year to the Dutch alone from the tusks they could obtain on their forays into the equatorial forest. Eventually, the impact of the trade on elephant populations began to be felt. By the 1660s Vili hunters had to undertake journeys of three months' duration in the middle Congo before they could return with the ivory needed.

AND WHAT OF the Africans?

Many of the peoples on the continent had been hunting the elephant from prehistoric times. The animal was an immense prize: meat from a single beast could feed an entire village, its hide could be made into shields, its tail hair made into fly whisks, and its great incisors carved into any number of handicrafts, jewelry, ceremonial objects, horns, prestige items, totems, and masks.

It's often claimed that ivory use on the part of African peoples never threatened elephant populations, but that may be due to less advanced technology more than to anything else. "It is an urban, and even subtly racist myth," writes John Van Couvering, "to credit indigenous peoples with an intuitive dedication to ecological balance," adding,

> The observed equilibrium is not always to the liking of the people who must participate in it, as witness the alacrity with which they abandon their wholesome way of life as soon as they can obtain more certain and effective methods of dominating the environment.

Before European colonization there were countless herds of elephants left in Africa, despite centuries of pursuit by Egyptians, Romans, and others seeking ivory. One obvious reason was that Africans found elephants hard to kill with primitive weapons. Hunting them was exceedingly dangerous and required great skill and planning, and of course the protection only careful rituals could provide. It was not undertaken lightly, and almost always was done by large groups. Some faced elephants armed solely with spears; needless to say, success was difficult to attain and conferred great status. Sometimes traps—pitfalls and deadfalls—were used as well as poisoned arrows or lances. Or hunters perched motionlessly in trees over elephant paths and plunged heavy harpoons into passing animals from above. Sneaking up behind an elephant to sever the hamstring tendon of a rear leg with a light ax could instantly anchor the beast to the spot, but at such close quarters an attacker risked a nasty demise. Whatever the technique, wounded animals that escaped had to be tracked, found, and dispatched if they hadn't already expired.

When an export market developed for ivory, indigenous peoples with elephant-hunting traditions like the Vili gained new economic incentives to pursue elephants specifically for their teeth. Skilled hunters were recruited on both coasts. As elephant herds thinned, hunting parties had to go ever farther afield, pushing into new regions and penetrating deep into the central forest. Elephants had to be located, pursued, and brought down and their tusks cut out and carried long distances to central collecting points before being transported in quantity to the coast for trading.

To improve their odds, muskets obtained in trade were added to African hunters' arsenals by the 1700s. The late-eighteenth-century Scottish explorer Mungo Park described how Bamana hunters of Mali would track a herd for days, following until one animal strayed from the rest and could be cautiously approached.

> They then discharge all their pieces at once and throw themselves on
> their faces among the grass. The wounded elephant immediately applies
> his trunk to the different wounds, but being unable to extract the balls,
> and seeing nobody near him, becomes quite furious, and runs about
> amongst the bushes, until by fatigue and loss of blood he has exhausted

himself, and affords the hunters an opportunity of firing a second time at
him, by which he is generally brought to ground.

These ivory-gathering expeditions constituted a considerable step
up from what had formerly been traditional and self-contained practices.
Elephants and their ivory were of great importance in a number of
African societies. In the Edo kingdom of Benin, which flourished from
the fourteenth to the nineteenth centuries in what is today southern
Nigeria, for example, ivory was a royal monopoly of the *oba*, a ruler at the
head of a system of titled chiefs who claimed divine origins and demon-
strated it through his art-laden ceremonies. It was the custom that the
oba had to be awarded one tusk from every elephant killed in his realm,
making ivory a kind of currency. In 1522 a female slave at the desirable
age of seventeen or eighteen was worth precisely two tusks. Huge stocks
of ivory were amassed, particularly after hunters gained access to European firearms, which precipitated the widespread slaughter of Nigerian
herds.

The *oba* supported craftsmen's guilds, including one responsible for
the inspired carvings of the court; these artisans were so skilled that they
worked directly on the raw ivory, disdaining preliminary sketches. Among
the most striking pieces of Benin ivory sculpture were huge ancestral altar
tusks, each one covered with elaborate surface carving and curving back-
ward out of a stolid head of cast brass. The evident skill and complex visual language in these pieces give them a timeless quality, but Benin art
was never static; it evolved in contact with neighboring peoples, such as
the Yoruba and, notably, the Portuguese, after the initial contact with
them in 1485.

Among the African products that the Portuguese took back to Europe in the fifteenth and sixteenth centuries were impressively carved
ivories, including oliphants, from the West African coast, the Sapi area of
Sierra Leone, and Benin, as well as the Kongo kingdom in Central Africa.
These treasures eventually made their way into the collections of the
Medici of Florence, Albrecht Dürer, and the elector of Saxony in Dres-
den, among others. Some of these ivories reflected African artists' efforts
to incorporate portrayals of Europeans into their art and iconography, and
included carvings made specifically for export that reflected European re-

quests for particular functions (spoons, saltcellars, pyxides) as well as imagery. Afro-Portuguese ivories, as these cross-cultural carvings are called, show a mix of European and African motifs, in which the long-haired, sharp-nosed, jut-jawed Portuguese stand out to non-African eyes.

What is less obvious is the African frame of reference through which these Europeans were reconfigured. For Africans, the arrival of Europeans was akin to having visitors return from the land of the dead: the sickly pallor of their skin, their strange ships and language and superior technology, their homes across the sea—they seemed to have reversed the journey the departed took westward toward the ancestors. The use of ivory adds another layer of meaning to these Afro-Portuguese carvings, particularly those from Benin. There its chalky color was linked to ritual purity, making it appropriate for offerings to Olokun, the god of wealth and the sea, as well as communication with the dead.

These themes mingle poignantly in the beautifully modeled pendant ivory mask in the Metropolitan Museum of Art in New York (and its nearly identical counterpart in the British Museum in London), believed to be a sixteenth-century portrait of the then *oba's* mother. The face, dignified and haunting, with scarification marks on the forehead, is surrounded by a tiara and a virtual choke collar composed of the bearded faces of Europeans who brought wealth from overseas—and took so much of it away in ivory and slaves.

FROM THE SIXTEENTH century on, the extraction of ivory from elephant-populous lands developed a new pattern that would often be overlaid on the basic trade in tusks. A portion of the ivory was handed back to local artisans to be carved to order for a ready market in the home countries of the colonial powers. The earliest examples of these hybrid art forms, when artisans wrestled with new uses and images, fitting them into their own craft, have the vitality of a visual struggle between different traditions. Later, when locals understood better what was wanted, artistic acquiescence resulted in increasingly formulaic production.

Anglo-Indian furniture is a particularly apt example. The British

East India Company based in Calcutta (Kolkatta) in West Bengal soon put the extraordinarily rich ivory-carving tradition in the subcontinent to use. At the beginning of the eighteenth century the company sent skilled workers from Britain with "great quantities of English patterns to teach the Indians how to manufacture goods to make them vendible in England and the rest of the European markets." The effort was so successful that English joiners petitioned against it, fearing the ruin of their trade. Many eventually gave in and signed up with the East India Company, then stayed on to open similar businesses in India, drawing on the carpenter caste for labor. These *vadrangis* copied the "muster" (model) sent from England "with the most exact and servile fidelity." At the low end of this imitative production were things like small workboxes carved out of ivory in the shape of English thatch-roofed cottages; at the top end, artful East-West fusions, such as the elegant and exquisitely carved solid ivory chair given to the first governor-general of India.

The ivory trade was now far more than commerce in raw material; it was a trade in ivory objects as well, sometimes highly specialized. The Portuguese used their outposts in India and Sri Lanka to put local ivory carvers to work producing Christian religious images for use in Portugal and Brazil. The Spanish took this trend even further, making the Philippines the leading producer of Christian art in ivory from the sixteenth century into the nineteenth. Carvers there made an entire array of somewhat Gothic devotional objects for the Catholic church in Spain, Mexico, and Latin America as well as in other Asian countries.

THE CHINESE HAD gone directly to Africa too, and they returned with ivory. That was merely one of many feats accomplished by Admiral Zheng He, the eunuch commander of the seven extraordinary armadas sent out by the Yongle emperor from 1405 on "to make manifest the wealth and power" of Ming China in foreign lands. That it must have done: there were two hundred ships in each armada and about a third of them were 385 to 440 feet long. Quite unlike the bellicose explorations of the Portuguese and other Europeans, these voyages around Southeast

Asia and across the Indian Ocean to the African East Coast founded no colonies, cornered no trade, toppled no rulers, and enslaved no one, despite the fact that there were twenty-seven thousand soldiers in the fleet (although the pirates encountered were crushed). The point was to impress any potentates along the way and draw them into the Chinese tribute system, in which whatever goods offered the emperor as gifts would be outdone by what he would bestow in return, a very grand and roundabout way to initiate trade contacts. Zheng He brought his largest ships back filled with ivory, gold, spices, and lots of exotic animals to amuse the Ming court—lions, leopards, ostriches, even giraffes.

These extravagant voyages came to an abrupt end, perhaps because of intrigues at court; in 1436 even building deep-sea vessels was banned. In any case they had been an aberration. China's traditional foreign policy was always most concerned with its territorial borders, and the empire turned inward for another six centuries. But goods went out—large quantities of Chinese porcelains were exported to the Middle East and the African East coast—and ivory came in.

China needed it, whether it was fresh tusks from Africa or mammoth tusks from Russia. In the late Ming Dynasty (1644) elephants were still found in Yunnan, Guangdong, Guangxi, and Hunan provinces, but their numbers were on the wane, pressed by the growing human population and the spread of agriculture that came with it. Unlike India and the countries of Southeast Asia, where elephants played an important role in religion and culture, in China they were widely regarded as crop-ravaging nuisances. But their tusks were highly desirable; ivory carving flourished during the Ming Dynasty, aided by increased availability from a variety of sources and widespread patronage for decorative arts. During the late Ming, the city of Zhangzhou in Fujian Province on the eastern coast enjoyed relative freedom from government trade constraints imposed on other centers. It had close ties with the Philippines, and some think that Chinese craftsmen there were also encouraged by the Spanish to provide Christian icons for the European market. That may have been the impetus for the ivory figure carving tradition of the late Ming and early Qing dynasties (1644–1911), which focused primarily on divinities associated with Buddhism and Taoism but also on other auspicious deities and legendary heroes.

During the Qing, ivory artisans turned out functional objects as well—table screens, wrist rests, intricately embellished brush holders, and other accoutrements needed for a scholar's desk. No material other than ivory permitted the minutely detailed and precise carving undertaken to satisfy the Chinese fascination for miniature worlds inspired by Taoist notions of paradise and the Buddhist ideal of "seeing the world in a seed."

Ivory retained its long-standing aura as a material fit for royal delectation. The twelve-leaf silk album *The Pursuit of Pleasure in the Course of the Seasons*, made for Emperor Qianlong (1736–95) by Chen Mei, one of his court painters, addressed the emperor's dual passions: his garden and his women. The coy depictions of court beauties promenading in the imperial gardens so touched the emperor that he commissioned a more permanent duplicate on twelve facing ivory leaves inlaid with jade and gold by five famous artists; the ivory ground, naturally, needed no coloration to depict flesh. (Qianlong apparently also ordered up a more graphic version as a personal pillow book—sex manual—for the instruction of his consorts.) With these kinds of distractions, it's no wonder that when Lord Macartney's delegation arrived at the Qing court in 1792 to discuss a commercial treaty with Britain they were told to go away.

Chinese ivory carving proceeded on its own track, reaching even greater technical refinement with the famous "devil's-work balls," intricate carvings of concentric balls within balls, a specialty of Guangzhou (Canton). These puzzle pieces captivated European viewers, who wondered how such surfaces could be carved, one inside the other. It was, of course, a matter of infinite patience. Conical holes had to be bored into a sphere of ivory, and then tiny, sharp, angled cutting tools were painstakingly worked in the holes to free up the inner sphere and then each successive sphere; finally, they were all incised with patterns in a similarly probing, maniacally obsessive fashion. European fascination with these objects helped inspire entirely new methods of working in ivory.

LACKING INDIGENOUS ELEPHANTS, the Japanese were late to ivory. They may have first become familiar with it in the form of carvings imported

from China in the sixth century. By the seventh and eighth centuries ivory
had been adopted by the elite as a precious material for sword scabbards,
official emblems, name seals, Go pieces, lids of tea caddies, and plectra to
play the samisen. By the sixteenth century a steady, if small, supply of raw,
unworked ivory was being brought into Japan (most likely from China),
although shipments must have been affected after 1639 when trade was
restricted, ports were closed to most foreigners, and the Japanese themselves were forbidden to travel under pain of death.

Not surprisingly, the ivory carving of the period was centered on domestic objects, primarily for the wealthy. There were the expected combs,
fans, boxes, and the like, but ivory was also a favored material for functional accessories of kimono dress. In the Edo (or Tokugawa period,
1603–1867) kimonos were common. Women carried small items in their
sleeves; men overcame the lack of pockets by tying personal items to cords
tucked up under the kimono sash and kept from slipping down by means
of a toggle. Among the paraphernalia that might be attached were medicine and writing kits, tobacco pouches, money purses, pipe cases, flints,
fans, and knives. The complete ensemble consisted of the *sagemono* (sus-
pended object), *ojime* (cord fastener), and *netsuke* (the toggle).

The making of netsuke—miniature sculptures with holes that allowed them to be threaded on cords—became an art form in itself, stimulated by exacting sumptuary laws then in effect that set out strict dress
codes for each social class, from aristocrats on down. Merchants, who
were constrained in the ways they were permitted to flaunt their wealth,
turned to netsuke, which were considered an acceptable form of display.
Ivory, like the rare woods and horn also used, was ideal for this purpose—
luxurious, but not on the level of the gems and jewelry forbidden to the
nonaristocratic rich. Netsuke makers were pushed to test their skills by
carving ever more complex items from a single piece of ivory. The range
of subjects was vast: demigods, urban scenes, bugs and slugs, fishes and
foxes, mythological monsters with wiggling tongues, grotesque hermits
and elaborate erotic couplings, a skull with a snake crawling through the
eye socket. Netsuke were appreciated for their auspicious references,
beauty, and humor, and above all the sheer technical skill of various master carvers.

The Japanese were captivated by the possibilities of the material; a few centuries later they would become the biggest consumers of ivory in the world.

CERTAIN USES OF ivory—combs, thrones, figurines—crop up in every culture and period. Conceptually, the way ivory entrenches itself in the imagination of various cultures follows its own well-worn set of tracks: its color makes it both a religious and a secular symbol of purity and perfection; its rarity and expense make it a marker of luxury and wealth. In European and Asian contexts, the literary counterpart to the sculptor's interest in its fleshy sensuality has long been ivory's use as a metaphor for pale, flawless skin. Shakespeare reached for the comparison in *The Rape of Lucrece* ("her breasts, like ivory globes circled with blue"). By the eighteenth century in Europe it had turned into a corporeal commonplace, routinely applied to faces, fingers, shoulders, thighs, and finally other body parts as well. In John Cleland's *Memoirs of a Woman of Pleasure* (1749), the heroine gushes over the "maypole" her lover brings to the coital fray ("such a length, such a breadth of animated ivory!").

In Europe, ivory's cluster of associations firmly fixed the importance of the material in its own social and conceptual sphere. Ideas about the elephant were also developing, but in an almost completely separate realm of discourse in which ivory figured little. In his *Historie of Foure-Footed Beastes* (London, 1607), English parson and naturalist Edward Topsell says of elephants:

> There is no creature among al the Beasts of the world which hath so great and ample demonstration of the power and wisdome of almighty God as the Elephant: both for proportion of body and disposition of spirit; and it is admirable to behold, the industry of our auncient forefathers, and noble desire to benefit us their posterity, by serching into the qualities of every Beast, to discover what benefits or harmes may come by them to mankind: having never beene afraid either of the Wildest, but they tamed them; the fiercest, but they ruled them; and the greatest, but they also set upon them. Witnesse for this part the

Elephant, being like a living Mountain in quantity & outward appearance, yet by them so handled, as no little dog became more serviceable and tractable.

The Asian and African elephants that were brought to Europe in the seventeenth century drew huge audiences and reinforced these admiring views. One was taken to Italy and was drawn by Bernini; another was displayed in the menagerie at Versailles (where it dipped bread into buckets of soup) and still more (from Samarkand) were shown at the court of the czars in Russia. By 1850 some fifty pachyderms had gone on view before transfixed crowds in Europe.

AFTER A PERIOD in which ivory carving in Europe seemed wedded to slavish imitation of other art forms, it came to life again in the baroque and reached dizzying levels of virtuosity. Various centers in Germany and Dieppe in France were the engines behind the revitalization of the craft in the early 1600s. A series of inspired carvers combined the refinement of Renaissance modeling with the emotional engagement and grandiose passions of the painting of the period (think Rubens) in a judicious choice of forms: small statuary, medallions, lavish furniture. They even began to sign some of their creations. The soft, satiny surface of ivory was put to striking use in portrait busts and relief medallions by artists such as David Le Marchand (1674–1726), an expatriate Huguenot who fled France for Edinburgh and then London. He developed a well-deserved reputation for creating a sense of monumentality in his small ivories, and Queen Anne, George I, Isaac Newton, Christopher Wren, and Samuel Pepys all sat for him.

Ignaz Elhafen (1658–1715), who worked primarily in Germany, was only one of many ivory-carving masters. His *The Death of Cleopatra* relief (ca. 1700) in the Victoria and Albert is a dazzling masterwork: picture looking at a large cylindrical section of tusk cut in half lengthwise and oriented to form a panorama of the last of the Ptolemies in her final agonies, all carved in deep relief within the tusk's concave inner form.

Cleopatra—who had once filled a tomb with ivory—is shown nearly nude and collapsing; tiny asps twine about her breasts, while no fewer than seven attending maids in equal states of undress prostrate themselves or writhe in despair. (All this, mind you, plus drapery, pottery, and foliage, in a piece seven and a half by four inches.) The material's own monochrome milkiness softens a scene that would have been garish in full color while bringing to mind the timeless whiteness of ancient marble friezes.

Some of Elhafen's other ivories, like those of his compatriot carvers, explore opposite extremes. At one pole is the marmoreal and rather chilly perfection of his *Venus,* and at the other the visual excess of his *The Rape of the Sabines,* a fat tankard encircled by a conglomeration of mythical figures that dissolves into a rather confectionary composition once you look past the superb technique.

In the late eighteenth century, Europe's last major artistic efflorescence in ivory ends. From then on the sculptural use of it will lapse back into a decidedly minor role. Ivory itself took on a different kind of importance.

PETER THE GREAT had been given Chinese silk hangings as an imperial gift from the Kangxi emperor (the mammoth-curious one) after settling a treaty. The designs were apparently not to his taste, but the czar found a use for them: in 1711 he bestowed seven pieces on Cosimo III de' Medici, in return for an ivory turning machine he wanted. He'd had one since 1698, and even ordered up two more six years later. Eventually he had dozens of these lathes, housed in an imperial workshop—the czar's Cabinet of Mechanical Equipment—manned by journeymen and master craftsmen, including the innovative machine builder Andrei K. Nartov.

Why? Peter the Great was a ruler with a passion for putting on a workman's apron, picking up a chisel, and spinning a piece of tusk on a mandrel, sometimes far into the night. Following Nartov's designs, the czar turned out "goblets, candlesticks, measuring instruments and sundials, openwork pyramids with polygonal stars inside, scepters, columns, engraved snuffboxes and polygons, all made of ivory." He wasn't unique in his passion. For some two hundred years, as historian Klaus Maurice has detailed, the crowned heads of Europe—in Austria, Bavaria, Saxony, Italy, France, Denmark—spent untold hours at their lathes turning ivory.

The lathe was not a new invention in Peter's time. Its basic form had been around as long as the bow drill and the potter's wheel, to name two other complex tools known to the ancient world. It was common in Rome and used in medieval times. Cutting a piece of wood, for example, into the desired shape by rotating it while applying a cutting tool was far more efficient than simply carving it. The later addition of the flywheel, which allowed whatever was being worked on to whirl continuously in one direction, was a huge advance. By the seventeenth century lathes had evolved into complicated marvels of metal and wood, full of intricate gearing and articulated parts. Lathes became "rose engines"—ones that had attachments for producing tricky circular and elliptical patterns. The development of adjustable cams that allowed the workpiece to be set at an angle or shuttle back and forth while being worked meant that all kinds of difficult shapes could be tackled.

It might seem surprising that these inventions didn't immediately jump-start the industrial revolution. At the time they were built, however, what they could do for the production of goods wasn't appreciated. They were regarded as useful for the amusement and elucidation of princes. Part of what the aristocracy was then taught (riding, fencing, dancing) went back to feudal times, and part of it (religion, study of the classics) was thought essential mental furniture for rulers. Increasingly, some practical grasp of art and science and manufacturing was deemed a useful addition to court education. Happily for them, the nobility could dabble in activities others worked at for a living. In fact, it was a marker of their class that they could acquire knowledge without the need for financial gain. Turning was an ideal way for fickle princes, beset by numerous distractions, to gain a sense of accomplishment, thanks to the assistance of a machine. And, given its rarity, costliness, and uniformity, what more princely material to play with than ivory? It seemed predestined for the lathe.

The courts of Europe embraced turning and filled their private "wonder cabinets" with hundreds of their own signed creations. Princes first tried simple receptacles that looked like the finials of fat bedposts, then progressed to ever more whirled and twirled ivory fantasies. "Art ennobles the ivory and the originator, Maximilian, Duke of Bavaria, ennobles the art, in the year 1608" reads the inscription on the bottom of his elaborate ivory candlestick. Everything about turning appealed to the nobility. Even the way the lathes could be set up to follow a predetermined course that would lead to an inexorable result seemed to replicate the apparatus of a well-ordered state under absolute monarchy.

As a prescribed noble activity it backfired somewhat: it was too successful. By the mid-eighteenth century advisers at courts began to consider turning a pastime just as idle as the traditional ones. "One must be patient if documents requiring signature remain unsigned for months because of a mistress, a foreign painter, or even a lathe, but is it laudable?" lamented a diplomat.

As might be expected there were always master artisans connected to these court workshops who were available to help the nobility spin their creations. Marcus Heiden, who served under several Saxon dukes and did turning of his own, wrote of his dizzily towering ivory chef d'ouevre—a drinking vessel balanced on an elephant and topped with a ship under full sail—which he began in 1637 and finished two years later. According to Maurice, "Heiden never mentions or describes technical difficulties in his book, other than that the ivory tusk was unusually large and heavy and had been selected in Amsterdam from 300,000 tusks!" The figure is surely an exaggeration, but no doubt an enormous amount of ivory was brought into Europe for the pleasure of princes.

In the end, ivory turning was no more than a courtly rehearsal for the nineteenth-century transformation of ivory carving from an individual undertaking to mass production. Two Frenchmen in particular helped that process along.

WHEN NICHOLAS GROLLIER de Servière (1596–1689), a military engineer who designed movable bridges and similar machinery and served in Flanders, Germany, Italy, and Constantinople, retired to his estate in Lyon he busied himself with the construction of models and machines. These included a "reading wheel" that consisted of a circular drum of shelves, each of which held an open book, a perspective machine for artists, floating bridges, water pumps, and regulator clocks. De Servière was also among the leading turners of his time, creating astonishingly unlikely forms on lathes of his own design.

These *pièces excentriques,* as he called them, "tended to be tall and precariously thin, like the circular steps that are attached to each other by tiny stems, looking like a pile of coins held together by bits of toothpicks, but all turned from a single tusk." They included a series of illusionistic carved ivory balls within balls, far beyond what the Chinese had ever attempted with their handcraft, some with needle-sharp points and fleurs-de-lis that baffle the imagination as to how they were carved. But de Servière's interest in turning was not centered on the creation of ivory fripperies. For him his *pièces* were important demonstrations of what could be accomplished through mechanical design, which inevitably focused attention on the lathes that made these fantastic forms possible.

Charles Plumier, a young friar from Marseille, was among those who came to goggle at de Servière's ivory figures and particularly the machines that made them. In his youth Plumier had been "hypnotized" by the lathe. He wrote a classic and influential work on the subject of turning, *L'Art de Tourner en Perfection* (1701), which revealed the construction of every lathe he could examine, some of whose blueprints were closely guarded secrets. Plumier's treatise managed to sum up the known technology of turning, thereby laying the groundwork for machine-assisted manufacturing. By the middle of the eighteenth century, interest had shifted from the ornamental products of the lathe—which had always been confined to singular individual objects—to the development of the machines themselves.

Once lathes capable of cutting metal had been harnessed to the production of parts that could be assembled, the possibility of the modern factory was born. The lathe, in all its variants, became one of the vital machines of the industrial revolution, which was shortly to transform the world—and, ironically, the manufacture of ivory products.

PART 2

IVORY UNDER THE SAW

4

PIANO KEYS AND
BILLIARD BALLS

There is no known portrait of Deacon Phineas Pratt, but one imagines he had much the same face that his youngest son, Julius, showed in his: firm-jawed, thin-lipped, full of high-collared rectitude, and with a piercing gaze fixed firmly on industry and enterprise. On April 12, 1799, Pratt, a goldsmith and clockmaker then resident in the Potapoug Quarter on the Connecticut River, was issued a U.S. patent for a hand-powered "machine for making combs." Like Eli Whitney's cotton gin and Samuel Colt's revolver, this Yankee invention proved to have far-ranging impact. An ingenious combination of flywheels and fan belts, thin circular saws and adjustable precision clamps on a wooden stand, it greatly shortened the time required to cut the teeth of combs, thereby mechanizing the manufacture of perhaps the single most popular ivory object in history.

A fundamental shift in ivory's importance had occurred, quietly and without fanfare. By demonstrating how it was possible to mass-produce ivory items, Pratt's invention initiated the transformation of world trade in ivory. The possibilities of what could be done with ivory were no longer limited by what the carver's tool, guided by the eye, could do, or even by the shapes that could be coaxed into being when it was turned on a lathe. From now on, tusks were fed like logs into indefatigable machines. Ivory, whose uses had formerly been restricted to artistic productions and handcrafted items for the wealthy and powerful, would now become a middle-class luxury material.

Now consider something else. Industrial use meant that ivory would be consumed at a startling rate. In fact, it was processed with such rapidity it began to smolder under the racing saws, which is why the blades in all the machines had to be water-cooled. Although very difficult to burn, ivory sometimes scorched anyway, as if in protest at the machine process. Workers described the smell as "animal" or "dirty" or the odor given off when a dentist drills a tooth, only on the vastly bigger scale of a factory floor.

PRATT SET UP shop with another son, Abel, in what is now called Essex Village. Within a couple of years a rival, Ezra Williams, had set up his own comb business at the mouth of the Falls River. In 1809 Phineas Pratt II and his brother-in-law, George Read, started a comb business and constructed a dam and a waterwheel in the nearby village of Deep River to supply power to their ivory-cutting machinery. A lawsuit and several mergers and improvements to Pratt's invention later, the foundations of an ivory manufacturing industry had been laid in the United States. The area was fertile ground for nascent capitalism. Essex Village, centered on a peninsula bordered by two coves on the Connecticut River and a short distance from Long Island Sound, was known early on for shipbuilding. Its yards turned out six hundred wooden sailing vessels between the American Revolutionary and Civil wars. Essex was chock-full of highly skilled artisan-entrepreneurs and ivory cutting in the area began to take hold, supplied by an increasingly steady stream of African tusks. Sailing ships brought them across the Atlantic to the deepwater ports of Boston, Salem, Newport, and New York, where they were transferred to steamboats and coastal packets that could breach the shoals at the mouth of the Connecticut River and finally dock at Essex or Deep River. There they were offloaded and stacked in horse-drawn carts like cords of firewood for the final, short step of their journey. New England craftsmen were now successfully competing with established British comb makers who still turned out their ivory products by hand; and, by 1839 the Americans had branched out into piano key manufacture—a move that would eventually make two Connecticut firms the world's largest producers of ivory goods.

NEW ENGLAND IS full of places like Bull's Bridge or Falls Village or Cheshire, named for prominent settlers or geographic features or appellations elsewhere on the globe. Ivoryton, Connecticut, isn't like that. A town document granting permission for the construction of the post office in 1880 has "West Essex" crossed out and "Comstock" inserted and crossed through as well and, finally, "Ivoryton" written underneath. Therein, in compressed fashion, is the history of "the town that elephants built." Local lore has it that the name was selected because ivory was brought there by the ton.

Driving off Route 9 and taking exit 5 toward Deep River, I had to slow down or risk missing the quick turns that take you to Main Street in Ivoryton. Unlike Essex a few miles down the road, which has just the right mix of upscale inns and restaurants, espresso bars, ice cream shops, antiques stores, and a marina full of yachts to attract crowds of weekend tourists, Ivoryton is decidedly lower-key: a playhouse, a couple of taverns, some shops, and a few grand houses on its leafy winding streets. If I hadn't been looking for traces of the extraordinary trade that once went on here, I might have missed Ivory Street—although I found more direct reminders, such as the chest-high crescent tusks in the entranceway to the Victorian gingerbread building that houses the local library. There, shelves of volumes on local history and albums of old photographs put faces to names in the story of ambition, greed, and achievement outlined in ships' logs, personal accounts, newspaper clippings, and corporate records.

Two more figures emerge from the pages of these volumes to join the Pratts as principal actors: Samuel Merritt Comstock, who largely shaped Ivoryton, and his partner, George A. Cheney, who strengthened the ivory industry's connection to East Africa via Zanzibar. Comstock— inventor, entrepreneur, paternal employer—was born in 1809 in West Centerbrook, a village of a dozen houses that, many decades and several name changes later, became Ivoryton. Comstock began making combs around 1834 and by 1848 had formed S.M. Comstock and Company and consolidated his ivory cutting in Ivoryton, making, according to his advertising materials, "Ivory Combs, Ivory Tablets, Ivory Tooth-picks and Toy Combs." A local history of the time reported that Comstock "was a man of enlarged views, honest and upright in his dealings with his fellow men, and endeavored strictly to obey the golden rule." Comstock's factory and its employees dominated the village. He built dormitories for his workers, opened a factory store, and drew up plans for the village's future development, making Ivoryton one of the first factory towns in the United States.

In 1860 George Arthur Cheney, a principal in the prominent New York ivory-importing firm of Arnold, Cheney and Company and a former ivory trader in Zanzibar, invested $4,500 to join with Samuel Comstock in forming Comstock, Cheney and Company. Based in Ivoryton, the new operation added production of ivory veneers for piano keys. Imports of tusks grew, and by 1873 the company had opened an even larger factory. A photograph from that year shows workers in bowler hats and smudged aprons lined up in front of the white-clapboard "ivory shop." A few prim-looking women stand on the lower steps; the shop foreman and two small office boys stand in the doorway, flanked—and dwarfed—by a pair of gigantic tusks, while Cheney and Comstock lean out of a side window.

The business grew rapidly and workers had to be aggressively recruited. After Comstock's death in 1878, it fell to Cheney to extend his efforts at welfare capitalism by building scores of factory houses for workers as well as a men's club and a library. There was a factory-sponsored baseball team with elephant emblems on the uniforms; it was said the children of the village cut their teeth on ivory rings and that even the outhouses had ivory doorknobs. At its peak, Comstock, Cheney and Company employed some seven hundred people, including a number of women, and in the process created the wealth that made the grander houses, still visible behind ironwork gates, possible. Ivoryton became the most affluent section of Essex township after the Civil War; shipbuilding was waning and other businesses in the area, such as the production of witch hazel and bicycle spokes, were easily overshadowed by the ivory industry. Today, the remaining two-story houses where Swedish, German, Italian, and Polish workers once lived have long since been sold and renovated and now house more mobile, middle-class employees who have a couple of cars each in their driveways.

Comstock, Cheney had competitors, even in its heyday. By far the most important of them was just up the road, in Deep River: Pratt, Read and Company, the substantial, well-positioned firm that resulted from a merger in 1863 of Pratt Brothers Company, George Read and Company, and the Julius Pratt Company of Meriden, bringing together businesses begun by the descendants of Phineas Pratt and their partners.

These factories in Ivoryton and Deep River became the colossi of the ivory-cutting industry worldwide. Between 1891 and 1903 they processed more than two and a half million pounds of ivory. By the beginning of the twentieth century the two firms together were processing 90 percent of the ivory imported into the United States—which had by then overtaken Britain to become the dominant consumer of ivory.

THE IVORY BUSINESS in the United States was born of technological revolution but remained dependent on a natural resource from halfway around the world. No other source of dentin but elephant tusks could supply the industry's needs. Walrus, hippopotamus, and boar ivory— none was uniform enough or available in sufficient quantities to be industrialized, although of course in modest amounts they still supplied individual carvers. Interestingly, it took until the nineteenth century, when elephant-based ivories were being mass-produced, for North Americans to become aware of the indigenous art that Inuit culture had developed out of walrus ivory. Along with such practical purposes as snow knives, sled runners, needle cases, and harpoon fittings, it was used for ear pendants, decorated pipes, and carefully worked amulets and charms, typically of marine mammals and worn to bring a hunter luck. Hippo ivory, though used for some princely turning in Europe and, given its hardness, for false teeth (including George Washington's), was destined to remain permanently in the shadow of the far larger units of workable ivory that elephant tusks represented. Boar teeth? Apart from their use for the handles of beer steins and corkscrews and the side plates of jackknives, these modest tushes remained of minor commercial interest.

On the other hand, the teeth of cachalots—sperm whales—which might have been regarded as a useful by-product of the whaling industry that grew to such prominence in the United States in the nineteenth century, never achieved that status. Although some two dozen teeth of *Physeter macrocephalus*, the largest toothed mammal, can be used for ivory, limited supply, a somewhat marbled appearance, and an internal double dentin layer like that of walrus all worked against its commercialization. Sailors on whaling voyages with spare time on their hands decorated these stumpy teeth, some as much as eight inches long and up to two pounds, by means of scrimshaw: incising lines on them with a sharp tool and then rubbing in various pigments to darken the etched design. Curios then and collectible now, these souvenirs of the short-lived age of what's been called blubber capitalism are, like narwhal tusks, intriguing but brief asides in the story of ivory. Still, the fact that sperm whale teeth (*tabua*) were revered and used to carve sacred figures in Fiji and elsewhere in Polynesia is yet more evidence that ivory in any large mass has sufficient seductive power to attract carvers of any culture.

IN NINETEENTH-CENTURY photographs of the wagons used to move the ivory from wharf to factory, there's usually a pair of patient farm horses harnessed to a low-sided, oak-slatted conveyance variously stacked with tusks, laid in clumps of scuffed crescents with their ends swooping up like arrested wave tops or stacked upright on their bases like gigantic bleached thorns. Some are longer than the hardworking driver—clad in overalls with a felt hat crushed on his head—is tall. These wagonfuls must have been an arresting sight on the winding rural roads that led to the doors of the factory vaults. The windowless stone-and-stucco buildings maintained the steady, cool, and damp environment necessary to keep the ivory in good condition.

The stenciling and notations on each tusk, added at various stages of its journey, indicated the importer's or firm's name, port of entry, source—Sudan, Mozambique, Abyssinia, and so forth—grade ("Zanzibar prime" and the like), and weight. But each had to be evaluated before use. An ivory selector, valued for his detailed knowledge and long experience in handling the material, weeded out cracked or otherwise damaged tusks and graded the rest into categories—"soft" or "hard," depending on appearance and workability.

Soft ivory from East Africa—so called because it was easily cut and worked—was preferred. Before being sent to the ivory-cutting department, tusks were washed, reweighed, marked with an order number, and soaked overnight in a peroxide bath. Throughout the nineteenth century the processing of ivory continued to stimulate the development of machines specifically for precision work on it. The first a prime African tusk typically fell under was the "junking" machine, a kind of band saw used to divide it along its length into four-inch-high cylindrical chunks. The operator clamped down a selected tusk, say of soft ivory, ideally around sixty pounds, to the bed of his machine. Because of the natural curve of the tusk, cutting a series of sections at right angles also created a series of circular waste wedges, wafer thin on one side of the circle, perhaps an inch thick on the other; such chunks created between the drums were salvageable for tool handles or inlays. "Junkers" worked carefully, mindful of the rare but real hazard of hitting a musket ball long buried in the tusk. After the long tooth was cut into segments, the parts were placed in a box covered with a damp cloth and left in the foreman's cupboard. He in turn had the responsibility of marking the tusk parts for further cuts and took each one to his bench for study. How best to cut the drum so that the maximum number of marketable items, above all piano key covers, could be produced was a matter for strong light, an eyeshade, and some reflection. There was no cut-and-dried method to extract all possible profits from it. Every tusk was individual, and each cylinder of it had to be examined carefully. Waste was to be avoided, but any leftover bits could be made into novelties or, if nothing else was possible, toothpicks. Once the foreman had scored the flat of the tusk part, he handed it over to the next worker, and so on. Yet even in the process of reducing the material to the smallest usable tiddlywink, ivory drew the workers' fingers to it. "As it is sorted, sliced, cut, and matched," one observer wrote, "each workman actually fondles and caresses it."

IVORY HAD BECOME the plastic of its age. That's the message embodied in the array of pale and faintly yellowed ivory products from Pratt, Read and other local manufacturers, laid out on the red felt of the display

cases on the second floor of the Deep River Historical Society's headquarters, a nineteenth-century house on Main Street. There were items
that could be turned on basic lathes, such as collar buttons, cigarette
holders, candlesticks, and doorknobs. Another group consisted of a selection of combs (including the ever-useful nit comb for picking lice)
and other flat sticklike machine-produced items: piano key tops, spatu-
las, dominoes and dice, folding fans, rulers, letter openers, and letter
folders that looked like ivory tongue depressors. The larger ones were
used to create neat creases in the weighty paper of official correspondence; "congressional" letter folders even came in a "senatorial" size that
was slightly bigger than the one designed for members of the U.S. House
of Representatives.

The exhibit included a clutch of specialty pieces, including fancy
folding toothpicks for a gentleman's vest pocket (what better tool for the
task than a minute bit of the mightiest tooth in nature?), hairbrushes,
snuffboxes, cuff links, and pistol grips, all intricate items that would not
easily lend themselves to rapid reproduction on machines. These custom
objects had been created from rough blanks supplied to specialty manufacturers such as jewelers and instrument, gun, and tool makers, whose
craftsmen fitted them to their products and finished them, much as furniture makers made use of the ready-made diamond-shaped ivory inlays
also on display.

Although there had never been a significant tradition of hand-carved
ivory in the United States, there had always been interest in imported ivory
handicrafts, particularly those from Asia. Chinoiserie, a fad in Europe and
America in the eighteenth century, had a brief recurrence in the nineteenth, and Japanese netsuke became available and collectible after Com-
modore Perry's 1853 naval expedition opened trade with Japan. For
Americans, the attraction of these ivory objects was their exoticism. Asia,
whose long craft traditions had found all sorts of uses for ivory, was able to
meet this interest with such oddities as *kan-handa* (Ceylonese ear picks),
Chinese cricket cages, and "doctors' ladies." The last were reclining ivory
medical dolls made so that a respectable woman, who was not permitted to
be examined directly by a physician, could point out the part of the body
that ailed her. These droll, tiny-footed odalisques, with their poppyseed
eyes and rosebud mouths, looked dumpy at first but became gradually

eroticized as the market for them grew, gaining svelte curves and enhanced bustlines for European and American delectation.

This trickle of craft trade from the East did nothing to slow the inexorable transformation of ivory from an individual carver's medium to a
deluxe material adapted to mass production. The growing middle classes
of the United States, Britain, and the whole of Europe increasingly encountered ivory in the reproducible forms of shaving brushes, cigarette
cases, saltshakers, poker chips, the handles of teapots (ivory is a poor con-
ductor of heat), even keypads on early telegraph transmitters that made
use of ivory as an insulator of electrical current. Ivory was incorporated
into an entire range of medical devices—urethral syringes, tooth extraction keys, surgical instruments. In the 1700s ivory had been used to create
amazingly lifelike medical models of the eyeball, and by the next century
it was used for prostheses, not just false teeth but artificial legs and noses,
and even a cosmetic ivory penis. Eventually ivory was incorporated directly into the body in the form of fracture pins, nasal implants, hip re-
placements, and the like.

Ivory was also used for advertising geegaws, in which the elephant
might appear as a logo. As symbols of exoticism far removed from everyday
life in nineteenth-century America, images of pachyderms, rather than
linking the product to the source, only separated them further. When the
connection was made, as in an 1864 advertisement for ivory products illustrated with a muscular African man in a loincloth extracting a tusk from
a kneeling elephant with a tooth puller, it was treated as a joke.

For Americans, the reality of the elephant was framed largely by its
appearances in U.S. circuses of the period. As early as 1804 two elephants
were touring the country, drawing crowds fascinated simply by the sight of
the creatures. Soon enough that wasn't enough, and by 1834 seven circuses and fourteen menageries were touring the Northeast and elephants
were performing tricks. By 1869 there were forty-two traveling shows. In
1881 showman extraordinaire P. T. Barnum purchased the famous
Jumbo, the London Zoo's African elephant, for $10,000 and exhibited
him to excited crowds for several years, until he was killed by a train. Even
then, Barnum found equal success by having Jumbo stuffed and towed
around the circus ring on a wagon to the strains of a funeral dirge. "Behind them," writes Shana Alexander, "plodded Jumbo's 'widow' elephant,

Alice, veiled and shrouded in black, and she was followed by all the circus's regular elephants, each animal holding a black-bordered bed sheet in its trunk, and trained to wipe its eyes on cue."

The mania for ivory had its matching elephantine excesses.

THE FERTILE FRICTION between the timeless natural treasure of ivory and the newly unleashed power of the machine gave birth to astonishing creations. A sheet of ivory, fourteen inches wide and *fifty-two feet* long, sawn from a single tusk, was sent by Julius Pratt and Company of Meriden, Connecticut (one of the forerunners of Pratt, Read), in 1851 to the Great Exhibition at the Crystal Palace in London's Hyde Park. Ivory veneer-cutting machines had been invented previously; a French patent was granted for one in 1826 and others were patented in England and France in 1844. One of the secrets of obtaining long sheets was cutting the ivory exquisitely thin. The machine Julius Pratt used was capable of producing an ivory veneer one-thirtieth of an inch thick, almost translucent. In fact, it was now possible to slice ivory so paper thin a newspaper could be read through it.

These machine methods for unwrapping the layers of a tusk with the ease of peeling an onion not only allowed for the production of ivory veneers for fine furniture but made it easy to supply thin plates of ivory for the painting of miniatures, by then a well-established craft on both sides of the Atlantic.

Portrait miniature painting had its start in sixteenth-century Europe as a way to keep or carry small images of loved ones when separated by lengthy travels, or to introduce people to each over long distances, say, for the purpose of proposing marriage. All sorts of materials were used: cardboard, vellum, chicken skin, copper, and, by the end of the seventeenth century, ivory. A thin ivory plate, no thicker than a couple of playing cards, was an ideal "canvas" for watercolor or gouache and often had a backing of glued-on paper to make it easier to handle when the painting was wet. Some commentators have suggested that since the surface would be covered, painting on ivory must have been a matter of underscoring the luxuriousness of the portrait through the use of extravagant materials—the specious addition of irrelevant value. That notion flatly ignores the artistic advantages of ivory. With its hydroscopic qualities, ivory responded to watercolor and gouache, even with its touch of gum, with nearly the thirst of paper. Its translucence returned light underneath thin washes of paint, suggesting depths impossible to achieve on a completely opaque ground. And of course its own softness and color could be put to direct use. Kunz reminds us that the prominent eighteenth-century English miniaturist Richard Cosway "frequently left parts of his figures entirely uncovered by the brush, depending altogether upon the delicate tones of the ivory to represent the hue of the skin."

The first American ivory miniatures were painted in the 1740s and the technique became popular for the creation of personal mementos occasioned by marriages, births, deaths, and extended separations. Ivory merchants sold tiny sheets of the material to itinerant portraitists and skilled artists alike, who used small easels and magnifying glasses to work on such an exacting scale. Later techniques for producing ivory veneers made larger sheets available for painting, but they were much more expensive. Page-sized sheets cut from tusk cylinders also had a tendency to curl. In some ways the jewel-like effects possible in painting on ivory were simply better suited for portraits that would be kept in small lockets and tiny keepsake oval frames under beveled glass. Still, it was only as minor a craft as the creativity that was brought to it. The possibilities inherent in the medium attracted early-nineteenth-century talents such as Benjamin West, Charles Willson Peale, and John Singleton Copley, and the gripping, dark images Goya managed to compress onto small plaques of ivory in the 1820s constitute one of the last great gasps of ivory in art, albeit in a supporting role.

The painting of ivory miniatures was one of the few avenues open for nineteenth-century women artists in the United States—the delicacy of the work and its confined ambitions were thought appropriate for female abilities. One of the most successful of these painters was Sarah Goodridge (1788–1853), who studied under the famous portraitist Gilbert Stuart before opening a studio in Boston and embarking on a thirty-year career, producing two or three miniature portraits a week until failing eyesight forced her to retire. Her coolly confident *Self-Portrait* (1830), a small watercolor on ivory, shows the artist in a three-quarter pose, a shawl around her pale neck and shoulders. Simple and striking, it looks like something she would show to her prospective clients as a sample of her work. But her most arresting miniature is the self-portrait painted two years previously, the one she titled *Beauty Revealed*. Painted in watercolor on a very thin rectangle of ivory, 2⅝ inches high by 3⅛ inches long, and presented as a gift to her most prominent client, the orator and statesman Daniel Webster, it is a portrait of her bare breasts, encircled in a swirl of pale cloth. Probably painted from their image in a mirror, they are rendered with great care, right down to a tiny beauty mark and the soft highlight under their fullness reflected from the twisted cloth below. Not only is the execution perfect, but so is the whole idea of it: painted on the very material that is the ideal simile for flesh, the artist used the thinnest of washes to allow the ivory to glow behind the pale pinkness of her tiny, daring bare-all message. The preserved correspondence between Goodridge and Webster does not confirm an intimate relationship but, as John Updike writes, she could have been simply offering herself to the recently widowed public servant: "*Come to us, and we will comfort you*, the breasts of her self-portrait seem to say. *We are yours for the taking, in all our ivory loveliness, with our tenderly stippled nipples.*"

Webster married money instead. But he kept the gift for the rest of his life in a leather case tucked in a drawer of his desk—as Updike puts it, "like a sugar-drop at the back of his mouth."

FROM 1850 TO 1910 Britain imported roughly five hundred tons of raw ivory a year. London was already a hub for a variety of animal-based commodities, and its trade network came to include everything from guano to cochineal, rhino horn, tortoiseshell, sperm oil, fur, antler, wool, hides, python skins, and ostrich feathers. The Port of London Authority's Ivory Floor—the ground floor—in No. 6 Warehouse beside a basin connected to the oily Thames became the central vault of the world trade in ivory. It arrived by ship at the lower docks of the Port of London and came in sacks of jute or hemp, holding one or two tusks each, to the Ivory Floor, where it was unwrapped, examined, classified, and stored before being sold. The tusks were grouped into lots from the "milk teeth" shed by baby elephants to the massive "hundred-pounders" of old males; workmen hefted and weighed them and then laid them out on the floor in nestled curves for inspection. Expert examiners passed an experienced hand down their lengths and looked into their hollows. Two parallel lines were marked on tusks with noticeable cracks, two wavy lines on those with long cracks. Honey-brown mammoth tusks took up a small section, as did the odd barrel of narwhal tusks and boxes of hippo teeth.

An increasing portion of what landed on the crowded docks and was stored in this high-ceilinged brick edifice built in the 1820s was auctioned off in the frequent sales held in Mincing Lane to foreign buyers and, in turn, exported to countries hungry for their own supplies. In 1859 a quarter of the ivory brought in went elsewhere; by 1913 some 70 percent of the million-plus pounds of ivory was bought for other markets.

Unquestionably, however, Britain was a huge consumer of ivory throughout the nineteenth century, absorbing much of it in its own newly mechanized ivory industry. Most of what was obtained went for brush and cutlery handles, for which the material was ideally suited. "Unlike bone or animal skin, which degrade with constant heavy rubbing," cultural historian David Shayt explains, "ivory generally retains its overall form and finish even under constant usage." The increasing wealth of Victorian England and the growing desire for decorative goods led to a vastly increased market for flatware, whose specialization became one of the important markers of class and refinement. After 1860, when food on the dining table was no longer laid out in dishes for guests to help themselves, but served à la russe, one course at a time by servants, the need for separate cutlery for these dishes created a market not just for knives, forks, and spoons but for entire matched sets that included lemon knives, sweetmeat forks, marrow spoons, ham bone holders, cucumber saws, grape snips, bonbon tongs—the list of specific implements could top one hundred. A service for twelve could require ninety-six spoons alone. Ivory was the material par excellence for the handles of these refined eating tools, and even for the bowl itself of a caviar spoon. How big a business was it? The cutlery firm of Joseph Rodgers and Sons, in Sheffield held twenty-six tons of better-grade ivory in its vaults in 1878 just to be sure of covering its yearly needs.

Ivory was a perfect Victorian substance, signifying both purity and prosperity; it was eminently suitable for parlor bell pulls, a lady's mirror back, the knob of a gentleman's cane, or the haft of his straight razor. It was flexible enough to be cut into knitting needles and riding whips. As in the United States, manufacturers wasted nothing; the smallest bits of tusk were turned into toothpicks, and the bagfuls of granular dust sprayed out by cutting tools were gathered up and used for fertilizer or burned and used in ivory black paint—Renoir's favorite formulation of the color— and India ink. Ivory shavings were even boiled with water to produce a jelly, which apothecaries hawked as especially nutritious and highly beneficial to invalids.

"I SHALL LOOK upon it as an altar upon which I will place the most beautiful offerings of my spirit," Beethoven replied in anticipation of the gift from Thomas Broadwood in 1818 of a London-built piano from his firm. By then nearly deaf, the composer appreciated the increased sonority that could be coaxed from the up-to-date English piano. The invention of a musical instrument whose strings vibrated when struck with keyboard-operated hammers seems to have been conceived in the fifteenth century, but credit for building the first one is given to Bartolomeo Christofori, a harpsichord maker in Padua, who accomplished the feat imperfectly around 1710. A number of English and German makers contributed badly needed design improvements, and by the end of the eighteenth century there were 454 piano makers in London alone. Broadwood and Sons produced six thousand square pianos and one thousand grand pianos between 1780 and 1800. The company added steam power to its factory in the early nineteenth century and began cranking out seven hundred pianos a year, easily distancing its closest Viennese rival, which could turn out only fifty.

The pianoforte, as it was called then, was embraced with alacrity by musicians and the middle classes alike, and Americans were quick to add their share of innovations to it. A novelty at the beginning of the Revolutionary War, the piano was an established concert instrument by the start of the nineteenth century. Most were imported from Europe when Jonas Chickering, the Henry Ford of his trade, was apprenticed to a piano maker in Boston in the 1820s. It was the right moment. "No house is considered properly furnished," a contemporary social observer proclaimed, "unless one of these instruments, polished and gilded in the most extravagant manner occupies a conspicuous place in the principal apartment." To make his meaning abundantly clear, he added, "The Piano-Forte is a *badge* of gentility, being the only thing that distinguishes '*Decent People*' from the lower and less distinguished kind of folks, known by the name of '*middling kind of folks.*'" Chickering industrialized his trade, shed his partners, and in 1829 produced forty-seven of the fat-legged, high-quality square pianos that were to be the mainstay of his growing market. In 1840 he was granted a patent for the iron frame he would use in most of his instruments to give them durability and sonority, and by 1852 his factory was making more than 10 percent of the estimated nine thousand pianos produced that year in the United States.

A year later, Steinway and Sons was founded in New York by the German piano maker Heinrich Steinweg and four of his sons. By 1860 the family business had 350 workers, their sweat assisted by steam power, producing thirty square and five grand pianos per week. These instruments incorporated a growing list of improvements, including the cross-stringing of grands. At the 1867 Paris Exhibition, the Americans' use of cast-iron frames, heavier strings, and powerful tone impressed the judges, who awarded gold medals to Steinway and Chickering. European makers duly noted what had been accomplished and copied the improved designs. Germany in particular developed a huge domestic and export business in these instruments.

It was outpaced, however, by the United States, which became the biggest maker of pianos in the world, producing some 350,000 in 1910, more than twice the output of Germany, its closest competitor. The piano became a fixture in most households that could afford one. "The piano in the parlor did not merely embody the ideal of the family at home," Richard Conniff writes, "it helped create it." Women were expected to play, children were expected to learn how, and sentimental sheet music (e.g., Stephen Foster) sold by the carload. In both urban halls and backwoods stations, flamboyant pianists on tour whipped audiences into frenzies.

Bone, boxwood, cedar, tortoiseshell, mother-of-pearl, even glass and porcelain all had their auditions as keyboard surfaces, but only one substance had the qualities desired by both piano player and manufacturer: ivory. With the minute porosity that gives their surface a faint stickiness as well as the ability to absorb perspiration, ivory keys were a boon to nervous pianists with damp hands. To drier fingers "it is yielding to the touch, yet firm," as ivory buyer E. D. Moore put it, "cool, yet never cold or warm, whatever the temperature; smooth to the point of slipperiness, so that the fingers may glide from key to key instantly, yet presenting just enough friction for the slightest touch of the finger to catch and depress the key and to keep the hardest blow from sliding and losing its power." Its availability made it de rigueur not just for top-of-the-line grands but for all save the poorest man's upright.

One of ivory's long-standing artistic uses had been its employment in musical instruments, from mammoth tusk flutes to the bridges of violins and connections for bagpipes. Now a single musical need alone came to overshadow not only other musical necessities but nearly every other use, period—that of piano key veneers. By 1913 the United States was using nearly two hundred tons of ivory annually just for the thin facings that were glued on the wooden keys. Each keyboard required a pound and a half of ivory; a sixty-pound tusk might yield enough ivory for three dozen keyboards.

George Read and Company in Deep River contracted with Chickering to supply ivory keys; in 1879 Steinway and Sons arranged to have Read's successor firm, Pratt, Read, supply the piano maker with portions of their keyboards. Neither Pratt, Read nor Comstock, Cheney in Ivoryton ever made entire pianos, but both created woodworking divisions to produce keyboards, actions, and sounding boards for some of their clients, such as Chickering, Steinway, Baldwin, and Everett.

Ivory "tops," "covers," or "veneers," as they were variously called, came in two basic forms: "heads," wide, two-inch-long rectangles that the fingers touched; or "tails," four-inch-long pieces that fit between the black keys (which were made of ebony, if possible). Junking, sawing, and slicing these little bits—essentially running them through a gauntlet of fine-toothed slitting saws—was only the first stage of the process on the ivory floors of the great factories in Ivoryton and Deep River. The steps required to turn tusks into the tops of piano keys were perhaps the most exacting and complex of any ivory manufacturing process.

In outline, it went like this. Graded by density, from the no. 5 coarse grain near the tusk surface to the prize no. 1 grade deep inside, these one-sixteenth-inch-thick "slips" were milled and squared in groups to the precise dimensions needed for piano key veneers. Once formed, they were placed in wood trays and allowed to dry out. Then, in groups, they were inserted in five-gallon glass jars filled with a preparation of peroxide and water for their initial bleaching. With some sun falling on the jars from factory windows, three days might do, but five would be required without it. Washed and dried, the ivory blanks would be placed in boxes—always segregated by order number, so that what came from a given tusk would be kept together—and taken to bleach houses and laid in trays.

This last stage in the production of piano key tops required that the ivories be placed under the windows of what looked like half greenhouses (or perhaps industrial skylights that had landed in rural fields) near the factory to stay exposed to the sun for four or five days, and up to a week in cloudy weather. Then, every little rectangle would be turned and exposed to sunlight for two more weeks. The aesthetic aim, and production goal, was uniformity of color: pure, creamy whiteness.

Sunbathing completed, the ivories were snapped out of their trays and delivered to the Ivory Matching Room, a veritable temple of precision. Here female factory workers—this being a task thought best suited to the fine motor skills and attentiveness of the womanly sex—sorted them. The goal was a keyboard whose ivory facings, if they revealed anything of their subtle grain under strong light, would exhibit a faint radiating pattern of matching grain across the keyboard. It was critical to know that these pieces came from the same tusk, whose inherent structure would be stamped on every slice of it, or sorting would be impossible. Even so, the women lined up at the counters under the room's windows, hair pulled up in no-nonsense buns, sleeves of their blouses pushed up, had to study each piece under the pale northern exposure, looking to eliminate those that showed flaws caused by injuries or strange swirling laminations occasioned by the varying diet of the creatures whose existence was reflected, ever so faintly, in these tiny, slice-of-life pieces of their great incisors. After initial inspection, heads and tails would be separated, sorted in six basic quality grades, and stored in cupboards.

Nearly ten thousand keyboard sets would normally be on hand to meet order requirements. To mate the ivories to the wooden keys entailed elaborate temperature controls and gluing procedures that sandwiched a piece of linen between the two; just the right amount of heat was necessary or the keys would fall off. Finally, to smooth out the join between the head and the tail to make it almost unnoticeable required the application of vinegar and a grailing machine, whose large abrasive drum ground down any microscopic misfitting to produce as close as one could come to a perfect piano key.

I have some of these ivory facings. Some years ago several of these heads slipped off the keyboard of my 1930s Steinway parlor upright in the living room of the Connecticut house where I live, casualties of the cold, dry New England winters that are so hard on furniture. A piano tuner persuaded me to let him substitute sturdier plastic tabs for the slightly chipped ones that kept flaking off, but I regretted the decision as soon as I saw the results. Next to the lustrous ivories, the inert, monochromatic modern stand-ins looked dead and lifeless, like poorly capped teeth. In angled sunlight the real ones show a delicate, wavy pattern, like faint watermarks in fine paper. Plastic keys sometimes show an ersatz grain meant to mimic the faint tracery of actual ivory, but it's not even close. As consolation, I've kept the heads in a box on my writing desk, so that I can take them out now and then and run a fingertip over their soothing surfaces and call to mind the silent stories summed up in them.

IT'S CURIOUS HOW many of the important leisure activities of the newly wealthy entrepreneurial class in the United States and Europe seemed, in one way or another, to involve ivory. It not only appeared on the keyboards of the now ubiquitous piano and the handles of the complicated cutlery of multicourse formal meals, but became essential in the production of billiard balls needed to supply the newfound fashion for the game. Billiards became one of the few important indoor sports of the late nineteenth and early twentieth centuries among those who could afford it.

Various forms of billiards—pocket games, carom games, English billiards, pocket billiards, pool, snooker—all have their origins in the late Middle Ages, when images of shepherds whacking at balls with sticks begin to appear in French tapestries. Louis XI brought the game indoors around 1470 with the purchase of a billiard table. James I ordered the first one built in England, and by 1666, billiards was available at fifty-seven licensed locations in Paris. Shakespeare mentions it, James Boswell was introduced to it, David Hume played it and pondered its meanings. Marie Antoinette had her own billiard room and an all-ivory cue, which she locked away with a key "that never left her possession." In America, as in Europe, the game was not confined for long to the homes of the upper classes. In colonial times it was popular in taverns, which accounted for its raffish association with drinking and gambling. When John Quincy Adams installed a billiard table in the White House, his opponents fulminated against his "gaming tables." Billiards became so popular in the nineteenth century that matches between top players drew huge crowds. In 1859 Michael Phelan, a billiards author and expert, played John Seereiter in Detroit for the first National Billiard Championship and a $15,000 purse. On the final night of the four-day event, four hundred fans paid $5 a head to sit in the gallery, while four thousand more milled outside to hear updates announced through a megaphone. Phelan won the close-fought match just before dawn with a run of forty-six balls.

In the United States, England, Germany, and France billiards became a national mania. The various related games didn't take their modern forms until the beginning of the twentieth century, but players had always been drawn by the blend of skill and luck and the intricacies of the evolving rules, and captivated by the attractive accoutrements—the perfect plane of green baize on warp-resistant slate, the massive carved table legs to support it, the cushioned rails, the sleek tapered cues. The social context had enormous appeal, starting with the amusing banter and chaffing and good-natured pontification possible with one's opponent. Then there was the game itself. After the ceremony of chalking the cue tip, a player got down to the serious business of squinting across the smooth felt and bent to his task of addressing the ball, lining up his cue, and beginning to piston it smoothly through his hands with a pendulum swing of the forearm. He faced at that moment the deliciously satisfying possibility of sinking a ball with the finality of a geometric proof or groaning inwardly at yet another fumbled stroke. "The game of billiards has destroyed my naturally sweet disposition," Mark Twain once said, only half-joking.

Billiard tables became a fixture in homes, clubs, and halls. When the Hotel del Coronado opened in San Diego in 1888 with the aim of becoming "the talk of the Western World," it boasted 750 rooms, an eleven-thousand-square-foot ballroom, and thirty billiard tables, four of which were reserved for ladies' use. In the first decades of the twentieth century, an estimated three million people in the United States played the game every day.

But without ivory, billiards would not have been possible.

"The billiard ball," writes historian Robert Friedel, "was the one object for which ivory was not only preferred, but required." The first indoor billiard balls were made of boxwood and other hardwoods, but by 1700 ivory had become vital to the game. It could be turned on a lathe to makes balls of nearly perfect sphericity and polish, with just the right amount of weight to roll with authority across the green. What's more, ivory was the only material that had sufficient elasticity or resiliency—"life," as it was called—to permit the full range of physical interactions between colliding balls. There was the delicate "kissing" of two balls in three-cushion billiards, as well as the showy displays French trick shooters were fond of incorporating in their games—spectacular caroms, back-spinning rebounds, even jumps—once the evolution of the cue came to include leather tips, which allowed sidespin or "cue ball english" to be deftly imparted. And there were the sensual aspects. When a player sent an ivory ball rolling down the length of the table into another, he heard a unique and gratifying *click* when they hit. Handling the balls, whose cool silken smoothness would slowly warm to the touch, was itself a pleasure. Billiards writers made the feel of cupping the hard orbs sound akin to caressing a young woman's bare shoulder.

It took the most skillful craftsmen using exacting ivory-working methods to produce balls that would meet the expected standards. A master turner such as George C. Britner, who worked at Comstock, Cheney before moving to Chicago, was considered a high priest of his profession and made the balls for a number of championship matches. Only the highest-quality, most uniform ivory from the center portion of a tusk could be used, and then only five short drums were normally cut for billiard ball production. Turners in the United States, England, France, and elsewhere used the same method. Each cylinder of ivory was clamped and turned on a lathe to rough out a hemisphere; the piece was reversed and clamped in place, and the other hemisphere carved. Because the tightness of the grain and thus the density of the ivory differed depending on its position in the tusk—and cutting it into a ball exposed it to a certain amount of shrinkage from loss of moisture—one side of the ball would typically shrink slightly more than the other. That meant that rough balls had to be set aside for a year, even five years, to season, before being turned to the precise size needed. And then there was the problem of the nerve channel, which passed through the center of the sphere. It was important that this minute opening (which would be plugged) ran through the precise middle of the ball in as straight a line as possible. Otherwise, the ball would not roll true; it would react erratically to a cue's poke and veer to the side as it came to a stop. In his authoritative 1896 treatise *Billiards*, Major W. Broadfoot, R.E., endorsed the view that a "good ball" would "pass muster" if it rolled straight and then stopped "motionless on the same line on which it was originally projected." If one was so fortunate as to possess a set of such paragons, he recommended locking them "jealously away." Billiard use put a huge premium on small tusks— "scrivelloes"—particularly those from female elephants, which are straighter than those of males and less likely to have a wavering nerve channel. They became, pound for pound, the most valuable tusks of all.

Turners made the balls as spherically exact as possible to ensure they would roll perfectly, but any inherent imbalance in their structure would cause them to be rejected—or sold as lesser grades. Five balls, say, 2$\frac{1}{16}$ in diameter (the standard for the English game), were the best a billiard ball maker could hope for from a top-grade scrivello, but none of them would weigh the same—their densities differed. To get three balls of the same dimension and weight for a set meant weighing and comparing every one produced; out of a hundred balls only five sets might be assembled, and only one set was likely to be up to match standard.

"Anyone who has served on the billiard committee of a London club," sighed Major Broadfoot, "may remember how his life has been made a burden to him by the never-ending complaints of members on the subject of balls." Though ivory was universally conceded to be the ideal material, it was organic in nature and so could never be perfectly uniform. Balls changed with the weather and with the temperature of a room (Queen Victoria had a heated billiard table to keep hers from warping), and over time developed an imperceptible but fatal egg shape. Wobbly balls were a curse. In Gilbert and Sullivan's *The Mikado* (1885), the Mikado proposes that the proper fate of a "billiard sharp" is to live out his days in a dungeon, playing

> *On a cloth untrue*
> *With a twisted cue*
> *And elliptical billiard balls.*

"CAUTION! DO NOT use these Balls before Reading the Special Notice on Inside of Cover." This notice appeared on the lids of the wooden boxes in which ivory billiard balls were shipped by the billiards equipment behemoth Brunswick-Balke-Collender of Chicago. The cautions included a dire warning that if the balls had been shipped in cold weather they would "split and break" if used immediately after receipt. This was only one of many drawbacks peculiar to ivory billiard balls. Another was price.

In the 1870s a perfectly matched set of three ivory billiard balls for tournament play could cost as much as $60, a substantial sum in the days when two glasses of beer could be had for a nickel. Demand for ivory increased when new games requiring more balls became popular: pool in the United States (sixteen balls) and snooker in Britain (twenty-two balls). In its 1908 catalogue Brunswick offered sets of top-grade ivory pool balls for $176. Regardless of price, ivory balls didn't last; they always needed replacing. Billiard ball producers had to keep twenty thousand to thirty thousand balls in stock in vaults with stable temperatures. Understandably, they feared that any kink in the supply would be devastating to their business. There was much dark talk of the "ivory problem," which was a decorous way of expressing concern that elephants might be on the decline.

Some had already looked ahead. In 1863 the American firm Phelan and Collender offered a $10,000 prize for the patent rights to a suitable synthetic material for billiard balls. The award is said to have "spurred the efforts" of John Wesley Hyatt, an American printer who was one of the pioneers of celluloid, the first synthetic material for manufacturing use. "Hyatt set out on his experiments," Friedel explains, "with the object of finding a replacement for ivory in billiard balls." Hyatt set up the Albany Billiard Ball Company with his brother to produce balls with a composition core and a coating of collodion or celluloid. In these balls, unlike ivory balls, the center of gravity was always the center of the sphere, but they had their drawbacks. A Colorado saloon keeper wrote to complain that if the balls hit each other hard enough, they made a sound like a percussion cap, which made everyone in the room draw his gun.

The Hyatt composition balls, which were advertised as not just stand-ins for ivory but better, were introduced to Britain under the name Bonzoline and were grudgingly accepted. At first they were regarded as suitable only where the climate might be difficult for ivory—the hill stations in India, for example. One might have thought players who complained ad nauseam about ivory balls that didn't roll true would embrace them, but no. "These men will tell you that there is no life in a composition ball, and that playing with these balls is like playing with stones," wrote one billiards expert in 1920. They even complained that "the click of them is dull and harsh," a dead thud. Rumor had it that if two composition balls smacked each other hard they would explode. This canard made the rounds because if the balls crashed together with sufficient force, their inner weight shattered the casing. Traditionalists didn't care to be corrected. For those addicted to their magic, only ivory balls could provide "the champagne of billiards."

Celluloid was an unsatisfactory substitute for ivory, but later materials, such as Leo Baekeland's Bakelite (1907), soon supplanted it for billiards—although ivory was used for some European billiards events until the 1990s. In historical terms, it is not a complete stretch to credit the drive to find a replacement for ivory in billiard balls as one stimulus of the birth of thermoplastic substances. Finding a substitute, as Friedel puts it, "was a long-standing objective of nineteenth-century inventors," even if what was discovered was soon appreciated for what else could be done with it.

EVEN IN THE nineteenth century some raised the question of whether there were limits to the supply of tusks needed for the staggering number of combs, piano keys, billiard balls, and hundreds of other ivory items produced. In 1876 one ivory dealer estimated the annual consumption of ivory at two million pounds and conceded that "the destructive war, carried on of late against elephants, tends gradually to decrease their number, and to accelerate their final extirpation." Ivory cutting was an industry only dimly understood by the public to depend on a natural resource. The 1889 image of James Burroughes of Burroughes and Watts, London, reclining on a haystack-size pile of rough-turned ivory billiard balls netted like so many bags of potatoes for warehousing and seasoning didn't immediately call to mind the mountain of dead elephants—some two thousand—it took to make the twenty thousand–odd balls in the photograph, much less how the tusks themselves entered the trade. Whenever the elephant cost of the billiards industry was raised, concerns were usually dismissed. In 1922 T. B. Wadleigh, secretary of the Illinois Billiard Association, commented that he was "safe in saying that 4,000 elephants are killed every year" to supply the ivory departments of billiard makers in the United States alone, adding,

> At first thought, some thin-skinned person might question the killing of this large number of elephants to provide a certain portion of the human family with billiards as a recreation, but on second thought, the charge of useless slaughter is wiped out. . . . All animals have been created for man's special use, and for his good, and this includes the elephant and his ivory.

5

"A TOOTH OF IVORY AND A SLAVE TO CARRY IT"

In 1882 Alfred J. Swann, an agent for the London Missionary Society at Lake Tanganyika in East Africa, saw for the first time a procession of Africans carrying tusks in what is now the Dodoma region of Tanzania. "As they filed past we noticed many chained together by the neck. Others had their necks fastened into the forks of poles about six feet long, the ends of which were supported by the men who preceded them," he wrote. "The women, who were as numerous as the men, carried babies on their backs in addition to a tusk of ivory on their heads." Swann groped for language to describe their whip-scarred state of filth.

> Feet and shoulders were a mass of open sores, made more painful by the swarms of flies which followed the march and lived on the flowing blood. They presented a moving picture of utter misery, and one could not help wondering how many of them had survived the long tramp from the Upper Congo, at least 1,000 miles distant.

When he pointed out to the headman that many of the slaves could barely carry their loads, he was told with a smile, "They have no choice! *They must go, or die!*" And if a woman was too weak to carry her child and a tusk? "*We spear the child and make her burden lighter.* Ivory first, child afterwards!"

Swann was not a completely disinterested observer. A self-described pioneer of "the gospel and the Union Jack," he professed outrage at what he saw and yet a decade later bought ivory in Ujiji, a slave trade outpost settled by Arabs, and sold it for profit, a practice forbidden by the missionary society. Still, his description of ivory being carried by slaves is

echoed in numerous accounts from the period that confirm the practice
in all its ghastly details.

What gives this particular tale out of so many similar ones special
interest is that the caravan Swann came across was that of the formidable
Tippu Tip, an Arab Zanzibari warlord and trader who ruled a 250,000-
square-mile empire of East African bush and single-handedly supplied
the majority of the ivory that made its way to America. Tippu Tip used
thousands of locally captured or bought slaves to transport the ivory plundered on his numerous expeditions to the markets of Zanzibar where both
would be sold. Ambitious and shrewd, Tippu Tip often aided explorers—
Livingstone, Stanley, and Cameron among them—and was as adept at
holding thoughtful discussions with his European interlocutors as he was
at burning and pillaging rural villages. He had spent thirteen years in the
interior when he crossed paths with Swann and, with his long-awaited caravan of ivory, had just brutally forced his way through a yearlong block-
ade of trade by an extortionist ruler east of Lake Tanganyika. "During this
year and more, when no ivory of consequence was arriving at Zanzibar,"
wrote E. D. Moore, "the Yankees in the Connecticut ivory-cutting factories were starving for ivory tusks." That is why, as he put it,

> The arrival of Tippoo, with tons and tons of ivory and the news . . . that
> the trade route was again open, were hailed with shouts of joy that rever-
> berated from the eastern coast of Africa to the inner shores of Long Is-
> land; and Tippoo was a hero in the streets of Zanzibar, in the
> houses of the Arab, European, and Yankee traders, and in the palace of
> Seyyid Barghash, the Sultan.

"UNCLE DWIGHT CALLED me up on the phone today and told me Arnold,
Cheney & Co. offered me a three years contract, [$]500 and expenses for
my first year, to sail for Aden next Wednesday. I told Uncle Dwight I
would be in New York Tuesday morning," Ernst D. Moore wrote in his diary on August 30, 1907. Two days later he confided in it that "I'm just beginning to realize now that I'm going, but I haven't any idea of all the

distance, the nights and days, and life in these coming three years. It will all seem short when it's over, but there will be bushels of things crowded into these years. I hope I make good."

In 1907 Moore was twenty-three years old and then known as Ernst R. Domansky. (Around 1912, after his parents had died, he followed his brothers in changing his last name to Moore, at the request of his childless uncle Dwight Moore, who wanted his family name continued.) Born and raised in Boston, he had thought of going to medical school but when his uncle, who had been U.S. consul in Aden and Zanzibar in the 1880s–90s, found him a position as an overseas ivory buyer he didn't hesitate. "Stories of adventures in Africa were almost a daily diet for me in my youth," he once said. His father had been a sea captain, and his mother's family, the Cheneys, had long been involved with the East African ivory trade. He went to work for the largest ivory importing firm in the United States, the New York–based Arnold, Cheney and Company, and served as its agent in Aden, Mombasa, and Zanzibar until 1911. Moore experienced ivory as few ever had. "I dare say I held in my own hands as many large ivory tusks as any man in the world in my time," he later wrote.

In the early 1930s Moore wrote a number of articles and a book about the ivory trade, but one of the most intriguing documents by him was never intended to be published: a diary in which he made daily entries nearly without fail during the time he was employed as an ivory buyer. Written in a legible, backward-slanting open hand, the yearly volumes, bound in black leather with the dates stamped in gold, rest in a locked trunk in the attic of his daughter's house in Haddam, a little farther up the Connecticut River from Deep River and Ivoryton. Their yellowing pages detail the life of an American trading in the outposts of the British empire and the evolution of thought of someone who came to be deeply troubled by the enormous human and animal costs of the ivory he traded in.

I MET RICHARD Moore, a white-haired, courtly eighty-six-year-old, at the door of a stone house covered with a profusion of ivy atop the crest of a knoll in Chester, overlooking the Connecticut River. On that crisp fall day he had a fire going, framed by an ornate stone mantel in the Italianate dwelling that his parents bought in 1924 and named the Ledges. He invited me out onto a terrace with a wisteria-wrapped pergola. Moore pointed out that the trees on the property has grown considerably since his father's time, but glints of the river were still visible in the distance under banks of gray clouds and occasional swaths of blue. "It's the only major river in New England that still looks much as it did a century ago," he told me.

The view from the terrace would have been much the same when his father, Ernst Moore, sat under the pergola and pecked out on a portable typewriter the manuscript for his exposé, *Ivory: Scourge of Africa*, published in 1931. Richard Moore went back inside for something he wanted to show me. It was autumn; the grounds were thick with fallen leaves and they rustled and stirred as the wind picked up. He returned, bringing a framed black-and-white photo. The glass was cracked but the image was clear enough. It showed his balding father in profile in a porch rocker, dressed in plus fours and a knit tie, typewriter in his lap, just where we were standing.

Richard Moore is one of five children, of which there are three surviving siblings—he and his two sisters. He wasn't here that often, he told me. Years ago, he had helped open the Paris branch of a New York law firm, and he lived in Paris now with his French wife. He came back to the house, now owned by his son, each fall and spring. The bits of ivory and related memorabilia that his father had kept—tusk tips, a scrivello—had been scattered, he told me as we went back inside, although he still had an ivory pestle in Paris. I asked if the dark mahogany Chickering baby grand in the living room was his father's piano. "Oh, yes," Moore told me. "He was a very good pianist—which was useful for someone who worked for a piano company."

Two years after his return from Africa, E. D. Moore married the former Elsie Warner of Chester and devoted himself to work and family. He became vice president of Pratt, Read, the chief customer for the ivory he'd once bought, in their subsidiary, the Pratt, Read Player Action Company, in Deep River. It produced player piano actions until 1928, when the growing popularity of radio put an end to the business. Richard and his sister Edith, with whom I had a brief follow-up telephone conversation, remembered a doting father and an indulgent husband. Starting in 1930 the shingle-sided Comstock, Cheney Hall in nearby Ivoryton, built originally for employees, began to be used for summer theater, and Moore's wife, who was "a bit starstruck," often entertained visiting New York actors, serving them strawberry shortcake on the terrace.

Moore told me his father had been "a proper young man from Boston" when he'd left for Aden and Africa. There is a picture of him standing with a tusk in the snow, but otherwise there was little hint among later family photographs of the extraordinary chapter of his life as an ivory buyer in Africa.

"THE LAND OF my adoption hove in sight about noon today, and at two-thirty we dropped anchor in the harbor. [I got] permission to land, and I tumbled ashore, after a preliminary row with the coolies who looked after the trunks. . . . The tropics here are as hot as anywhere else," Moore wrote of Aden in his diary entry of September 27, 1907. The week before he'd leaned excitedly on the rail of the ship's deck and watched camels and water women and children running along the banks of the Suez Canal shouting *"Baksheesh!"* but by the time he arrived in "Arabia"—Yemen—he understood why explorer Richard Burton referred to Aden as the "coal-hole of the East."

The heat was stultifying and the days began to blur into one another. He fell into the rhythm of long periods of boredom at the agency office ("Worked hard today. I translated a two-word cable from New York."), watching the sun set in the harbor and local boys kill large rats. His uncle Dwight advised him to "pick up the threads of the local business" by making some social connections. "I'm butting into Aden sassiety [*sic*] with a sickening thud," he writes by early November. "Tonight I dined with the Bank-wallah and the missus. Uncle Dwight's old boy Abdul butlered. . . . I am in the midst of historical scenes." But it wasn't all tennis and drinks with friends at the Union Club.

He was expected to perform. Moore, like his fellow agents, traded in all the local commodities, from tortoiseshell to goatskins, coffee, and civet. But their main interest was the ivory brought in by Arab, Abyssinian, and East Indian traders. Some days were packed with transactions. "Smith and I spent the morning figuring ivory, and closed a deal for 18 bundles in the afternoon. I got 38 tusks of it—one weighs about 90 pounds." The next day, a Sunday, was just as busy. "Certainly worked today. Those two cables this morning put my day of rest clean on the blink. . . . Then in the afternoon I found out there was a boat for NY tomorrow. Smith and I hustled over to Liverato's, weighed the 18 bundles, I took my 38 teeth, and we started things right away. After dinner I came downstairs and worked until half past eleven. That's going some for this burg. We get the stuff away tomorrow all right."

The U.S. demand was growing enormously. Joseph A. Jones, secretary of Arnold, Cheney, wrote to George L. Cheney, then general manager (and soon to be president) of Pratt, Read in Deep River, in early September of that year, "Yours of the 3rd, advising sales for August, is indeed surprising—it seems as if there is no limit to the growth of the business. You will probably have to set a new limit shortly, on which you will pin your eye, and throw that million dollars a year sales into the rear." A month later Jones wrote to Cheney to advise that, given Pratt, Read's sales, they would need about thirty-one thousand pounds of ivory over the next three months to be able to start 1908 with at least two months' worth of supply on hand, and he summarized world ivory market conditions with an eye to eliciting a substantial order. "Ivory at Zanzibar is strong in price, but the arrivals have been abnormally light for the period—we think that the scarcity is the reason for the increase in the price. . . . At Aden, we know there is a stock of Abyssinian, but have not yet succeeded in purchasing it. Antwerp stocks are now large, 170 tons. . . . London, as far as I can as yet find out, shows but a small sale, though parcels of Egyptian were looked for and may be on time. . . . We ought to buy at least 20,000 lbs. Congo at Antwerp, to carry you on." Jones adds a nudge: Arnold, Cheney will also be buying for Pratt, Read's Ivoryton competitor Comstock, Cheney in the London sales and is not anticipating a decline in prices.

By mid-December of 1908 Moore had been transferred to the port of Mombasa in British East Africa to replace an agent ill with fever. He found the agency house smaller than the one at Aden but equipped with imposing, beautifully carved doors. "This is rather a pretty place, from the outside, anyway. I'm not in a position to know much about the inside, as yet," he wrote on his arrival. "It was quite charming after the dull monotone of Aden. It was all palm trees and those big branchy fellers, and purple and white and red flowers. Looked mighty nice. But vegetation brings bugs, and rains and fevers, and I think the Aden rocks are to be preferred, despite their somberness. The gharris here are a funny proposition—they have no horses here, and the gharris consist of covered trucks, seating two people which run on rails to all parts of town. The motive power is supplied by two Swahili boys, who 'push it along.' . . . Everybody seems to like it here. Perhaps I will in time." In Aden he had volumes by Balzac and George Eliot, a bottle of Moët et Chandon to toast the New Year and ward off homesickness, and a dog, but he found himself "rubbing the varnish off the chairs at the Club" during boring conversations on the veranda. He had higher hopes for the Mombasa Club.

In little over a year's time Moore became one of Arnold, Cheney's principal ivory buyers and, depending on staffing, often the only one in the markets in which it operated—Aden, Mombasa, and Zanzibar. The ivory he dealt with was of various kinds, or "descriptions," as the trade called these groupings. There were names referring to geographical origins (or ports): Congo, Zanzibari, Uganda, Ambriz, Angola, Mozambique, Sudanese, Egyptian, Abyssinian, Gaboon, Sengalese, etc. Another set of names referred to the uses to which the ivory would be put, such as "ball" and "bangle." Others names included "scrivello" (small tusks under fifteen pounds), "bagatelle" (small-diameter tusks), "cutch" (under forty pounds), "gendi" (brownish or spotted). Physical condition added further descriptors: "prime," "defective," "diseased," "shaky," and "perished." Above all were the two main classifications into which all ivory fell: soft and hard. Soft was the more desirable of the two.

"It has a more compact texture within the tusk," Moore would write decades later, "so that it has a milky or creamy texture in its natural state, in contrast to hard ivory, which has more the suggestion of skimmed milk. Cut into wafers, the soft ivory is opaque, the hard ivory, translucent. The soft ivory contains more of the oil or waxy substance that contributes to the polish and, probably for the same reason, is more amenable to the working tool than the hard." Roughly speaking, East Africa produced soft ivory, West Africa hard, but Central African ivory could produce either. During the working day, Moore was surrounded by tusks, stepping over them on the floor of the walled godowns (warehouses), sorting them, handling them, calculating what he might have to pay. "All I can see in front of me is elephants' teeth, yellow ones and black ones, striped ones and plain ones, big ones and little ones, long ones and short ones, and curved ones and straight ones," he confided to his diary. "If I don't have a nightmare with a long prehensile nose tonight, it'll be a marvel."

Moore became familiar with sellers' tricks, such as the soaking of ivory in water to make it heavier. As a consequence, he never paid for ivory unless it had sat in the godown long enough to dry out, and he always probed the hollow of each tusk assiduously with a pointed rod to dislodge any hidden lead or stones shoved into the apex of the pulp cavity to boost the weight, or to uncover the little "beans" that indicated disease and, therefore, waste ivory. He had to be sure of what he was buying, or he would be certain to hear about the quality or weight of the tusks not matching the expectations of the ivory cutters back in Connecticut. Moore had a healthy respect for the business acumen of the Indian ivory traders, the great middlemen of the business, who were masters "in the art of juggling prices, grades, and proportions." He found them invariably "too smart for the white man," who was left trying "to trick a competitor of his own hue. There were no ethics in the ivory business."

Like the other ivory agents, Moore employed scouts to shadow the ivory that arrived by dhow or steamer, bribed traders' underlings for information, and had spies count the tusks that went in and out of his competitors' godowns. He learned to read the Gujarati numerals that the Indians marked on their tusks ("if the white man's weight was the higher, there was a trick to be uncovered"). He also learned the art of bidding—or getting others to bid secretly on his behalf—at the British East African government ivory auctions in Mombasa. An old photograph of one such auction shows Moore in his white suit, sun hat in hand, seated with a dozen of his competitors—a few Europeans in similar attire but mostly Indians variously garbed, capped, and turbaned. In front of them is a sprawl of massive curving tusks; off to the side several Africans sit on a pile of smaller tusks, ready to drag out another lot for inspection.

Of course, Moore was expected to drive as hard a bargain as possible. He didn't have unlimited funds at his disposal; he complains frequently in his diary about the limits the New York office was always putting on what he could pay. "I cabled the local ivory situation home last night and this morning there was another drop, with the proviso that I could use a couple dollars more if our rivals up the street got gay. Visram swears he won't sell at the price and says he'll send it home. That's where it all is now!" Still, Moore could brag about how much ivory he was shipping. "We're the kingpin ivory wallahs in these parts," he wrote at the beginning of 1909. His May 22 entry is exultant. "We shipped a mere 101 tusks by the *Herzog* today. Our rivals shipped nineteen, all they'd collected in the past three months, while we collected ours within three weeks. This shipment brings my ivory values over one hundred thousand real dollars since the first of the year. Put that in your smoke and pipe it." Four months later, he writes, "We preserve our proud boast of sending ivory home on every German [ship] this year. A shipment every boat is more than our rivals have made—they've made about four this year. Our score is twenty or more." When he is able to add up the figures for 1909, he finds they've shipped 1,034 tusks of ivory, weighing a total of 66,054 pounds, and worth $187,688.76.

Moore thought he could ask for a raise for the last year of his contract. He was ecstatic to receive a message from New York telling him his salary had been doubled to $1,000 but was brought up sharp by being told he needed to better cultivate his trading relationships: "It is imperative for us and you have been told so, to hold Ali Visram as the most important native merchant in your territory. We do not suppose that you or anyone else, could get Visram to sell you good[s] for less money than others, but your cables for the past four or five months would look as though we could only get goods from Visram if we paid more than Childs & Co. [a New York rival importer] were offering." Moore answers with assurances that "my prime duty in Mombasa is the maintenance of cordial business relations" with Ali Visram, and lets New York know that Childs and Company ends up with what Moore has rejected, as its agent doesn't know to probe the hollows of the tusks with a metal rod.

He worked harder than ever. Moore wrote out an elaborate description of ivory classifications on five oversize sheets, which included details of how many points should be subtracted for particular shortcomings and defects (cracks, streaks, spots, age, etc.) and the percentage that could be added for straightness and gradual taper. Using these tables he could determine, for example, that for piano keys a forty-one-pound hard ivory tusk with twelve points off for defects would be worth 84.48 percent of the value of a sound sixty-pound hard ivory tusk. He put these tables to use. In Mombasa, he later reflected, he "saw and handled more ivory there than I had thought existed in the whole world. Mombasa was then, due to the construction of the Uganda Railway, probably the greatest ivory port in Africa, and streams of bloody, smelling tusks flowed through our godowns. I traded for ivory in Arabic, sold *merikani* (American cotton cloth) in German, bought rhino horns and hippo's teeth in Kiswahili, and chilli peppers in Hindustani."

While stationed at Mombasa Moore also ventured into the interior after ivory, meeting hunters, poachers, and traders. "I had at and under my table some of the most rascally ivory thieves (from the Belgian and Portuguese viewpoints) or most eminent sporting adventurers (according to the British idea) who graced the eastern half of Africa," he recalled. But for him the high point of his stay was acting as one of the hosts for Theodore Roosevelt at a dinner at the Mombasa Club the evening of the day the former president landed in Africa to commence a yearlong safari. There is a photograph of the two of them in pith helmets, TR in jodhpurs, speaking with Moore in the doorway of the club, April 21, 1909. The safari porters quickly took to calling Roosevelt *Bwana Tumbo*, which meant "big-belly boss." Moore felt the locals were a little kinder to him; he was *Bwana Pembi* — "ivory boss."

Mombasa had been a success. But the place Moore had heard about from boyhood, the one he regarded as his "destiny" — Zanzibar — was waiting.

"THE SHORES ARE simply lined with the thickest and greenest mass of palms and other vegetation that I ever saw," Moore wrote in his diary of a week-long preview he had of Zanzibar. He'd grabbed his chance to get a berth on the S.S. *Bürgermeister* to Tanga, a small Indian Ocean port in what's now northern Tanzania, and then across to the island where in the coming year he would take up his new posting. "Zanzibar has always had a romantic sound to me, and I find the place just as interesting as I expected.

The streets here in town are only about six feet wide—in fact, there are only one or two through which a rickshaw will pass. The roads, those like the one out to the sports club, are beautifully lined with all sorts of tropical foliage." That night Frank W. Vining, whom Moore would replace at the end of Vining's agency contract, brought him along for a tour of the local tenderloin. Moore took it all in. "There were bars galore, and ladies of dead-easy virtue on every corner and stoop," he wrote, quickly adding, "They were hardly what could be termed tempting, however."

The next day the two of them hopped the island's narrow-gauge train in front of the sultan's palace. Moore marveled at how it passed through the town and its bazaar so close to the buildings on each side that he could touch them with an arm thrust through the window. They rode it for several miles along the shore until it reached the settlement of Bububu. "It is useless," he writes, "to describe the beauty of it. The white beach and clear blue water on one side, and the groves of palms and mango-trees on the other, with the clear blue sky overhead, make a picture not easy to forget." The island had cast its exotic, perfumed spell over him; Mombasa, he decided, couldn't be compared to it "for a minute." He returned to the theme on the boat trip back to the mainland, scribbling thoughts like "Gee whiz, but I am stuck on Zanzibar." The images of glaring whiteness, from sandy beaches to city walls and buildings to white-robed people, had dazzled Moore.

BUT THE HISTORY behind the whitewashed facades of the spice island included some dark shadows that Moore would come to terms with only decades later. Before Zanzibar's rise to prominence in the ivory trade, Africa had been bled of ivory and slaves from both sides of the continent for several centuries. After elephant herds were thinned along the west coast, the supply of ivory dwindled during the eighteenth century; slaves became the important export. Hausa traders from northern Nigeria as well as Arab merchants shifted much of the ivory trading in West Africa in the nineteenth century from the Upper Guinea coast to Cameroon. There, ivory was for a time transported by camel caravan across the Sahara to North African ports for export to Europe, but by the early twentieth century the trade had largely sputtered out.

Using the same routes that had operated for the export of slaves up to the 1850s, those supplying the seemingly insatiable European demand for ivory opened up whole trade networks deep into the Congo basin by the 1880s, seeking to exploit the herds there. At the tip of the continent, South Africa's elephant population south of the Zambezi was virtually eliminated by the end of the nineteenth century. On the East African coast, there had long been ivory trading links between the Lake Nyasa region of southeast Africa and Indian traders on Mozambique island just off the coast, with shipments going to India. But Portuguese dominance in the region and increasing taxation collapsed the ivory trade there by the end of the 1700s; ivory coming from the interior was diverted to Zanzibar, which had come under the rule of Omani sultans. The island archipelago became the central collection point for East African trade and a major commercial entrepôt for the Indian Ocean, attracting American, French and German trading houses.

One of the forces driving these transformations in the African ivory trade in the early nineteenth century was the *tenfold* rise in the prevailing European price of ivory between the 1780s and the 1830s. The East African coast, which had for millennia exported ivory to Asia, became the focus of intensified European—and soon American—demand. In 1840 Sultan Seyyid Said moved his capital from Muscat in Oman to Zanzibar, where he had profited mightily from the clove plantations he'd set up previously with slave labor. Ivory trading there was in full swing. In 1858, when Burton and Speke became the first Europeans to reach Lake Tanganyika, they met caravans returning to the coast loaded with tusks; later, Burton encountered one transporting twenty-eight thousand pounds of ivory. In the 1860s and 1870s elephants, like fish in the sea, were "there for the taking." Explorers' accounts of the ivory available stoked the dreams of many. Lieutenant V. L. Cameron, who crossed the continent in 1874, wrote that ivory was said to "be used for fencing pig-sties and making door posts." Livingstone wrote of people in the Congo basin bringing "tusks by the dozen till traders get so many that they carried them in relays," and Stanley dubbed parts of East Africa "the El Dorado of ivory seekers."

With the United States and European countries eager to acquire East African ivory, and India remaining a steady customer, the intensified demand precipitated something like an ivory rush: herds all along the lengthy coast were devastated, and new areas for elephant hunting far in the interior became worth exploiting. This drew increasing numbers of local men away from traditional labor, including agriculture, and concentrated power in the hands of those organizing elephant hunting and ivory caravanning, which allowed domestic slavery to flourish.

East African commerce in human lives was a long-established Middle Eastern trade, the Indian Ocean version of the grim Atlantic slave trade. Sultanates used African slaves for agricultural labor, as soldiers, and in the household, and the growth of French sugar and coffee plantations on Réunion and Mauritius and, later, clove plantations on Zanzibar, as well as the growing need for ivory transport, helped drive the increased demands for slave labor. The trade became a specialty of the Swahili culture that developed from the mixed Arab and African coastal settlements, and slaves were one of Zanzibar's principal exports in the nineteenth century—perhaps as many as thirty thousand a year at its peak. On a visit to the island in 1839, one Englishman wrote in his diary about how slaves were purchased not far from where ivory was sold.

> [I] walked back to the market where as usual at that hour a number of slaves were exposed for sale. The purchasers to view their paces threw a stick to some distance that they might walk to pick it up. It was rather an animated though a disgusting scene.

However, slaves weren't typically used to transport ivory. In many parts of Africa, ivory porterage was a prestigious activity that actually attracted labor. The Wanyamwezi of Tanzania specialized in it. The place of honor in these marches was right behind the flag bearer of the caravan and was bestowed on the man who could carry the heaviest tusk. Why use people to transport ivory? As Abdul Sheriff points out, the endemic "tsetse fly prevented the use of beasts of burden in the transport of goods and necessitated their being carried on human shoulders."

The total wages for a 350-mile march through the bush from Tabora to the coast, carrying a fifty- or even eighty-pound load, might be the equivalent of two and half American dollars, hardly a vast sum even in the nineteenth century but appealing enough. At Unyanyembe (now Tabora)

in central Tanzania, Arab traders coming from Zanzibar met up with caravans coming from Ujiji, bartered for ivory, and rehired porters laid off by
a previous caravan. By 1885 these caravans had swelled in size, reaching
up to two thousand porters apiece.

Bartering for ivory might require a supply of colored beads, copper
rings, or cloth. "There is a record," R. W. Beachey writes, "of one caravan
in the 1880s carrying 27,000 yards of *merikani* made up in loads of 30–40
yards each, and, in addition, thousands of yards of other kinds of cloth."
Scissors, cavalry sabers, pots, and parasols were also popular, and gun-
powder and firearms were much in demand. One missionary turned ivory
trader exchanged Martini-Henry rifles and Winchester repeaters with a
Ugandan chief at the rate of one weapon per seventy-five pounds of ivory.

Ivory was heavy to transport. If it was moved by slaves, both could be
sold at the coast, increasing the profit of the trading venture. But many of
the slaves brought to Zanzibar were women and children, who made poor
carriers. What confused European observers was that some porters were
slaves who had been hired out by their masters. "The intertwining of ivory
porterage and slaving," Alpers writes, "was not typical of the ivory trade in
general, but represented a late development that reflected the increasing
pressure of intensified profit taking on the eve of European colonial conquest."

Indeed, as the ivory trade intensified, traders found it too tiresome to
bargain endlessly for every tusk, from the pair scavenged from a carcass
stumbled on by a farmer to what a canny chief might have on offer from his
trove of tribute ivory—an ivory cache could simply be taken by force. If
porters couldn't be acquired from a tribal leader for a few muzzleloaders,
men could be press-ganged into service by using the weapons. The age-old
practice of enslaving the conquered and shackling the prisoners to transport
the available booty was always something a trader could fall back on. Besides, ivory became more valuable than the humans who carried it to ports
on the coast such as Mombasa, Tanga, and Bagamoyo. Before the shutting
down of Zanzibar's open slave market in 1873, the tusk bearers who had
made it that far faced a further trip to the island. The emaciated bodies of
those who died there awaiting sale would be thrown on the beach, Moore
wrote, "to rot until the tide carried their bloated bodies out to sea."

Tippu Tip, whose real name was Hamedi bin Muhammad el Marjebi—"Tippu Tip" was what many in the interior called him, after the sound his armies' guns made—was the most notorious of these Swahili traders. Born in Zanzibar, he began trading in ivory and slaves at age eighteen. By 1880 he and his men ruled an empire that penetrated a thousand miles inland from the coast. Tippu Tip left his own account of his activities in his 1903 autobiography, but his history is augmented by the accounts of Livingstone, Cameron, and other European missionaries and explorers. When Tippu Tip penetrated into new territories, he and his followers were often seen as "agents of opportunity." Even Livingstone, who regarded the slave trade as "slaking thirst for blood and catching free people," noted that among local peoples "some, to ingratiate themselves with the Arabs, became eager slave-hunters." These Africans were often converted to Islam by circumcision and a crash course in the rudiments of the religion—just enough to set them apart from those they would now join in oppressing in a straightforward policy of pillage. One British observer wrote in his journal in 1887:

> The Arabs attack and capture a village, kill the grown up men, and make prisoners of all the boys, girls, and women they can; these they carry on with them on their marches, selling women where they can for ivory and bringing up the boys for raiders and the girls for their harems—the system is a good one, though one which destroys the country they pass through.

Tippu Tip claimed that his suzerainty was often accepted. In the eastern Congo, he said, "there are no hereditary chiefs; into the country come folk from other areas and offer wealth to those who own the land. These, in turn, make one of the strangers chief." He had scant regard for judgments from colonizing Europeans on his slaving practices and his rule over the interior. Swann tells of a heated and prescient exchange with Tippu Tip over differing concepts of European and Swahili Arab territorial possessions some eight hundred miles deep in the interior. Swann remembered it this way, beginning with the slave master's remarks:

"I came here as a young man, fought these natives and subdued them, losing both friends and treasure in the struggle. Is it not, therefore, mine by your law and ours?"

"It is only yours so long as you govern and use it properly!"

Tippu Tip rose up and demanded, "Who is to be my judge?"

"Europe!"

"Aha!" he replied. "Now you speak the truth. Do not let us talk of justice; people are only just when it pays. The white man is stronger than I am; they will eat my possessions as I ate those of the pagans, and . . . *some one will eat up yours!*"

THEY KNEW, DIDN'T they? Those comfortable captains of the Connecticut ivory-cutting industry must surely have been aware that the tusks that arrived with clearly stenciled shipping marks also came with an invisible but indelible stain: the terrible human cost of getting them out of the African bush. It's possible—just possible—that Julius Pratt and George Read, who were pioneer figures in the early days of the industry and whose firms folded into the Deep River colossus Pratt, Read in 1863, might not have known all that much of how the swoops of ivory that reached their factories made the journey from elephant to their doorsteps. They never went to Africa; early on both depended on imports of tusks through Providence, Rhode Island. One of their suppliers, however, John Bertram of Salem, Massachusetts, had shipped directly from Zanzibar and could not have been ignorant of the use of slaves in ivory transport. What makes the question of what Pratt and Read knew about the ivory trade in Africa of considerable interest is that they both held antislavery views—and acted on them.

Julius Pratt was a strict Puritan who eschewed most amusements. A rigid disciplinarian, he once threw his four-year-old son into the river after catching him singing at the local grocery store. He was also an abolitionist in a town where such sentiments were in the minority; when he joined others to invite an antislavery speaker to address the Congregational church in Meriden, Connecticut, in 1837, opponents broke through the church doors and threw eggs at the audience.

George Read was taciturn, abstemious, and a deacon of his church, the kind of upright character his clear-eyed portrait in the Deep River Historical Society suggests. By 1828 he was working for the Underground Railroad. That year, Richard Conniff writes, "a fugitive slave was directed from New Haven to seek refuge with Read in Deep River. Read put him up in the family home for the next twenty years."

One can't really know about these men; there simply is no hard evidence. But there doesn't seem to be much mystery about their successors in the ivory-cutting business two decades later. They had to have known that their business was intertwined at various points with the slave trade. If nothing else, there were all those published missionaries' and explorers' accounts, by Livingstone and others—some of which became best sellers on both sides of the Atlantic—which painted shocking word pictures of miserable wretches shackled together in long lines, tusks bobbing on their shoulders and heads as they shuffled toward the coast. ("Every tusk," Stanley fulminated, "has been steeped and dyed in blood.") But many of these men didn't have to read about it. They would have seen it for themselves—they'd been to Zanzibar.

Before George Arthur Cheney joined Samuel Comstock's ivory business to form Comstock, Cheney in Ivoryton in 1860, he'd made four voyages to Africa and lived in Zanzibar. Americans had been quick to set up shop in East Africa; in 1823 the first U.S. ship landed in Zanzibar and Mombasa and traded for copal (a tropical tree resin used in varnish) and ivory. Serious American trade started when Captain John Bertram arrived in Zanzibar in 1831 on the first of many voyages; he became a prominent (and immensely wealthy) trader. Between 1827 and 1835 nearly three dozen American merchant vessels visited East Africa. The United States managed to strike a deal with Sultan Seyyid Said to remove what it considered obstacles to the expansion of trade—this was the first commercial treaty between Zanzibar and a foreign power. In 1836 the first U.S. consulate was established. In the beginning, Americans were making annual voyages, but that soon changed.

George A. Cheney, who became the son-in-law of Rufus Greene, a Providence, Rhode Island, shipping merchant anxious for a share in the Zanzibar trade, first sailed there in 1850 and apparently purchased ivory on the voyage; more important, he helped Greene establish a trading firm in Zanzibar, in partnership with Greene's two brothers, W. S. and B. R. Arnold, the firm that became Arnold, Hines and Company and eventually Arnold, Cheney. By his third voyage there in 1853, Cheney had married Rufus Greene's daughter Sarah and took her with him to Zanzibar. In a surviving letter to her family from that year, she wrote of her "servant problem."

> The one I have now is rather stupid and lazy and has already had to receive a dozen lashes for running away and stopping all night. I fear you will consider us hard-hearted, but you can know nothing of it at home. George has never struck one himself but stands by to see it done and is pale and sick for hours after.

I think about what this scene says about the American ivory trader's attitudes. George Cheney doesn't wield the whip himself—clearly that would be personally repugnant—but he is complicit in the punishment, which, while excessive by his own standards, is the way things were done on the island. As Stanley later wrote, "Men experienced in the ways of oriental life need not be told in detail how people live in Zanzibar." There were infinite gradations of servitude and slavery, and the practice appeared omnipresent, from the home to the marketplace. As late as 1873 Sir Bartle Frere, who had been sent from London to negotiate a new slave-trade suppression treaty with the sultan, had to admit that there was no one in the East African trade who could "feel sure that no part of his commercial transactions is connected directly or indirectly with the slave trade." In any case, whatever Cheney's personal misgivings over what he saw there, they clearly didn't interfere with his mission, which was to buy ivory, or with his later career with Comstock, Cheney.

For those Americans in the ivory industry—especially after the Civil War, when international efforts were made to end slavery in Africa—it wouldn't have been a matter of ignoring what was happening, much less excusing it. The unpleasant fact that obtaining ivory cost human lives may have been little publicized but it had to have been faced by the factory owners, importers, and traders time and time again. Doubtless they thought it was one of those regrettable things, but one that fortunately went on halfway around the world. And, after all, what could one be expected to do? It was the Dark Continent, hopelessly mired in mankind's past. Besides, hadn't the Connecticut ivory cutters been economic visionaries who had found a way to give a common substance in Africa's forests—Livingstone himself said ivory was used for *fence posts*—whatever value it possessed? It took immense effort and huge capital every step of the way. Grasping heathens demanded extortionate sums for tusks that still had to be shipped across oceans and cut and shaped and bleached and polished until the softly glowing material bore not one blemish, just as it no longer resembled anything that recalled a tooth. And, yes, remember that it took another mountain of enterprise to sell all those piano keys and billiard balls, by which time one could feel justly rewarded in taking a profit proportionate to the enormous risks required. This vast undertaking took colossal enterprise and admirable industry. No, it wasn't perfect, those merchants would have said, but the ivory-cutting industry represented progress, in fact, a particularly American brand of progress— didn't it?

WHEN MOORE FINALLY became Arnold, Cheney's man in Zanzibar at the end of July 1910, he moved into the agency's historic house, "a maze of passages and bridges, and the rooms like a village of small houses instead of one big one." But the building (Nyumba Pembi, Ivory House) took up an entire block and was redolent with history. Burton, Speke, and Stanley had walked through its great carved teakwood doors. The high-walled complex had a thick-walled godown with barred windows directly under the living quarters where for decades tusks had been brought by Indian merchants and Arab traders—including Tippu Tip—to be weighed in heaps in the giant scale and then kept stacked in vaults away from light and moisture and the gnawing teeth of rats. It was also headquarters for a succession of American consuls, including his uncle, Dwight Moore, who knew Tippu Tip well.

It must have seemed an almost impregnable business. Americans dominated the Zanzibar trade until the Civil War dampened the U.S. ivory market and threatened shipping, but they steadily recovered their position afterward. By then Europeans also had a strong presence. Germany was already represented by Wm. O'Swald and Company, later joined by Hansing and Company and representatives for H. A. Meyer of Hamburg, buying for their own substantial domestic consumption of ivory for piano keys, billiard balls, and the new fashion for carved ivory flowers. In 1870 German firms secured nearly a quarter of Zanzibar's foreign commerce, from spices to ivory, as had the Americans; the Indian and Arab firms, the island's ever-present commercial presence, were just behind; the French and British trailed. By 1874 Stanley was reporting a phalanx of firms and supporting consulates.

> Close to the water battery is the German consul's house, as neat as clean whitewash can make an Arab building, and next to this house rises the double residence and offices of Her Britannic Majesty's Assistant Political Resident, surmounted by the most ambitious of flagstaffs. Next comes . . . the agent of the great house of John Bertram & Co., of Salem, Mass., and . . . in neighborly proximity, is seen the snow-white house of Mr. Frederick M. Cheney, Agent of Arnold, Hines & Co. [later Arnold, Cheney], of New York.

Although there were more Europeans than Americans in Zanzibar in the 1880s, Americans held on to their commanding lead in the ivory business; their firms had orders for twelve thousand pounds of ivory a month and no problem filling them. Zanzibar was awash in ivory, reaching the point where tusks had become a kind of currency. Particular lots would often move from one merchant's godown to another's for several years as security for various transactions until someone would settle on a transaction that shipped it out. In 1878 merchants on the island had so many caravans leaving for the interior that there was an acute labor shortage; porters' fees went up 100 percent. These in-demand laborers were another example of the confusingly blurred line between captives and freemen—they were slaves whose owners hired them out and in turn paid them.

Substantial quantities of ivory had been exported from Sudan through Khartoum from the 1850s to the early 1880s. When uprisings and conflicts there shut down the trade, Zanzibar became not just the dominant ivory market for East Africa; it ended up providing three-quarters of the world supply by 1891, a year after it became a British protectorate. Ivory remained a top export for American traders. In 1894, 80 percent of the soft ivory exported from Zanzibar went to the United States. The next year, a single huge shipment of 355 tusks weighing 22,307 pounds left for New York.

Business was good all around. By then Tippu Tip, who had retired, was said to have accumulated seven *shambas* (plantations) on Zanzibar and ten thousand slaves. Presumably, he made full use of them, at least up until 1897, when the newly installed sultan submitted to British demands and ended slavery. The photos taken of Tippu Tip show a dark, dignified Zanzibari in a neat swirl of a turban, often dressed in a spotless white tunic with a jeweled *khanjar*, or curved dagger, in his sash. He blinked a lot, was sarcastic, and never deigned to haggle; it was take it or leave it as far as price went, and for the ivory he brought to Nyumba Pembi he would be paid with boxes of newly printed Zanzibar dollars, or *merikani* if he chose. He died of fever in Zanzibar in 1905, before Moore came to the island, but the ivory buyer came to know Muhammed bin Khalfan, Tippu Tip's old partner.

By the turn of the century only one American business was left in Zanzibar: Arnold, Cheney. Rivers of ivory flowed through the spice island, and more often than not the majority of it still went to the United States—and, of that, the lion's share went to Ivoryton and Deep River. At the same time, those Connecticut factories were buying additional ivory stocks from London and other markets; between 1884 and 1911 ten million pounds of raw ivory were brought into the United States. It's clear that during the 1890s and early twentieth century, Pratt, Read and Comstock, Cheney were the largest individual buyers of ivory in the world. E. D. Moore probably purchased most of the ivory these firms used during the time he was overseas—in any event, he bought enough ivory to have covered the keys of most of the pianos sold in the United States in that period.

Moore settled into the life he had already come to know from Aden and Mombasa. He had his room "whitewashed and fixed up pretty slick." He had accounts at the Mnazi Moja and English clubs, where he could play with ivory in the form of billiards and the piano and enjoy a good meal—his own cook put sugar in the mayonnaise. "Took a rickshaw ride around the market this morning. Never'd been there before. It was quite a sight, full of color and Swahili girls and vegetables," reads one diary entry. He got a cable from New York that R. H. Comstock himself, president of Comstock, Cheney, would visit Zanzibar for a few days with his "frau." "Gee whiz, that's a big order," he confesses. "This joint must be slicked up some."

He is buying steadily, and as much Zanzibari—"the softest and loveliest of all ivory," as he later called it—as he can get his hands on. Tanzanian in origin, such tusks were the ultimate trader's "tooth": "gracefully slender and beautifully shaped, with wide, sweeping, out-turned curves; the skin is a light cream-yellow or the slightly lighter color we know generally as 'ivory,' and fine light-blue hair lines run lengthwise in the tusk."

Moore was now a cannier trader than ever. "We got a little ivory from Champu Bhanjie," he writes. "He's that Banyan with the toe on top of his foot. I soaked him with five rejects out of 19 tusks and after about an hour's weeping and wailing and gnashing of teeth he finally tumbled to the fact that it was really so. He took 'em back." But Moore slipped up three days later, passing one defective tusk as prime in a rush to get a shipment ready; it would come out of his margin.

After playing host and sightseeing guide for the Comstocks on their visit—days packed with seeing the shops and the market, having tea with distinguished islanders, picture taking, and various dinners—he takes them back to their ship on the last day of 1910 and ends up celebrating New Year's with his old colleague Smith, who's just arrived. Moore started counting the days before he could leave.

The old Zanzibar was fast disappearing when Moore sailed home in February of 1911. The sultan, Sayyid Ali bin Hamud Al-Busaidi, abdicated before the year was out, bringing to an end such traditions as maintaining a harem of a hundred or so concubines with attendant eunuchs. His successor, demoted by the British to a constitutional monarch, adopted other amusements, such as playing tennis. In 1915 the American consulate in Zanzibar closed, only to be reestablished in Mombasa, which overtook Zanzibar in importance as an ivory market.

IT WAS THE end of an extraordinary era in Zanzibar, well documented in photographs. The Western world's romantic fascination with all points East pushed pioneering photographers to Africa almost immediately after the invention of the process. Louis-Jacques-Mandé Daguerre's invention of the first practical photographic process was described to a session of the French Academy of Science in January of 1839; by November of that year daguerreotypes of Egyptian antiquities were being taken. Bulky equipment, slow shutter speeds, unpredictable chemicals—not to mention conditions that included mold, dust, and heat—at first gave uneven results, but within a decade startling images were being captured.

Zanzibar was a camera magnet. It offered an irresistible visual mix of African and Arabian colors and fabrics and people, lush tropics, a whitewashed polyglot island with a sultan's palace and a teeming port. Some of the earliest photographs, dating from the 1850s, were taken by German merchants (Wm. O'Swald and Company) and show slaves aboard Arab vessels as well as daily life. Later in the century, professional photographers, such as Coutinho Bros., P. De Lord, and A. C. Gomes and Sons, opened studios there. E. D. Moore bought postcards from the latter, but that's not why the name is worth remembering.

Many of the extant photographs (as well as magic lantern slides and even stereo views) of crowded street scenes are riveting reminders of the ivory trade—Africans in loincloths holding huge tusks or perched on piles of them, turbanned Arab and Indian merchants posing next to their wares, European and American buyers in white linen suits and pith helmets. Two in particular are indelible. One is the image of two Africans in white tunics steadying the Kilimanjaro tusks in front of the ornately carved teakwood door of Nyumba Pembi. It was taken in 1898 by A. C. Gomes, who possibly took the companion photo as well, an image of two Africans in a courtyard holding up each end of one of the Kilimanjaro tusks while two more are bent over under the great *mzigi-zigi*—a tusk so heavy it took two porters to carry it—using their backs and shoulders to help support the weight. Markings in Gujarati indicate a weight of 228 pounds.

Moore had first heard about the tusks when he was in Mombasa. "We got two tusks out of Zanzibar about eight years ago that are 'world beaters' still," he wrote in his diary. "One weighed 215 lbs.—the other 220. They were two valuable bits of dentistry, me boy." Every account of these tusks gives a slightly different set of weights (even Moore differs with himself, later stating their poundage at 228 and 232). These discrepancies doubtless have something to do with their drying out over time. Still, each tusk is over ten feet long and nearly twenty-four inches in circumference; when fresh, the two of them together amounted to nearly a quarter of a ton of ivory. Moore later reflected that had he been at his post a few years earlier he might have been the one to purchase them. "The then Zanzibar agent of the writer's firm bought them for a thousand pounds sterling—nearly five thousand dollars—the greatest price that has ever been paid for the tusks of a single elephant."

They were shipped to New York and exhibited at Tiffany and Company. They were sent to London two years later, by which time their weight had "diminished to 226 pounds and 216 pounds respectively," according to G. F. Kunz, who was Tiffany's gemologist. The heavier tusk was purchased by the British Museum (Natural History) in 1901, for £350, and the "small" tusk was bought by Joseph Rodgers and Sons of Sheffield for £325. Spared the fate of being turned into knife handles, the latter was exhibited in the entrance hall of the firm's showrooms. In 1933 the two were finally reunited when that tusk was purchased by the Natural History Museum (as the London institution came to be called), for an "unspecified amount." These two giant gleaming curves went into the permanent collection. Think of them, if you will, as a pair of massive parentheses around an age that did not yet know how fast it was passing.

MOORE RETURNED TO the United States and continued to work in the ivory industry at Pratt, Read in Deep River, Connecticut. He married and moved to nearby Chester. He played Liszt on his Chickering, a make of piano Liszt himself was said to favor, and he began to collect books on Africa, ordering many of them from London. They're still on the shelves around the fireplace of his old house: Livingstone and Stanley, of course, as well as less familiar ones such as T. A. Barnes's *Tales of the Ivory Trade*. At some point in the late 1920s Moore decided to go on record to describe what he had seen and heard. He began to write.

Twenty years after his return from Africa, *Ivory: Scourge of Africa* was published. The dust jacket bears a striking image of an ivory slave coffle: yoked and chained Africans bearing tusks, a black and white procession whose art deco style brings to mind all too well an ebony and ivory keyboard. "During all the turbulent period of which I write my people lived and traded there for the ivory spoil the Arabs brought out from the depths of the mysterious interior," he wrote in the foreword. "Some of the sweating blacks who laid the ivory before me had been the Arabs' slaves, had carried their stolen tusks, shouldered their loads and guns. From them, in large measure, I gathered the story of the ivory treasure that was garnered in the blood of beast and man in a welter of cruelty and carnage that the world will never see again."

Although Moore states that he'd heard these stories firsthand, their moral sting didn't sink in until long after his return to America, if we go by the evidence of his diary. In all those little volumes there's scant evidence he had any qualms about the impact of the enterprise in which he was engaged. "Our lives were so crammed with our business and adventure," he once told an interviewer, "that we were perfectly content to take what we had and make the best of it." Perhaps at the time he was in Aden, Mombasa, and Zanzibar, what he saw and what he came to know of the cruelties of the ivory trade appeared inseparable from the exotic backdrop of the countries in which he worked. He might have seen himself as part of something inevitable, a historic period in which he was swept up, like someone who has been in a war and only later is able to write about horrors barely understood at the time. Yet clearly there was a point when he grew uncomfortable enough with what he knew, what he had been witness to, and what he could piece together to want to put it all down. He was hardly the first to assert a link between the ivory and slave trades—that accusation was a staple theme in much of the writings of nineteenth-century explorers and missionaries— but in his book he connected it to the inner workings of the ivory business.

In his diary he sometimes lapsed into using a shorthand of cultural and ethnic stereotypes typical of his time, but it appears more unthinking than deeply felt. As his outrage over the intertwining of the ivory and slave trades and the endless slaughter of elephants boils up at the end of his book, however, he unleashes a jeremiad that focuses blame squarely on the Swahili middleman.

> The once great river of ivory tusks, sprinkled with the life blood of unhappy slaves as well as of the animals who bore the treasure through the distant forests, is now a trickling narrow ribbon, and the dagger of the perfumed Arab has been snatched from out his bloody hands.

Yet he was perfectly aware of what had really driven the commerce, and pages before he had looked out at his own backyard, writing that ivory "still bobs up and down in the long lines of marching men on the weary trek. . . . And finally much of it is put ashore on the banks of the Connecticut, just a little way in from the Sound, at a little village which, curiously enough, considering the tragic connection of ivory and the black man, bears the same name as that of an old Negro spiritual—Deep River."

Moore's book also dealt with "another phase of the bitter story": the elephant. When he had first arrived in Aden he was far more flippant after shipping two hundred large tusks, worth over £7,000, inside of two weeks. "By gum, I wish those things were mine," he wrote in his diary. "It's slightly exasperating to think a bloody elephant, without having worked a day in his life, can bring about a dozen times the amount of a man's hard earned savings of a lifetime, just for a couple of jaw ornaments that never cost him a [cent] in the first place." After he was posted to Mombasa, he was surprised by the flow of ivory that was always there to meet New York's demands. "More ivory in today. The way that stuff comes into this burg is amazing. There must be a pile of elephants nosing around upcountry, and no mistake." He was also impressed by how big the tusks could be. One of them brought into his godown was "a Congo weighing 111¾ lbs. That's the biggest one I've seen," he wrote in his diary. (The biggest ones he ever bought in his career were a pair of "blunt-pointed, chunky 'gendi' teeth"—hard ivory from the Congo; one tusk weighed 164 pounds, and the other 168 pounds.)

Later, what had been happening became clear to him. He remembered the ivory markets he had been in.

> At Aden, where I secured tons of Abyssinian ivory collected as taxes and tribute by Menelik, King of Ethiopia, little of the ivory showed signs of having been recently in a living head. On the other hand, this condition apparently was reversed in the country to the south. At Zanzibar and Mombasa, the greater number of the tusks were small, under thirty pounds in weight. I paid little attention to the freshness or staleness of the small teeth laid out in rows on to godown floors, because I was buying only the larger tusks. In regard to these, the evidence of decay, dryness and cleanliness, on the one hand, and of recent bloodstains, dried tissue and the like, on the other, could not be overlooked.

More and more, ivory was coming from freshly killed elephants. The pious hope of those concerned about the impact of the trade on elephants had always been that much of what ended up in commerce was "found" ivory, recovered from elephants that had died of natural causes. This notion is an old one, particularly among the British. In 1810 the African Society in London was told that "the demand on the coast . . . induces [the traders] to sell to the Negroes who traffic there, the teeth which in the course of their journey they find in the woods."

Lewis and Peat, Ltd., ivory brokers at 6, Mincing Lane in London, took the same reassuring line in its 1921 brochure *Ivory: General Information:* "It is perhaps not generally known that Ivory for the most part is found dead in the jungle, and collected by natives from the 'Cemeteries,' so called because the herds of Elephants which inhabit particular regions and wander round from place to place for water and food, are supposed to have chosen spots in which to die, and when these cemeteries are discovered a good haul of Ivory results. Only a very small percentage of Ivory is shot by hunters."

Moore knew better. "You may be sure," he told his readers of the 1930s, "that your bit of ivory comes from an elephant expressly slaughtered for the ivory it carried." In the beginning, he explained, it was easier to raid the accumulated ivory stocks of villages in the interior than pursue ivory in the forests, but when those sources had been exhausted Arab ivory traders would send out indigenous hunters to wrest what they could from local herds. Elephant populations were being devastated.

What's more, big tuskers were being killed off—that was clear from the steadily falling average weight of "prime" tusks, those over forty pounds. In the 1880s these teeth used to fall between eighty and ninety pounds, by the late 1920s they were averaging fifty-five pounds apiece. The trend was apparent. To make it clear that the desire for the luxurious, satin-surfaced material used for the backs of ladies' hand mirrors resulted in the "sickening" slaughter of elephants, he estimated that thirty thousand African elephants had to have been killed each year between 1905 and 1912 to satisfy the demands of the ivory trade. This figure seems so large it almost fails to register in the mind, although he works out the dimensions of just how big a pyramid all those dead pachyderms would make. The example he gives of how brittle ivory could react to sudden exposure to cold on the London ivory docks by cracking with a noise like a gunshot seems a more tangible reminder of the cost of each pair of tusks.

Yet, astonishingly, it turns out that Moore's figure is actually too low. Ivory trade researcher Esmond Bradley Martin's recent analysis estimates that nearly forty-four thousand African elephants were killed annually between 1850 and 1914. Put another way, at least seven hundred tons of ivory were shipped from Africa every year during that time frame—and this meant that 2,800,000 elephants were killed. Moore had concluded that the appetite for ivory was insatiable. He admitted there was no substitute for it.

> Compare its "feel" with any substitute—celluloid, for instance; there is
> no comparison. This same "touch" and grace of ivory in toilet sets
> pleases the sensitive hands of femininity; and even in coarser male hands
> an ivory billiard balls feels like one apart from the common kind and
> prompts inquiry and compliment.

Moore feared "the killing for ivory" would go on "until the elephant is exterminated throughout the whole continent of Africa."

If Moore ever felt any remorse over his participation in the ivory trade, he seems to have kept it to himself. In fact, he once said in an interview that

"I would not exchange those years in Africa for anything in the world." The
dedication to his book

> *I, too, have slept in the arms of Zanzibar, have been her slave, am her*
> *lover still. To her, lovely and cruel mistress, I dedicate this volume of her*
> *misdeeds*

has been construed as a veiled confession, but to what? A man who be-
rated himself in his diary for the moral failing of putting his arm around a
married woman (at her request, no less) is not someone who is likely to
have wallowed in "the fleshpots of the East." It's more plausible to read
this as an admission that his seduction by the island he had longed to see
all his life could not keep him from laying bare its pivotal role in a commerce that had cost Africans and their elephants so terribly much.

Moore had experienced Zanzibar before its exoticism faded into
faintly perfumed history and looked back at his time there with mixed
feelings. "I saw it at the end of the old Arab era," he wrote in the early
1930s, "before its old romance had been outgrown or destroyed: but now
the old slavers are all gone, the elephant poachers are curbed, the ivory
comes down in driblets and trickles instead of the solid stream I saw; and
the country generally, from the viewpoint of an old ivory man, has gone to
hell." He'd seen it as he cared to remember it, and he didn't want to go
back.

Ernst D. Moore died in 1932.

6

Ivory Hunters

"Fitting cartridges between my left hand fingers and with full magazine I approached as quietly as possible, fully prepared to give anything heading my way a sound lesson," W. D. M. Bell wrote of stalking an elephant herd in the Lado Enclave on the Uganda–Sudan border in 1910. He had already shot two bulls in a clearing and was hoping for a third.

> Looking into the brilliantly lit open space from the twilight of the forest, I saw over the backs and heads of the cows between us the towering body of a large bull well out in the centre of the herd. His tusks were hidden by the cows but it was almost certain from his general mass that they would be satisfactory. Just the little dark slot above the earhole was intermittently uncovered by the heads, ears or trunks of the intervening cows, which were still much agitated. At last I got a clear slant and fired. The image was instantly blocked out by the thrown-up heads of several cows as they launched themselves furiously towards the shot. . . . I myself had been badly scared once or twice with their barging about, and it was now time to see about it. My shot caught the leading cow in the brain and dropped her slithering on her knees . . . in time the space was clear of living elephant.

Walter Dalrymple Maitland Bell was neither the first nor the last ivory hunter, but he may have been the most successful. He slew more than a thousand ivory-bearing elephants before finally retiring, in the 1930s, to Scotland, where he purchased an estate and, later, an eighty-foot yacht with the proceeds of his ivory-hunting safaris.

E. D. Moore's hope that slavery had been suppressed, poaching controlled, and the slaughter of elephants at least partly curtailed by the early decades of the twentieth century was not entirely misplaced. Slavery, while proving difficult to eradicate, was no longer the open trade it had been. And the "scramble" for Africa—the final post-1880 race among competing European powers to carve up the continent into colonies—did bring, in the wake of vast social changes, the first efforts to regulate hunting and establish game reserves. But elephants were still being killed in huge numbers. The combination of scant enforcement of early game laws, the development of modern firearms, and the increasingly high prices paid for ivory allowed for one final phase of unlimited elephant pursuit: that of the lone ivory hunter.

Ivory hunting in the late nineteenth and early twentieth centuries could flourish only in poorly governed regions and in some cases had to compete with powerful states equally interested in the trade in tusks. As Arab-led ivory and slave trading faded, a new, even more powerfully extractive commerce took its place: state-sponsored ivory grabs by ever more effective colonial administrations. None was more openly rapacious than that of Leopold II, king of the Belgians, who treated the Congo basin as his personal fiefdom. His wholesale looting of the natural resources of the Congo cost some ten million lives. "As the 1890s began, the work whose sanctity Leopold prized most highly was seizing all the ivory that could be found," Adam Hochschild writes. "Congo state officials and their African auxiliaries swept through the country on ivory raids, shooting elephants, buying tusks from villagers for a pittance, or simply confiscating them. Congo peoples had been hunting elephants for centuries, but now they were forbidden to sell or deliver ivory to anyone other than an agent of Leopold."

In many ways Leopold's "command economy" was simply an updated, more thorough version of the cruder ivory-gathering methods employed in mid-century in the Sudan. Then Khartoum merchants obtained Egyptian monopolies of districts they could farm for ivory by backing "penniless adventurers, loaning them money at 100 percent interest, and requiring repayment in ivory at one-half its market value." Leopold offered his agents in the field a commission, based on ivory's market value, making it worthwhile for them to obtain ivory by any method they thought they could get away with. Joseph Conrad's *Heart of Darkness* paints an unsparing portrait of Europeans' ivory lust in the Congo, when the spectral pallor of a white tusk had the significance of a death's-head. (*"The word 'ivory' rang in the air, was whispered, was sighed. You would think they were praying to it. A taint of imbecile rapacity blew through it all, like a whiff of some corpse."*)

Not content with exploiting the entire Congo, Leopold, in 1894, managed to secure by treaty a lifetime lease over a huge portion of East Africa on the Sudan–Uganda border. It was run by Belgians in his personal employ, and all revenue was streamed into his royal purse; in effect, it was the king's private estate. The terms stipulated that six months after his death the entire region—220 miles long, 100 miles wide, extending along the banks of the Nile up to the borders of the Belgian Congo—was to be handed over to Anglo-Egyptian Sudan, as it was then known. In June 1910, after Leopold's death, the Belgians began to move out before the Sudanese could establish effective control. For an ivory hunter, this legal gray zone, a no-man's-land full of elephants—including older bulls carrying substantial ivory—was a magnet.

Before Leopold's demise, Bell had obtained an unlimited elephant hunting license for the Lado Enclave (for £20) from the local *chef de zone*, who spent much of his time at his remote post holding drinking contests. This formality hardly seemed necessary after the king's passing. A horde of adventurers arrived, dreaming of making their fortunes in elephants' teeth. They had been infected by "ivory fever," the way miners caught gold fever. In the nineteenth century, many African explorers had succumbed to it. Sir Samuel Baker, the discoverer of Lake Albert, couldn't pass up the 2,000 percent gains possible in "ivory transactions" in Bunyoro in Uganda—at one point he had accumulated so much ivory he "required 700 porters to carry both tusks and provisions." He predicted that "the future was tinged with a golden hue. Ivory would be almost inexhaustible." Ivory prices, which had remained remarkably stable through the mid- to late nineteenth century—there always seemed to be fresh supplies from previously untapped regions to meet growing demand—were climbing impressively in the early twentieth: in New York top-grade ivory had doubled in price from 1895 to 1905 and was now almost $4 a pound.

There was nothing to prevent someone with enough adventure in his soul from amassing his own vast treasure pile direct from the source: elephants. And the Lado Enclave had enormous herds, all for the taking and with few questions asked. "Finding themselves in a country where even murder went unpunished, every man became a law unto himself," Bell wrote. Attacked by renegade soldiers while traveling in his canoe, he managed to escape after exchanging gunfire. Bell regrouped his porters and pushed off for the "primeval forest" of the backcountry, where he collected so much ivory he had to bury it in caches to be dug up later.

Bell was following in the tracks of previous European hunters who had gone out on their own for ivory. In the mid-nineteenth century R. G. Gordon Cumming had hunted elephants in South Africa—in a kilt and deerstalker, no less. Noted for his cold-bloodedness, he thought nothing of brewing coffee before bothering to finish off a dying elephant he'd wounded. In the 1870s Frederick Courteney Selous financed his numerous safaris across southern Africa with the ivory extracted from the elephants he shot, returning from one hunting trek with five thousand pounds of tusks. Selous, who later accompanied Theodore Roosevelt on the first part of the ex-president's grand safari, had a naturalist's instincts as well as a hunter's and pursued butterflies as well as big game. He shared this quirk with Arthur H. Neumann, another fabled Victorian ivory hunter, who netted three new species of Lepidoptera on his elephant safaris, the last one of which, in 1904, also netted him ivory worth £4,500.

Ivory hunters, as opposed to those who picked up a few tusks as a by-product of their explorations or hunting trips, were professionals. They worked for themselves and outfitted their own safaris. They were like nineteenth-century whalers: they made their fortunes by slaying great beasts in remote places and were often gone for a year or more. Unlike whalers, however, they had smaller crews and simpler equipment—a couple of trusted trackers, a gun bearer, a cook, a headman and a string of porters that could be hired as needed, rifles, camp gear, and sometimes a wagon and oxen or river craft were normally all that was required. The job description for an ivory hunter included a lust for danger, a disdain for authority, bottomless stamina, and the ability to shrug off the hardships of the bush: venomous snakes, crocodile-choked rivers, fever-carrying insects, blistering heat, bone-shaking cold, thieving porters, treacherous chieftains, and corrupt officials. There were rewards, to be sure. A successful ivory hunter might make £3,000 to £4,000 from a six-month safari. But it was a high-risk business. Not all of them returned from their long treks to a comfortable retirement and wrote of their adventures.

W. D. M. Bell had the right résumé before he ventured into Lado. Born in Edinburgh in 1880, Bell was the second youngest of ten children and orphaned at the age of six. Raised by his older brothers, he ran away from several schools and was finally allowed to fulfill his dream of going to Africa. At the age of sixteen he arrived in Mombasa with a beat-up rifle and eked out an existence as a meat hunter for a railway survey party. Broke, he went to the Alaskan Klondike to join the gold rush and then fought in the Boer war, where he was taken prisoner and escaped. He went back to Britain and finally returned to Africa at the beginning of the twentieth century. Bell spent nearly five years hunting elephants in the Karamojo region of northeast Uganda, which earned him the moniker "Karamojo" Bell.

It was difficult, dangerous, messy work. Once an elephant had been slain, there was the onerous task of getting the tusks out. Bell would set his Karamojan men to work to hack and slice away the flesh of the head and expose the huge bone socket of the uppermost tusk. "A very long and tedious job it is to get the skin and gristle away," Bell wrote. "Nothing blunts a knife more quickly than elephant hide, because of the sand and grit in its loose texture." After the skull was exposed on one side the neck had to be cut, "a herculean task," as he put it. "The vertebrae severed, the head is turned over by eight or ten men, and the other side similarly cleaned." Then came the critical task—always left to an expert native equipped with a sharp ax—to chop the tusks free from the clutching sockets in which a third of their length was typically embedded without losing large flakes of precious ivory. He would test the tusk from time to time, finally wresting it free with a great sucking snap, like a large tree limb breaking off. Understandably, Bell's men much preferred to let "sun and putrefaction" do the work—within three days the uppermost tusk could usually be worked loose from the carcass, the one underneath the following day.

Held with its point up, a blood-streaked tusk would relinquish the last clump of animal flesh that had been clinging inside, a wet sack of tooth pulp that slid out onto the grass. Once the ivory had been sorted out, the always protein-hungry trackers and porters—their ranks invariably swollen by local villagers who always seemed to come out of nowhere—could have their fill of meat. At this point many hunters would leave the huge remains to be dismembered by an excited swarm of people, not caring to watch the scramble for chunks of fat and other raw tidbits and the piercing of the abdominal wall when the entrails would spill out, as one put it, "like the blossoming of a great opalescent flower, flowing and growing in pastel hints of appalling beauty, until the whole mass quivered five or six feet above the carcass." But Bell wanted to study the innards, the vital points, heart, lungs, brain, in relation to the animal's exterior, and he would peer into the huge cavity of the massive rib cage. "I had spears thrust through from the direction from which a bullet would come," he wrote, "and tried to commit it to my memory."

Bell was persistent, observant, and methodical, always looking for ways to improve his skills and increase his ivory take. It was one thing to find elephants, another to sneak up on them. But given an elephant's size and power, not to mention a hide an inch thick in places, it wasn't easy to kill one. Bell was well aware that an indiscriminate spray of bullets was no guarantee the animal would go down unless a vital organ was reached. He quickly learned that wounding a big bull, even fatally, in the middle of a herd would scatter the rest of the animals, but they might cluster around an animal that fell dead in its tracks, milling in confusion, thereby allowing additional kills. To understand exactly where he should aim, he once had his trackers use a two-man saw to split the skull between the tusks of one of the elephants he'd shot so he could determine the exact location of the brain: a small, foot-long loaf in the center of the skull, just forward of the ear holes. A gifted draftsman, he made careful sketches of the dissection to work out different shooting angles. Bell became a master of the brain shot, which he would use on elephants at the edge of the herd so that they wouldn't topple over on the others and panic them. In areas where the animals had not been hunted with firearms before, the sound of a shot might—at first—be taken for a thunderclap.

Most ivory hunters put their faith in big bore armament, typically double rifles newly devised in London for African pachyderms such as elephant, rhino, and hippo, chambered for cartridges the size of small cigars and loaded with bullets weighing an ounce or more. The recoil of these heavy shoulder cannons was almost enough to knock a nimrod out from under his pith helmet, but the downrange impact was thought to provide extra insurance. Sir Samuel Baker, who pondered the issue of weaponry at length in his book *Wild Beasts and Their Ways* (1891)—in which he posed questions like "What is the duty of a bullet?"—came down firmly on the side of the mighty .577 Nitro Express as "quite equal to any animal in creation."

Bell preferred to use a .275 Rigby (7×57 mm) bolt action rifle to kill elephants with surgically precise shots—as he would certainly have to do, using a caliber regarded as more suitable for shooting deer. His "wicked" little weapon weighed just over five pounds; he carried it everywhere, until it became an extension of his arm, and his marksmanship, he admitted, achieved "automatic accuracy." Bell's reputation as a crack shot was never questioned by his contemporaries. He was known to be just as deadly when sitting on the swaying shoulders of a porter in high grass or, almost unimaginably, when six tons of enraged elephant was bearing down on him. None of this was for show. Bell was in business. He thought in terms of the tusks he could collect, not the mighty-hunter posturing that was to become a major feature of the future safari business. He picked off elephants with exactitude, but not because it would be less traumatic for their herds than the sloppy carnage a less skilled shot would cause; Bell dropped them on the spot so he could shoot more.

It was all about ivory. Sitting around a sputtering campfire in the rain in the African night, picking at a bowl of larvae-flecked maize, bone-weary ivory hunters dreamed of striking it rich by finding the so-called elephants' graveyard, the place where old tuskers supposedly went to lay down and die. Was it to be found in the bottom of rivers or lakes, the end of the road for fatally thirsty elephants? Perhaps a secret trail into a mountain lair? Despite their size, few elephant carcasses last long, whether on the savannah or in the forest, and their tusks, if not gnawed away, were quickly collected. All this fed the legend: where had they gone? Bell himself thought he might have stumbled across it, or one of them, anyway, north of Lake Rudolf (Lake Turkana) in Kenya, at the end of a well-worn elephant path—a grassy plateau dotted with "lava-strewn hill-slopes of the most forbidding description." The grass was dotted, Bell recalled, with sun-bleached elephant skulls and the whitened posts of partly buried leg bones. Three pools of clear green water glistened in the oasis, ringed with a white powdery residue marking higher water. Bell tasted the water and recoiled from its bitterness. The locals told him that a great drought had brought elephants, and people, to drink from these deadly salty pools, whereupon they died. "So much for the elephant cemeteries," wrote Bell.

The ivory hunters never found the elephants' graveyard. Instead, of course, they created their own.

IN 1902 BELL and his men walked into Mani-mani, a slaving settlement in northern Uganda, and encountered a motley lot of Arab, Swahili, and African traders, one of whom they all deferred to: Shundi, a "great coal-black Bantu" whose extraordinary calm and dignity made him appear to Bell "like a lion among hyenas." A Kavirondo by birth, he had been captured and sold into slavery but converted to Islam to obtain his freedom and had risen to become a great slaver and now a prominent ivory trader. Bell discovered that Shundi had owned the Chagga hunter who four years before, on the slopes of Kilimanjaro, had slain the elephant that carried the now famous colossal tusks. Although Shundi had wealth, respect, and whatever comforts the eighty Masai women in his retinue could provide, he thought himself a fool for selling those mighty ivories for their weight instead of for what they were: the greatest tusks ever recorded.

AFTER TAKING TIME out to become a fighter pilot in World War I, Bell married. He made two more trips to Africa before finally retiring to an estate in the Highlands of Scotland. There he wrote several books detailing his African adventures, illustrated with his own sketches, and commissioned a steel-hulled sailing yacht, which he raced and cruised with his wife before his death in 1951.

W. D. M. Bell was among the last of his breed, although there are a surprising number of books written by people claiming to be the very last of the "last of the ivory hunters." The image is still potent, carrying a distinct whiff of pungent, half-illicit adventure, even if it lingers largely in the form of dimly remembered scenes from the film version of H. Rider Haggard's *King Solomon's Mines*. Legal ivory hunting on the grand scale that was possible in the Lado Enclave in 1909–10 was no more. That period overlapped neatly with the first of the great organized safaris, Theodore Roosevelt's. "He advertised East Africa as no other could," Moore later reflected. "Following him came a veritable flock of big game hunters, globetrotters, nabobs and upper crusters." The safari business had been born—the very prototype of "adventure travel." Books abounded with advice on what to take, from sun helmet to snake-proof English puttees, and offered useful Kiswahili phrases: *Nguo wangu wapi, boy? Nataka kwenda kupiga nyama sasa hivi* ("Where are my clothes, boy? I will at once go out to shoot animals.").

The image of the professional adventurer that "ivory hunter" once summoned up was supplanted in the public imagination by the "white hunter" (later "professional hunter," or P.H.): a European in a wide-brimmed khaki fedora with a leopard-skin hatband who guided clients on motorized safaris to knock off a variety of game on license (backing them up if the animals didn't keel over as planned and things got a bit sticky), and entertained them with tall tales and sundowners served by black Africans in fezzes as they sat around a crackling acacia-wood campfire under the bowl of the vast and starry African night.

Elephants were the biggest of big game, one of the "big five"—the short list of large animals that might take serious exception to being turned into taxidermy. There was no end to the argument over which was the most dangerous quarry: lion, leopard, buffalo, rhino, or elephant? If things went wrong, a client could be bitten, shredded, stomped, gored, or flattened, possibilities that added a certain frisson to stalking through the tall grass, although the P.H. would do everything in his power to ensure his meal ticket wasn't endangered. Still, if size mattered, the largest living land animal had no rival as a trophy. A hundred-pounder—meaning a bull elephant carrying tusks that weighed more than a hundred pounds apiece, a rarity even in the old days—would be something to brag about.

In fact, just flanking the fireplace back home in London or New York with a pair of man-tall swoops of ivory would say it all for you.

HUNTING, AS IT had been done in Africa from time immemorial, became something that colonial powers structured according to European ideas of property, boundaries, and rights, with all the attendant licenses, bag limits, seasons, and permissible methods such regulation required. A *mzungu* (white man) knew how to stay within the hunting laws (or bend them to his needs), but the African who hunted as his grandfather did could easily discover himself jailed as a poacher. This states baldly, of course, what was an enormously complex, decades-long process by which different colonies (at a later stage countries) sorted out acceptable versus unacceptable taking of game from the European point of view.

In the early twentieth century, wildlife management invested in game control schemes to reduce or eradicate certain species to allow for ranching, railway lines, agriculture, fences, and settlement in general. As the game warden of Kenya put it in the 1930s, the game laws were intended to "retain as much game in the Colony as is consistent with the varied human interests—white settlement, and native husbandry, development and evolution."

John A. Hunter, one of the most prominent East African professional hunters in the first half of the twentieth century, helped shoot nearly a thousand unwanted rhinos in a single year for the Kenya Game Department— merely one of many such tasks. Hunter was famous for his steely nerves. In 1931, when pursuing cattle-killing lions with his friend Denys Finch Hatton (Karen Blixen's lover), Finch Hatton managed to nail two of them together with a right and a left from his double rifle. "Good effort," Hunter commented. "I'd take any chance with you behind me, J.A.," Finch Hatton replied. For decades up to the 1950s Hunter guided European aristocrats, American tycoons, movie stars, Indian princes, and hundreds more on safaris that became increasingly luxurious. But when he grew tired of clients, he went off ivory hunting on his own. Back then there were few restrictions on the numbers of elephants that could be shot in outlying districts.

> At that time ivory was selling for twenty-four shillings a pound—say an
> average of £150 for a pair of good tusks. An experienced hunter could
> drop an elephant with nearly every shot, and a .450 No. 2 cartridge cost
> only one and sixpence. I was enough of a Scotsman to like a bargain like
> that.

Hunter was also asked to assist in gathering evidence in cases of ivory
poaching. To him it became a familiar story of nabbing the perpetrators
and fining them a goat, but to no effect. The money that could be realized from poached ivory was worth the risk, if they could find a buyer,
who would be at the end of a long chain of contacts, each taking a commission. So Hunter had to forge a parallel chain of bribed informers to arrive at the usual suspect: an Indian shopkeeper in a riverside village.
"Poached ivory," Hunter wrote, "always begins its journey to India in a
dhow hired by the buyer who conceals his prosperous smuggling activities
behind the façade of a store filled with junk."

Europeans, settlers or visitors, had or could make use of legal access
to the ivory. They could hunt for it and sell it or keep it as trophies, while
the colonial government controlled the sale and export of tusks. The "natives" and the shopkeepers who kept up what remained of the ancient Indian Ocean ivory trade simply went underground.

DURING THE FIRST half of the twentieth century, elephants were seen as
far more than quarry or a source of ivory; in fact they appeared in a proliferation of personas—or, more precisely, had these roles thrust upon
them. Long-standing symbols in art, elephants now multiplied on postage
stamps, on matchbox covers, and in a wide range of advertising. They
populated hosts of children's books (Rudyard Kipling's *Just So Stories* in
1902 and Jean de Brunhoff's *Babar* series, which began in 1931, to mention but two). They began appearing in films (Robert Flaherty's 1937 *Elephant Boy*, Walt Disney's 1941 animated feature *Dumbo*, and so on), and
both African and Asian elephants became staple exhibits in zoos all
around the world. At first they were typically housed in terribly cramped

conditions, the equivalent of jail cells for animals used to roaming vast distances. Many were reduced to rocking in place, although some got to move about by being put to work giving rides to children.

As they had in the previous century, elephants continued to perform in circuses on both sides of the Atlantic, taught to do unnatural tricks such as headstands or feats like walking on tightropes through persistent conditioning and the judicious application of the elephant hook. Sometimes what was asked seemed charming enough, at least to human audiences. In the 1940s the Ringling Brothers, Barnum & Bailey Circus commissioned George Balanchine to create choreography for elephants; Balanchine in turn persuaded Igor Stravinsky to write the music. *Circus Polka* premiered in New York in 1942, performed by fifty elephants in pink tutus and jeweled headbands, each with a ballerina on its back. The star was Modoc, the largest Indian elephant in America, ridden by ballerina Vera Zorina. The ballet ran for 425 performances.

Away from the glitter and music of the ring, however, circus life for elephants was often considerably darker, and sometimes literally crushing. When adult elephants go into *musth* — a condition that is thought to be associated with sexual behavior but isn't perfectly understood — they secrete a fluid from the temporal glands on both sides of the head between the eyes and ears and dribble urine. These glands are much more active in males than in females, and captive animals in musth can become irritable, uncontrollable, aggressive, and dangerous. In the early years of the circus in the United States, there was a string of incidents in which trainers or bystanders would be thrown, gored, trampled, or otherwise extinguished by male elephants in musth. If a townsperson met this unpleasant fate, local outcry demanded the elephant's execution, which was usually accomplished by a hail of police gunfire. Circus bulls in this condition were sometimes shackled at all four feet or even draped entirely in chains. In the late 1920s that was the fate of Tusko, billed as "the most chained elephant in the world." Owned by the Barnes Circus in the United States, he was paraded around the ring as a kind of bound monster. In an effort to control his musth, he was put in a "crush cage" — a sort of giant clamp made of railroad sleepers that held him immobile for three or four months at a time. Unable to lie down or move a foot, he broke his tusks in desperation. Surely a bullet to the brain would have been kinder than being buried alive this way, but Tusko was eventually purchased by a sympathetic trainer and rehabilitated.

Ivory source, big game, gentle giant, circus act, film star, children's ride, maddened rogue—the actual elephant was getting hard to see behind the guises created by these often incompatible roles.

IVORY TOO WAS starting to become as much an idea as an actuality.

It was still revered and valued as an artistic medium and had uses, such as piano keys, for which there were no satisfactory substitutes, but widespread applications that had been found for it in the late nineteenth century were in many cases now being better served by modern plastics. Natural substances like ivory could effectively only be cut or carved, but there were no such limits with plastics. They could be molded into complex shapes, flowed with ease into fantastic forms, given eye-catching colors, and endlessly reproduced. Initially, celluloid was the most common substitute for ivory, but by the 1890s branded synthetic materials such as Eburnea, Xylonite, Ivorene, Bakelite, Implex, and dozens of others led to yet more refined and specialized plastics. Plastics arguably became the defining material of the twentieth century.

Whether plastics could function as substitutes for ivory seemed increasingly irrelevant. They had their own exoticism—daring and modern. "By the 1920s the introduction and use of plastics like Bakelite, celluloid, and others had begun to change the appearance and 'feel' of life," as Robert Friedel explains it. For the first time in history, the "touch" of organic materials was on the way to becoming less familiar, even uncommon. By the 1930s advances in the field of chemistry "combined with the ambitions of giant companies, both in Europe and the United States, to push ahead the development of a whole host of 'polys,'" as Friedel puts it: polyethylene, polystyrene, polyesters, polyvinyl chloride (PVC), polymethyl methacrylate (acrylics). Plastic coffee cups, "popcorn" packing pellets, shopping bags, food wrap, and all the other disposable plastic conveniences that now litter modern life would not be long in coming.

The success of plastics even knocked the bottom out of the modest market for an organic ivory substitute discovered in Victorian times, tagua—"vegetable ivory." The hard, cream-colored seed endosperm harvested from the nuts of two palm species in South America is attractive and carvable, but tagua's inch or less size limitations restricted its use to buttons and minor jewelry. Nearly forty thousand tons of the material were shipped to Europe and the United States from Colombia and Ecuador annually until cheaper plastics wiped out the tagua trade in the 1940s.

Even the real thing started to look old-fashioned. Like grandmother's good silver that was brought out only on special occasions, ivory began to be put away in cupboards and attics. Still, when extravagance was called for, it fulfilled its timeless role of seducing the eye and hand. Before independence, Indian princes ordered bespoke Rolls-Royces that featured, alongside gun racks and hunting lamps and purdah glass for limousines, ivory steering wheels and control knobs. For some uses, it was still highly preferred. What made ivory the peerless material for piano keys—its smooth but nonslippery touch under the fingers—also made it the perfect material for pistol grips. When a clammy hand needed a firm grasp on a tense situation, a man wanted a fistful of ivory. Wild Bill Hickok carried two ivory-handled .45 Colt six-shooters, butts forward in open holsters for a cross-body quick draw. During World War II the equally flamboyant General George S. Patton also carried ivory-handled .45 Colt single-action revolvers. A reporter once made the mistake of referring to his guns as "pearl-handled," incurring the general's retort: "Only a New Orleans pimp would carry a pearl-handled gun."

Unquestionably, ivory still held allure. Heiress Nancy Cunard, fascinated by all things African, was famous for her thick, inches-wide ivory bracelets; Man Ray's photograph *Ivory Shackles* shows her wearing them. For Cunard's *Negro Anthology* (1934), her collaborator Raymond Michelet had "originally planned to include an article in which he would have claimed that ivory when warmed by body heat gives off the smell of semen, indicating his belief in erotic motivations to African art." And, of course, writers kept finding metaphorical uses for ivory's inevitable tactile associations. Consider how Vladimir Nabokov in *Lolita* (1955) has his protagonist describe a caress.

> The hollow of my hand was still ivory-full of Lolita—full of the feel of
> her pre-adolescently incurved back, that ivory-smooth, sliding sensation

of her skin through the thin frock that I had worked up and down while
I held her.

Yet none of this potent array of use and meaning could prevent the slow
slide of ivory's primary importance in modern culture toward its final resting
place as just another name in the color wheel. When everything else about it
was forgotten, a substance could always linger on in a poetic afterimage. Because the term "ivory" carried such rich associations, those who gave names
to sample chips in displays of house paint were either drawn to it or, because
of them, weren't. Ivory suggests age, antiquity, importance, dignity. It's white
with patina. It's old lace wrapped in memory. Yes, it's creamy, but there's
more than mere milkiness to it. It easily overshadows the modest cluster of
meanings that accrue to "eggshell," "vanilla," and "beeswax," respectively,
and in gravitas it easily trumps the blandness of "beige," the desert-dryness of
"bone," the powderiness of "chalk," or the lifelessness of "off-white." Among
serious shades of white, there's simply no contest. Ivory has weight, which is
why it is the color of diplomas, decrees, and proclamations.

Ivory is the color of German taxis and the underparts of the largest
breed of domestic cats, the Ragdoll. It's the description given to the center portion of lesions as well as to the rind of ripe casaba melons. Ivory is
the tint of the clouds given off when ice water is added to a glass of anise-
flavored Turkish raki and is the lightest acceptable color of authentic
Swiss grade A Emmentaler cheese. It's the color a bride would choose for
her gown if she wanted a very traditional look for her wedding. Of course,
one must not forget Ivory Soap, a product that dates from 1879 and since
1882 has been advertised as "99 and 44/100% pure." But all this use of
"ivory" as a descriptor to be slapped on this or that by latter-day copywrit-
ers, decorators, and marketers has had the effect of further diluting it—
not just taking the material itself out of it but whiting out any unpleasant
associations with elephant deaths.

ONE MIGHT HAVE thought that the rise of plastics would rescue ivory from
its absorption into industrial use and restore it to its original stature as a

rare, precious material and artistic medium. But the conquest of plastics failed to refocus artistic ivory use. It seemed to hang on only in jewelry and cue sticks and fine furniture, although in that sphere it had one last brilliant encore in the hands of art deco masters, such as *ébéniste* (cabinet maker) Émile-Jacques Ruhlmann, whose 1920s creations celebrated the new industrial age and modernist forms while drawing on traditional materials, including ivory. Ivory carving on the continent persisted in Germany and France in such places as Erbach and Dieppe, but the trade waxed and waned with fashion. Seemingly marooned by history, these centers were condemned to repeat old forms. In Erbach, craftsmen turned out figurines, tankards, and intricate re-creations of flower blossoms; in Dieppe, where Napoleon himself had shopped for ivory, carvers turned out endless small ornaments and *articles de Paris*, but the craft was dying; by the mid-1960s there were only two carvers left.

THE IVORY-CUTTING industry in the Connecticut River Valley, so heavily dependent on the importance of the piano, was living on borrowed time. New marvels like the gramophone, the radio, the automobile, and motion pictures distracted the middle class and undermined piano sales, and the Great Depression knocked the weak legs out from under the wobbly market. Pratt, Read of Deep River could boast sales of $2,105,470 in 1925; by 1932 sales had fallen to $147,928. The company entered into talks with its nearby longtime rival Comstock, Cheney, which had suffered a similar decline. Descendants of the founding families of the two firms had sometimes worked in each other's businesses; starting in 1936 they would join forces, merging the companies under the Pratt, Read name, which was better known, but moving all production facilities to Comstock, Cheney's factory in Ivoryton, which was more up to date.

   In World War II piano production virtually ceased. Pratt, Read made wooden gliders for the government, even reopening the Deep River factory to meet demand. After the war the company resumed piano action production but sought to streamline its business and diversify. Celluloid had been offered as an inexpensive piano key covering as far back as the 1880s, and as use of synthetic materials continued to grow Pratt, Read saw the future and went out of the ivory business. It brought in its last shipments of ivory in the mid-1950s. At one point, it did investigate the possibility of importing mammoth ivory from the Soviet Union as an alternative, but nothing came of this. By 1958 its last ivory stocks had been used up. From then on the "ivories" on its keyboards were made of plastic.

J. A. HUNTER LEFT a fascinating account of guiding an Indian maharaja on a grand safari in colonial Kenya in the 1950s. Not wanting to be indiscreet about a former client, Hunter was coy about his name but described him as the ruler of a southern Indian state, fabulously wealthy and inclined to corpulence. Looking for some needed outdoor activity out of sight of his subjects so that he might dispense with the expected pomp and ceremony and get about on his own two legs, he settled on an African safari. Hunter, who thought he'd seen everything on previous extravagant excursions in the bush, was taken aback by the arrival of a fleet of vehicles that included an armored car, a mobile wireless station, a van set up as a movie theater complete with plush armchairs, an elaborate kitchen on wheels, a medical unit complete with X-ray equipment, and a royal caravan with a lavish bedroom and separate drawing room holding a small, exquisite piano.

The sheer magnificence of the London-built guns the prince had sent on ahead made Hunter's eyes grow moist, but he was especially pleased when he finally met his client, every inch a maharajah, already dressed in tailored khaki drill, wearing a jeweled turban and exuding impeccable manners. "We'll have a splendid time, Hunter," he said. "I feel it in my bones." Enthusiastic and curious, he "could have gone round popping off guns here, there and everywhere," as Hunter put it, but he turned out to have little taste for indiscriminate killing. Still, each day's bag was duly recorded by the prince's secretary and typed overnight on gold-edged paper and bound into a red-leather book, which the maharaja kept beside him.

The prince didn't overlinger in the bush; he wanted to get back to his caravan each evening and play his piano. Devoted to music, he kept a

The Kilimanjaro tusks—at a combined weight of 464 pounds, the largest pair ever recorded—in the doorway of Nyumba Pembi (Ivory House) in Zanzibar in 1898.

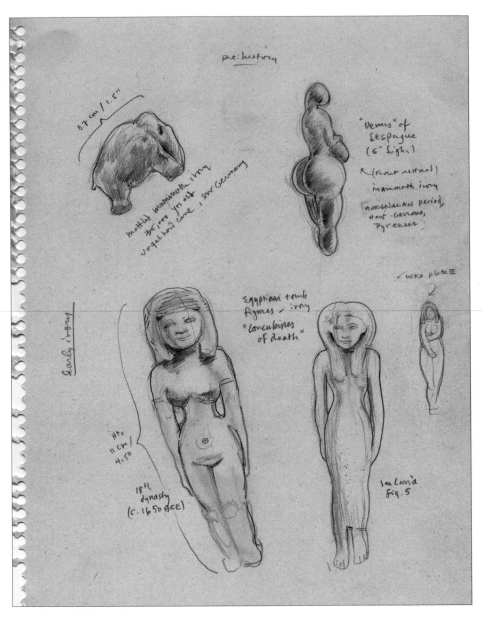

pre:history

37 cm / 1.5"

mottled mammoth ivory
35,000 yrs old
Vogalherd cave, srr Germany

"venus" of
Sespugue
(6" high)

(front restored)
mammoth ivory

AURIGNACIAN period,
Haut-Garonne,
Pyrenees

Egyptian tomb
figures — ivory
"concubines
of death"

ucko, plate III

early ivory

Ht:
11 cm /
4.5"

18th
dynasty
(c. 1650 BCE)

see Land's
fig. 5

Author's sketches of an inch-high 35,000-year-old figure of a mammoth,
carved from that species' ivory, Pleistocene mammoth ivory "venus" figure,
and ancient Egyptian ivory "concubines of death."

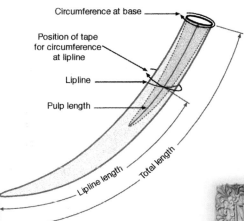

Circumference at base

Position of tape
for circumference
at lipline

Lipline

Pulp length

Lipline length

Total length

Simplified diagram of an elephant tusk
showing conical tooth-pulp hollow and
lip line—the point at which the tusk
emerges from an elephant's head.

SYMMACHORVM

The foot-high Symmachi panel,
a late-Roman ivory diptych leaf, ca. 400.

Ivory pyxis (cylindical container) from the workshops of
Madinat al-Zahra in Islamic Spain, ca. 968.

English ivory triptych (ca. 1330-40) made for John de Grandisson, Bishop of Exeter.

Ming dynasty ivory medallion, late-sixteenth, early-seventeenth century.

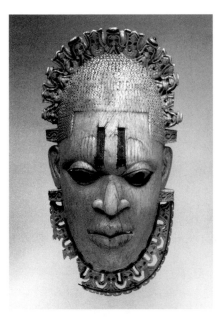

Benin ivory pendant mask
(sixteenth century).

Ivory figure of the Hindu god Ganesha
(India, fourteenth-fifteenth century).

The Death of Cleopatra, ca. 1700, a German ivory relief by Ignaz Elhafen.

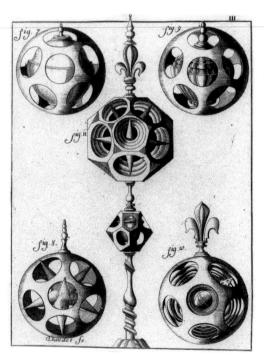

Ivory turner Nicolas Grollier de Servière (1596-1689) created "*pièces excentriques*" from single pieces of tusk using complex lathes—machines that later made possible the industrialization of ivory.

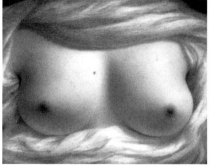

Beauty Revealed (Self-Portrait), an 1828 watercolor on ivory by Sarah Goodridge.

George Read and Co.'s nineteenth-century ivory-comb manufactory
in Deep River, Connecticut.

Julius Pratt, a prominent figure in the American ivory industry and his mid-1800s ivory-
goods catalogue emphasizing the growing importance of ivory piano-key production.

Letterhead of Harvey and Ford, ivory merchants in Philadelphia, 1860-70s.

An 1889 photograph shows James Burroughes of Burroughes and
Watts, London, resting on 20,000 ivory billiard balls produced by the firm,
a stock which required the demise of two thousand elephants.

Tippu Tip, a Swahili-Zanzibari trader, ran a vast East African empire built on ivory and slave trading in the last half of the nineteenth century.

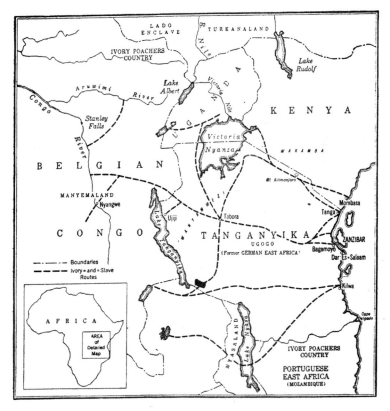

Ivory and slave routes of the period.

An ivory hunter (possibly James Ward "King" Rogers), ca.1908-1911.

An ivory hunter's caravan fording a stream in the Lado Enclave west of the upper
Nile on the border of the Belgian Congo, ca. 1908-1911.

Weighing tusks in the godown (warehouse) of Ivory House in Zanzibar, ca. 1910-1911.

Ivory buyer E. D. Moore, center right, in the godown displaying two large tusks, ca. 1908-10.

Elephant teeth en route to Connecticut ivory factory; the inscription reads "32 Tusks of Ivory worth $9000, Deep River, Conn. Sept. 20, 1906."

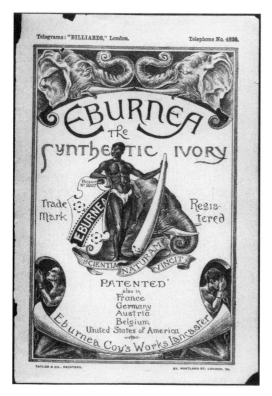

The 1890 trade booklet cover of George Wright and Co., London, promoting the superiority of "synthetic ivory," especially for Africans and elephants; substitutes, however, did not always gain acceptance.

Elephants find refuge at a waterhole in
Botswana's Chobe National Park in 1986.

In 1988 Angolan rebel leader Jonas Savimbi sent Defense Secretary Frank Carlucci
an AK-47 replica carved from ivory and wood in appreciation for U.S. support of his
movement, which was partly funded by his vast ivory poaching operations.

One of a series of advertisements from the African Wildlife Foundation's "Don't Buy Ivory" campaign. International efforts to combat ivory poaching helped bring about a global ban on cross-border trade in ivory in 1989.

Tons of tusks recovered from elephants that die of natural causes pile up in the ivory vaults of Kruger National Park in South Africa.

Few Japanese craftsmen still use hand tools to make ivory *hanko*.

Author's sketches of orphaned baby elephants at the
David Sheldrick Wildlife Trust in Nairobi, Kenya.

A large bull startles a motorist in Kruger Park.

private orchestra at home to accompany him. "The ease with which he used to switch from the aesthetics of hunting to the aesthetics of music never ceased to amaze me," Hunter wrote. "He would hand his rifle to his bearer or secretary after his final shot of the day and murmur, 'I shall approach the *Polichinelle* tonight.'" He once complained that "trigger work on his Purdey was bad for passage work on his Scriabin." However, the prince's piano technique was not always adequate to cope with the Chopin and Liszt pieces of which he was so fond. "Sometimes he was brought to a standstill by the mountainous difficulties of the B-minor Scherzo or *Campanella*; then he would scramble all the notes together, throw up his hands and cry, 'Bothersome, very! Not nearly so simple as hunting.'"

After stopping in an isolated village and learning that a trio of elephants had been raiding the local crops, the maharaja was very keen to pursue them, seeing that "this time he could really be of use." After tracking them for two days they surprised the bulls in a thicket; Hunter dropped two and the prince took the third with a classic ear shot and then strode over to his quarry and straddled its neck. "His pleasure was like a schoolboy's—and well-merited, for he'd timed and aimed his shot splendidly," Hunter recalled. "There was a simple satisfaction in putting one's foot on the carcass—the 'alone-I-did-it' feeling." The trackers cut the tails off the elephants to be used in making lucky bangles for the hunters. The two returned to camp, and the next day Hunter's men showed up with two sets of tusks—hundred-pounders—and the unnerving news that the maharaja's elephant had risen from the dead and walked away without his tail. Hunter was horrified at his lack of caution. Clearly the elephant had only been stunned, but the prince was left with the gratitude of the village and the bracelet of elephant hair from the one he'd shot. Besides, he'd lost a stone in weight.

Hunter long remembered how the prince had played on into the African night, the pianissimo notes gently struck on the ivory keys competing with the mad cackling of distant hyenas fighting over the remains of a carcass.

It was the end of an era.

PART 3

THE ELEPHANT DILEMMA

7

RESEARCHERS AND POACHERS

The bull elephant appeared blue-gray in the hazy midday glare of the parched, still landscape. I watched him slowly and methodically drink his fill at the muddy hole, drawing up the dark water with his dripping trunk, curling it up to empty in his mouth, over and over. This oasis, if one could call it that, was almost devoid of greenery that year. It was 1986, and Botswana's Chobe National Park was in the middle of an extended drought. I leaned out of the door of my vehicle with binoculars and then followed up with a few sketches and notations in my journal, curious why the antelopes that had also gathered in the shimmering heat stood back from the water's edge while the elephants drank at this rock-rimmed water hole. Then I saw the lions, stretched out here and there, half-hidden in the scraps of shade behind bushes and logs at the water hole's edge. Their presence, even in repose, was keeping dozens of thirsty impala and kudu from approaching, though they took turns creeping forward before losing their nerve and retreating to a safer distance.

The elephant stepped back from the water's edge and flapped his ears before starting a slow, stately circuit around the hole's perimeter to join a group of cows and juveniles on the opposite bank. The large male lion sprawled resting in his path rolled his yellow eyes as the looming bull, swaying with each stride, closed the distance between them. The dark-maned lion growled, flipped to his feet, and slunk away like a house cat fearing a kick.

I was on a magazine assignment that had already taken me from Botswana's Kalahari Desert to the Okavango Delta, but this was the first day when I'd really had a chance to view elephants up close. Earlier that morning I'd seen another bull push over an entire tree with his forehead, just to get at bunches of the tender topmost leaves, then rest his trunk over one tusk the way someone might drape a towel over a peg. His power startled me, although perhaps it shouldn't have. A door of one of the Land Cruisers I'd recently ridden in had a ragged hole the diameter of a coffee can punched through it, the result of a run-in with an elephant unafraid to use his tusks as weapons.

It's one thing to read about elephants, another to see them in zoos, but something altogether different to observe them in their own environment. I found myself as fascinated as I had been as a child when I was taken into a tent behind the big top of a small traveling circus outside Detroit to see the elephants. In that confined space I had been overwhelmed by their presence, the heat and smell of their massive bodies and their amazing, probing, snuffling trunks. There were several of them, doubtless all tractable Asian females, chained by at least one leg and watched closely by their handlers, and I got to lean over the thin rope that was all that separated them from the crowd and drop a peanut into one of the upturned nostrils of an inquiring, warmly breathing trunk with its few bristly hairs. I was astonished to hear the peanut rattle up the nasal hose, as if being vacuumed. I imagined it was being ingested that way, not realizing that the reason the creature then put its trunk in its mouth was to blow in the tiny tidbit; I had thought that, lacking a thumb, the pachyderm was simply sucking its trunk.

This time I was better informed for my visit with the elephants. I'd been reading books on African wildlife and various animal studies, absorbing elephant lore and information about their life cycle and the social structure of herds. I didn't think about it then—I was too caught up in the moment—but later I realized that I hadn't given much thought to the larger context of my experience, from the evidence of how drought conditions were affecting elephants to the oddity of people rumbling up to and away from elephants in motorized vehicles, when for all previous history humans pretty much had to approach them on foot. While I was there, a zebra-striped tourist van arrived at the water hole, stayed the fifteen minutes necessary to let its passengers shoot a few rolls of film, and then bumped off trailing clouds of dust on the way to the next photo opportunity. What I regarded then as a peripheral annoyance—ignoring the fact that I'd also arrived in a vehicle—has of course become one of the most common ways humans now interact with African wildlife.

In postcolonial Africa, elephant environments changed dramatically in just a few short decades. Many, though certainly not all, elephant populations were now clustered in if not confined to parks and reserves as the populations of sub-Saharan countries soared and open bush gave way to roads, cities, and modern agriculture. The wildlife policies put in place by colonial powers were often just as oblivious of African realities as the national borders that were drawn during that period. The peoples of Africa and their wildlife are still feeling the effects.

"THE ONLY THING of value the interior of Africa produces at present in any quantity," wrote Professor Henry Drummond in his 1889 *Tropical Africa,* "is ivory." Drummond fully expected the disappearance of the elephant in a matter of a few years; as a source of ivory the animal had been "too great a success." He saw no development of "legitimate industries" in Africa "so long as a tusk remains," and put the matter in the bluntest possible terms: "The sooner the last elephant falls before the hunter's bullet, the better for Africa."

That grim assessment, underscored by concerns that as long as there were elephant herds "the brutal hunting of natives as slaves to carry tusks" would continue, seems to have been all early British and German colonialists in East Africa needed as an excuse to arm indigenous groups with modern weapons and commence clearing entire districts of the troublesome giants while at the same time relieving them of their valuable teeth, which, coincidentally, could be used by the same locals to pay their newly imposed taxes and fines. But overriding economic concerns checked short-term greed.

Britain established the Uganda Protectorate in 1894 and a year later the British East Africa Protectorate (modern Kenya) to counterbalance German advances in East Africa (modern Tanzania). In British East Africa, ivory accounted for almost half of export earnings. Fearing elephant eradication, the colonial administration prohibited shooting female elephants and any whose tusks weighed under ten pounds each—the first wildlife conservation laws in Africa outside the Cape Colony. In 1900 foreign ministers for colonial powers in Africa met in London and signed the Convention for the Preservation of Animals, Birds and Fish in Africa. This, the first international conservation treaty, was motivated partly by alarm that the spectacular fauna of the continent was disappearing but also by concern that animals whose hide, meat, or ivory was of value—as well as those whose hunting provided sport—might not be around much longer. This broad agreement set the tone for wildlife policies in the colonies, which were intended to ensure the survival of wildlife for future generations—but, as Captain Keith Caldwell, who helped establish the wildlife departments of Uganda and Kenya, put it, "in such a way that it does not in any way retard or interfere with the economic development of the country, or place any difficulties in the way of stock-breeding or crop-growing." As Raymond Bonner points out, colonial administrations were primarily concerned about white settlers, not indigenous Africans.

> Throughout the continent, it was usually their land that was taken for parks and reserves. And although hunting was allowed, a license was necessary, and white colonial administrators did not issue many licenses to Africans, who could not have afforded one anyway; moreover, for political reasons, the governments prohibited Africans from owning rifles.

Although some groups were allowed to continue to hunt as they always had hunted (i.e., with "crude weapons" but not "cruel methods," such as pitfalls), others found that their traditional practices were now considered poaching. What's more, actively ensuring the survival of wildlife by restricting hunting also meant that it often had to be managed and "controlled" (i.e., shot) when it interfered with agriculture. Indigenous Africans were rarely allowed to take matters into their own hands; they had to seek help from the authorities, or once again find themselves poaching.

When it came to species with economic value—and elephants, with their ivory, topped the list—there was an effort to have it both ways and temper slaughter with protection. If the number of elephants killed did not exceed the reproduction rate, it was thought possible to preserve them in locations where they were wanted (parks and reserves), while profiting from their demise where they were not wanted (on farms, feasting on crops). Captain Caldwell, who disdained "making money out of the destruction of game," made an exception in the case of ivory: its sale financed the Kenyan game department. "In 1923," Bonner writes, "the department earned £16,000 from the sale of ivory; the cost of running the department was only £4,000." This early example of using game to fund game management was a forerunner of finding ways to let wildlife "pay for itself" by what came to be called sustainable utilization.

In 1970 ivory was trading at around $3.40 a pound. It reached $32 a pound less than ten years later, with catastrophic consequences for elephants. As I watched elephants around the water hole that day in 1986, I was unaware that the entire continental population of these animals had fallen by 40 percent in the previous five years.

TO WATCH ELEPHANTS in their natural habitat is to come to appreciate their intelligence, their complex social system, and the evident care they have for their young. A vast multicultural lore has accumulated from earliest times about these animals, grouped around such enduring themes. The oldest information, when it was not fanciful, was often conjectural (Aristotle thought elephants could live to be two hundred years old), and even up to the twentieth century much direct observation (by ivory hunters, for example) was largely anecdotal, a few dissections notwithstanding. This would all change. By the mid-twentieth century field biologists had initiated basic and long-term studies of these fascinating mammals, aided by technological advances such as immobilizing drugs and miniaturized radio transmitters that allowed them to be tracked. In the space of a few decades it seemed as if more had been discovered about these creatures than had been gathered in the previous millennium.

Martin Meredith lists a number of the post–World War II pioneering researchers and their results: John Perry carried out the first modern dissection of an African elephant; Irven Buss discredited the notion that elephants were led by bulls (they're led by closely related cows); Richard

Laws undertook fundamental research on elephant growth, diet, habitat, and population dynamics. By the 1960s elephant research was no longer something undertaken solely by game or park departments; it was done by Ph.D. candidates looking to discover something fresh for their dissertations. Iain Douglas-Hamilton, for example, was an Oxford graduate who studied elephant social structure in Lake Manyara National Park in Tanzania. Those drawn to elephant research didn't always begin as biologists. Cynthia Moss was a former *Newsweek* journalist in New York before she set up her research project in Kenya's Amboseli National Park, just north of Mount Kilimanjaro, to document elephant family life in detail. She was joined by biologist Joyce Poole, who worked on musth males, and in 1985 by Katherine Payne, who had uncovered the hitherto unsuspected world of elephant communication by using infrasound.

Listening more closely to elephants is especially emblematic of the contemporary interest our species has taken in the worlds of other living things. While observing Asian elephant cows and their calves on a zoo visit in Portland, Oregon, in 1984, Payne noticed "a palpable throbbing in the air like distant thunder, yet all around me was silent." She recalled how when she was a choir girl the entire chapel would throb when the organ "blasted out the bass line in a Bach chorale." Elephant vocalizations had been studied before, but Payne was able to demonstrate the animals' ability to generate in their nasal passages sound waves that fall below human hearing. This discovery helped explain previous observations of behavior that seemed coordinated by some mysterious form of communication over distances of two or more miles. These included how female elephants in estrus (heat) manage to let far-ranging male elephants know they are receptive to advances (a window of opportunity that might be as infrequent as two days every four years), how elephants seem to be able to let one another know the location of water holes, and how a culling operation in one region can alarm herds miles distant.

There was one more aspect of these studies that came to have an important impact on the public's perception of elephants. Douglas-Hamilton's careful observations required keeping track of individuals, which led to naming them (Virgo, Boadicea, etc.). Other elephant researchers adopted this practice. Cynthia Moss had her Slit Ear and Tallulah, Katy Payne had Miss Piggy. Subsequent documentaries on these researchers' studies focused on such pachyderm "personalities," which, for a large television audience, had the effect of giving previously anonymous creatures an emotional significance usually reserved for pets.

THE GAME MANAGERS in Britain's African colonies thought they could balance wildlife and people, both settlers and "natives," by promoting game sanctuaries alongside programs for the eradication or reduction of problematic animal populations in settled areas. With regard to elephants and "native gardens," however, it wasn't just the pachyderms that needed control; lack of supervision over "native settlements" meant local populations had inconveniently dotted their houses and agricultural plots in elephant territory. But elephants could always be shot and entire settlements relocated.

"Control," as researcher Stuart Marks points out, began with belief in "elephants' superior mental abilities and assumed that they would learn quickly to associate cultivation with danger and sanctuaries with safety. Teaching them to stay in their new places demanded coordination. . . . Half measures, such as shooting only one elephant from a marauding party or leaving a herd close to a damaged field, could not be tolerated." Before the 1960s these grand control schemes included the creation of some two dozen parks and reserves in sub-Saharan Africa. Unfortunately, efforts at control did not always go as planned. In 1935, 1,796 elephants were killed by rangers in Southern Tanzania, most in the Liwale and Kilwa districts. The Kilwa district was then thought to be entirely free of elephants, but a year later crop raiding was just as bad in these, and an additional 669 elephants were shot. "It would seem that, until elephants were trained to read the GAME RESERVE notices," Wilson and Ayerst drily observed, "they would continue to wander at will in search of food and water."

Increasingly, however, elephants clustered where they were relatively undisturbed. In 1929 elephants could be found in 70 percent of Uganda's territory. Thirty years later, they inhabited only 17 percent of the country. Why? The rise in the human population in the same period from

3.5 million to 5.5 million helped push herds into remote areas and the refuges that had been set aside for them. There, elephants' ability to transform their environment—second only to that of the human species—also contributed to their insecurity. Under ideal conditions, elephant populations can grow 6 percent a year. An elephant consumes 4 to 6 percent of its body weight daily; a big bull requires around six hundred pounds of forage a day, as well as fifty gallons of water. Thanks to the milling action of their ridged molars and ever useful trunk, they can feed on practically anything they can reach from the ground on up—grass, fruit, nuts, leaves, bushes—and can strip bark and branches off trees and uproot them (or just push them over) to get at what they want. Their ability to live off a varied diet allows them to survive in an impressive array of habitats, from desert to savanna, woodlands to swamp, floodplain to forest. A herd of elephants, bulldozing their way as they feed, will open up thick brush and forest, allowing it to regenerate and cycle through stages of plant life, a boon to other species. Widely roaming herds crisscross vast regions in search of food and water, following much-used routes; it's said that many of today's highways across the continent follow these efficiently laid out ancient elephant trails.

Game managers discovered that if elephants are confined to a park, their increasing numbers can turn a lush environment into a desert. Uganda's Murchison Falls National Park, which had been created in 1952, had its thick woodlands turned into open grassland by its burgeoning elephant population. When plant life changed, chimpanzees, forest hogs, and much of the birdlife also disappeared. Alarmed that elephants were reducing the diversity of the habitat as well as their own food base, park authorities inaugurated, in 1966, a culling operation that killed two thousand elephants out of a population of fourteen thousand. Richard Laws, who amassed the data from careful analysis of each carcass, found that almost all the mature elephants showed evidence of stress-related diseases of the cardiovascular system.

Culling operations were employed in Zambia, Zimbabwe, and elsewhere in an effort to keep down swelling elephant numbers, even in the absence of actual habitat destruction. In Zimbabwe, elephants were utilized as a natural resource, not just to pay for culling operations but to generate profits to support the park system, among other purposes. There was more to elephants than ivory—their hides, which could be turned into leather products, were quite valuable. Even the meat was sold. But the growing unpopularity of killing elephants to maintain their numbers at specific levels came to a head over the elephant problem in Kenya's Tsavo National Park.

Tsavo was established in 1948, and at some eight thousand square miles constitutes the largest park in Kenya. In order to achieve gazettement—that is, make the park boundaries legal—indigenous peoples who had long used the region for hunting, such as the Waliangulu, the Kamba, and other groups, had to be expelled. For centuries the Waliangulu had lived off elephants migrating from the swamps of the Tana River to the north down through their homelands to Kilimanjaro. They used powerful longbows with hundred-pound pulls to shoot iron-tipped arrows dipped in poison deep into elephants' spleens, resulting in rapid death. Originally, the Waliangulu used every part: skin, meat, and tusks, the last for trade. By the beginning of the twentieth century they were exchanging ivory for alcohol and *bhang* (cannabis) from coastal traders.

Eventually, they turned to pursuing elephants primarily for tusks. Those who continued to hunt in the newly declared park were now, of course, poachers. Aided by a military-style antipoaching force drawn from the parks administration, game departments, and police units, the park's warden, David Sheldrick, managed to suppress the Waliangulu holdouts. Hundreds were jailed and the rest resettled outside the park's boundaries in an area set aside for them. There, a trial program was set up whereby they were allowed to continue elephant hunting, but even with the strict limits imposed professional hunters and safari operators were alarmed at the prospect, fearing loss of business if "natives" should be permitted to do what they had always done: hunt. In their view, the wildlife was for colonial whites and rich foreigners to shoot; the locals should stick with (or convert to) agriculture. The plan called for letting the Waliangulu benefit from the sale of meat and trophies, although they were cut out of any share in ivory revenues. Naturally, they eventually returned to poaching.

Inside the park, meanwhile, the number of elephants climbed to forty thousand. The strong savanna woodland and "wait-a-bit" thorn scrub seen by the first white hunters were transformed by the 1960s into a degraded environment that reminded observers of a battlefield dotted with smashed trees, some of them ancient baobabs tusked open to provide access to the moist spongy wood inside.

Sheldrick put Richard Laws in charge of a research project to cull three hundred elephants to determine their reproductive trends, following the methods Laws had used at Murchison Falls National Park in Uganda. In 1969 Laws announced his recommendations: a cull of three thousand elephants with possibly more to follow, warning that Tsavo was on its way to becoming a desert. As word of these findings got out, many conservationists around the world "recoiled in horror," as the science writer Boyce Rensberger put it. "Killing the animals they were trying to protect hardly fit the traditional conservation ethic." Sheldrick had a change of heart. Culling was no longer an option for him; he thought it preferable to institute a hands-off policy, even if it meant that a great many elephants would starve. Park authorities supported Sheldrick; Laws resigned; nature took its course.

In 1970–71 a severe drought—months went by without a raindrop—sent Tsavo's ecological decline into a tailspin, turning it into a habitat that couldn't support all the elephants (not to mention scores of other species) crowded in there. Fires seared the vegetation that might have hung on, had there been fewer elephants. While arguments over culling raged, Rensberger wrote,

> Elephants began dying by the hundreds, not of thirst—there were still a few permanent water sources—but of starvation. The grasses and leaves they needed had long since gone. In desperation, many elephants ate the bare twigs and branches that remained. The elephants starved to death with their stomachs full—of wood. The first to go were the youngest and the oldest. Unable to keep up with the herds as they ranged farther and farther in search of food, the weakest ones dropped. For most of the little ones that died, their nursing mothers died also. When her baby falls, a mother elephant will rarely abandon it. Park rangers reported seeing many mothers desperately trying to raise their dead babies, nudging with their feet or lifting with their trunks. For hours they struggled hopelessly, themselves growing weaker. Refusing to abandon their calves to find food

or water, somewhere between 2,000 and 3,000 nursing mother elephants
died . . .

That estimate was one of the low ones. Others put the final death
toll somewhere between nine thousand and fifteen thousand. In any case,
the grim aerial photographs of Tsavo elephant carcasses in Peter Beard's
The End of the Game tell the story better than figures do: skeletons dis-
assembled in dust, parts of their hides stuck to the bones like torn tar-
paulins, pointing tusks dried and split in the sun. African elephants will
spend time examining the skulls and ivory of their own species, and there
was plenty for the remaining survivors to look at—a veritable elephant
Golgotha.

In the bitter assessments that followed what happened in Tsavo, advocates of culling pointed out that their dire predictions had come to pass.
Had culling taken place, they argued, fewer elephants might have died.
What's more, the ones that did die yielded no worthwhile scientific information, and the $3 million that could have been gained from the sale of
hides and ivory from the proposed cull could have been spent on helping
drought-stricken subsistence farmers around the park. Besides, a cull
would have yielded much useful meat for the locals. All the carcasses that
littered the landscape simply rotted in the sun when the vultures and hyenas couldn't finish them fast enough. For advocates of culling, the hands-
off policy in Tsavo was itself an action whose consequences led to
appalling waste. Noninterventionists said it showed how natural events
keep elephant populations in balance, though some scientists wondered
if what had happened was anything like a natural cycle.

Still, those who argued for letting an elephant die-off occur in Tsavo
were tapping into one of the deepest of human beliefs: that the processes
and the cycles of nature can be trusted to establish an equilibrium. Left
alone, nature would right herself; all the forces of disease and weather, the
availability of food and water and predation, would come to bear on the
elephants and the trees and all the other species and paint an entirely new
picture within the artificial boundaries of the newly created park. If the
scene that resulted did not look like what was expected or desired, so be it.
What came to be was meant to be. The mass die-off of female elephants
created a generation gap that took the pressure off the land, making way

for the regeneration of the trees. David Sheldrick's widow, Daphne, later described the events in Tsavo this way: "It was all over in three months, at no cost, and with no disruption to other wild communities—no profiteering—just a cataclysmic natural tragedy soon obscured by the mists of time." For her, the natural selection of a die-off "surely must be more humane than an annual cull."

Proponents of these two opposing points of views on elephants would clash again and again.

"MOMBASA IS SLOWLY taking over the role of the world's main ivory centre from London," proclaimed the *Mombasa Times* in January of 1961. During 1960–61 virtually all East African ivory, some seventy-five tons, passed through the port of Mombasa, as did one hundred tons from the Congo.

In 1970 the scene on auction day at the Mombasa Ivory Rooms didn't look much different than it did when E. D. Moore was purchasing ivory. "The unprepossessing warehouse close to the waterfront was thronged with a varied collection of more or less shabbily dressed men, alike only in their wearing of that completely disinterested look affected by all professional dealers," Wilson and Ayerst wrote of their visit there. "Swahilis in robes and turbans, Indians in long jackets and skullcaps, here and there an occasional European buyer—all wandered with catalogues and pencils from pile to pile of carefully graded tusks and 'pieces.'" Together, the dealers paid more than £100,000 for the day's lots in heated bidding, especially over two magnificent pairs of hundred-pound tusks; nothing remained unsold, they wrote, including dirty cracked ivory and a handful of hippo teeth—"such is the demand for African ivory throughout Asia."

Wilson and Ayerst found that about a quarter of the forty thousand pounds of ivory in the sale was confiscated from poachers, another quarter came from game department culling programs, and the rest came from elephants shot on license by hunters and "pick-up ivory" recovered from elephants that had died of natural causes. Under East African colonial rule, Mombasa had become the preeminent center of the continent's ivory trade; following independence in the early 1960s, most countries made their own export arrangements—Tanzania was sending virtually all its ivory to the People's Republic of China. Nonetheless, ivory in the sale room had came from the Congo, Uganda, Sudan, and Ethiopia as well as Kenya. It stayed in the government warehouse for several weeks after purchase while the agents resold the ivory by cable, telex, and telephone, almost all of it to China, Hong Kong, India, and Singapore, with small parcels going to the Persian Gulf and Europe.

Ivory's value had been remarkably stable for decades before it rose in the 1920s and then fell sharply during the Depression. Afterward, it recovered its previous levels and started climbing steadily once again. Following World War II, the demand for ivory from newly prosperous Asian countries pushed prices to historic highs and, from the 1970s on, to dizzying new heights.

In the 1970s the Asian market was led by Hong Kong and Japan—together, they were importing three-quarters of the world's annual ivory supply. Hong Kong reexported raw ivory to other Asian countries and, like China, produced endless ivory knickknacks for the international curio business, even sending some of its worked ivory back to Africa to be sold to tourists as African carvings. Hong Kong had three thousand craftsmen, who by then had adopted electric tools, especially handheld drills, to carve ivory, vastly decreasing the time required to turn out, say, a Cantonese concentric ball. India, which had imported ivory for centuries from East Africa, had imposed import duties on the material after 1947, sending its carving industry into a decline. Imports fell from nearly two hundred fifty tons to twenty tons, although there were seventy-two hundred ivory carvers as late as 1978, manufacturing baubles and back scratchers for foreign sale; except for bangles, little worked ivory stayed in the country.

Japan became the driving force behind Asian demand. The century before, Japan's historic attraction to ivory had been satisfied primarily by imports of tusks from Thailand and other parts of Asia because Japanese craftsmen preferred to work with harder Asian ivory. In the 1890s, however, dwindling elephant populations in Southeast Asia forced Japanese traders to turn to African sources. In the 1960s Japanese imports averaged ninety-five tons a year. As the country's growing economy increased the wealth of its middle class, they bought more than cars, clothes, and modern appliances; they bought traditional items as well, including those made from a long-revered substance: ivory. In the late 1970s, when Japan became the largest consumer of ivory in the world, imports swelled to more than two hundred fifty tons a year.

JUST AS HUMAN understanding and respect for elephants was deepening, large-scale organized ivory poaching emerged. It took time for this renewed threat to elephants to become more visible. Culling was hotly debated, taking attention away from what else was happening to elephants in the early 1970s. Warnings that ivory poaching was increasing were often dismissed. If elephants were so numerous that they had to be shot, many people seemed to think, how could they also be under grave threat?

The signs were there. The informal but complex network of East African coastal traders who dealt in ivory had never really disappeared. Dealers in the interior bought ivory (as well as skins and rhino horns) from black and white poachers alike at a fraction of the legitimate market price and brought it to the coast in cars, trucks, trains, and river craft, hidden under crates of chickens or tucked into cloth goods. There it was loaded at night onto dhows, whose owners often smuggled spirits, tobacco, and other dutiable items into African ports at the same time. Wilson and Ayerst cited an example.

> In July 1968 a mixed force of Kenya Game Department officials and police, acting on information received as a result of several months' detective work, raided a warehouse in Mombasa. They opened up crates of "Jaggery" (a sugar product) ostensibly from Uganda and found an estimated £52,000 worth of trophies, mainly ivory. This huge cargo was destined for the Persian Gulf. This single consignment, roughly equal to the total sales at the Mombasa ivory room for a whole year, was just one that happened to be caught. How many got away?

The sharp rise in ivory prices that was about to begin would rejuvenate ancient trade networks in a brisk smuggling business. In the absence of knowing anything more about the situation one might have thought high prices were an indication that antipoaching efforts were working, making illicit ivory that much scarcer and more valuable. But expanding demand for ivory was far outpacing the increasing amount of illegal ivory entering trade channels, encouraging even more poaching. The decline in elephant numbers was ominous. Kenya's elephant population fell from an estimated 167,000 in 1973 to 59,000 by 1977. Drought and continued human pressure on elephant habitats certainly played a part in the falling numbers, but this was a precipitous and alarming drop.

Kenya wasn't an isolated case. When a 1971 military coup brought Idi Amin to power in Uganda, government officials backed poaching in the national parks. The number of elephants in Murchison Falls National Park fell from 14,300 in 1973 to 2,250 two years later; the country's entire elephant population of some sixty thousand had been reduced by 90 percent.

THE RESEARCHERS WHO'D been patiently following Africa's elephants now had unwelcome company: poaching gangs who were openly tracking the herds. Funded by illicit ivory traders, they were typically equipped with military weapons left over from numerous African conflicts. Early European traders had exchanged firearms for the ivory they wanted from the continent's peoples, but in the colonial period more caution was used; there was an effort to keep the latest in modern weaponry out of "native hands," almost as if Europeans instinctively anticipated the wars of independence to come. Those inevitable conflicts left the continent well supplied with caches of up-to-date weaponry, notably the ubiquitous Soviet-designed AK-47 assault rifle. Armed with it, four men could take down a herd of twenty elephants in several minutes. It wasn't sharpshooting—it was more of a fusillade of automatic weapons fire and very messy—but it worked well enough for ivory poaching, the revenues from which, in countries like Angola, were used to fuel ongoing civil wars. To remove the elephant carcasses that came inconveniently attached to the ivory, poaching gangs turned to another modern tool: the chain saw.

In 1971 well-armed poachers, including Somali *shifta*—bandits—moved into Tsavo and began shooting elephants. There were long-standing smuggling networks in Kenya's Northern Frontier District but this was big business, conducted in the open. Sheldrick's modest park forces resisted but were finally outnumbered and outgunned by these gangs. The beleaguered warden estimated that during 1974–75 Tsavo had lost fifteen thousand elephants, almost half the park's remaining population. Ivory poaching was now a phenomenon that went far beyond traditional hunters equipped with bows and arrows, or even the few better-equipped infamously successful freelance poachers who often eluded capture.

At a time when newly formed African nations had to confront falling commodity prices and shaky national economies skewed by colonial demands, ivory looked like a natural (and renewable) resource that could be exploited, this time by Africans for Africans. But it didn't work out that way. Instead, in the rush to profit from higher and higher prices, a nineteenth-century-style ivory grab ensued. "At a different level, given the enormous profits that could be made, equivalent to well over a year's wages from one tusk of ivory," Alpers writes, "poaching of elephants was a temptation to African men who were either unable to obtain jobs for wages or who sought greater return for their labor than they could find through agriculture or employment."

At the government level, corruption began to undermine antipoaching efforts and hijack the mechanisms of the legal ivory trade. The scale of the ivory poaching operations that had arisen would have been hard to hide from the authorities, unless they were deliberately looking the other way or even assisting in it. Smuggling always works more smoothly when corrupt officials are involved, and just who was behind it in Kenya finally emerged. In 1975 the government denied there were irregularities, much less corruption, in its ivory trade and criticized foreign media for "dragging in" President Jomo Kenyatta's family in discussions of the issue. However, London's *Sunday Times* ran a three-part series on corruption in the East African country that implicated the Kenyatta family in the export of tons of illegal ivory. The government announced a crackdown on ivory dealing, but officials were still making money from ivory. Sheldrick, who reported massive poaching in Tsavo in 1976, was removed from his post. The wardens who followed couldn't or wouldn't stop the slaughter, and finally the rangers themselves became the main poachers. As a grand gesture, Kenya banned all hunting in 1977. "When that didn't achieve the desired goal of halting the poaching," Bonner writes, "the next year the government put an end to the sale of any wildlife products, such as zebra skins and impala horns, as well as ivory carvings, which was a blow to many small shopkeepers in Nairobi." The oddity of being the only country on the planet with these kinds of laws would take time to reach its full effect.

In the meantime, the Convention on International Trade in Endangered Species of Wild Fauna and Flora (CITES), drafted in the early 1960s, was just coming into being. Eighty countries finalized the wording of this sweeping conservation agreement; now more than double that number of countries belong. Its effectiveness stems from its structure. To meet its obligations under CITES, each country passes its own legislation to come into compliance and is responsible for enforcing these regulations. The basic mechanism of CITES is the imposition of controls over international trade in specimens of certain species; endangered species are listed in the three appendixes of the convention according to the degree of threat they face. A species that appears in Appendix I is threatened with extinction unless trade is halted. A species placed in Appendix II isn't necessarily threatened but might be if it weren't listed; hence trade requires a permit. Appendix III is used for listing species that need some control over trade, hence appropriate permits.

The Asian elephant, whose numbers had dwindled to perhaps fifty thousand animals, was already in Appendix I; in 1976 the African elephant was placed on the Appendix II list, although it was clear to most observers that ivory exports were easily manipulated. What policy makers, conservationists, and biologists needed was solid information on what was happening to African elephant populations. Elephants in Kenya and Uganda were being killed in increasing numbers, but was this also true for the rest of continent? If so, why was this so, and what were the implications? "Two leading authorities on elephant conservation and the ivory trade presented diametrically opposed views on these questions," wrote researchers Tom Pilgram and David Western in the *Journal of Applied Ecology* in 1986, "based on the same information." The frustrated note they sounded referred to the comprehensive reports in 1979 by Iain Douglas-Hamilton and Ian Parker, which came to different conclusions on the emerging elephant/ivory issue.

With support from a number of conservation organizations, Kenya-based biologist Douglas-Hamilton had spent three years gathering information from parks and reserves, game wardens and scientists, aerial counts and questionnaires. Some of what he gathered was hard facts, the rest the best that could be estimated. He came up with a figure of 1.3 million elephants for the whole of Africa. When one considers that alarms over the numbers remaining of other charismatic species—pandas, tigers, gorillas—had not sounded until their populations were down to a few thousand or even a few hundred, well over a million elephants sounded healthy enough. But Douglas-Hamilton was convinced poaching was reducing their numbers at a devastating rate, something like a hundred thousand a year, except in South Africa, Zimbabwe, and Botswana, where, confusingly enough, elephant populations were actually on the increase.

Ian Parker, also Kenya-based, was commissioned by the U.S. Fish and Wildlife Service to write an exhaustive report on the ivory trade. Parker had been a game warden and in the 1960s had started his own wildlife consulting firm, which had undertaken the original culling operations in Murchison and Tsavo. He concluded that perhaps 630 tons of ivory had left Africa annually in recent years, the equivalent of 45,000 elephants, a huge number certainly but presumably sustainable, given that a substantial portion of the tusks shipped were the results of natural mortality. Hunting for profit was not a threat, except in certain areas; besides, he argued, Douglas-Hamilton's figures for the total African population had to be low by a million or more, considering how many elephants must be hidden in the central rain forests.

Douglas-Hamilton countered that Parker had exaggerated elephant deaths due to natural mortality, that elephants were overhunted almost everywhere, and that the reason elephants were being targeted at levels that recalled the late-nineteenth-century slaughter was the same as then: ivory. But Parker's views, which were rooted in the obvious, that elephant habitat was everywhere on the decline, held sway among conservationists until the mid-1980s. By then other researchers were refining the available data. Pilgram and Western were able to run computer simulation models incorporating additional information from other researchers and mine the data for the processes that appeared to be at work. Current elephant hunting patterns, they concluded, would drastically reduce their numbers. In addition, Parker's position that "range compression" accounted for the increase in elephant deaths was weakened by the fact that these deaths were outstripping "the increase in either human population or land under cultivation. The number of tusks appearing in the ivory trade between 1979 and 1983 increased more than 100 percent," they wrote, "while the rural population of Africa grew by just 13 percent." Even more telling was their finding that to sustain the high volume of ivory exported, more and more elephants had to be killed. Steady harvests coupled with increasing deaths "most resembles the scenario which leads to population collapse." The upshot? If the trend continued, the African elephant population would be cut in half within a decade.

THERE WAS A legal ivory trade, to be sure, but it seemed dogged more than ever by an underworld of poaching and smuggling and now laundering of the CITES permits required for the export of tusks. As ancient a trade as any, it had started being regulated very, very late in its history. In fact, determining precisely where ivory came from had never been easy. E. D. Moore had been open about this.

> A considerable portion of the ivory exported from Zanzibar and the east coast from 1900 to 1912 and thereabouts, was stolen ivory. The European and American traders knew it for that when they bought it, and the government officials, too, knew it was stolen ivory when they put their customs seals upon the tusks as they were brought across the borders. But the customs stamp of the territory in which the trader purchased the ivory made it honest ivory, technically, for commercial purposes.

These practices were still going on, albeit in a different form. As an inducement to get nonmember states to become parties to CITES—an understandable priority—the CITES secretariat would, in certain instances, allow countries sitting on dubious stockpiles of ivory to register their tusks for sale, giving instant profits to those who had colluded in shady transactions. Somalia and Singapore benefited handsomely by joining the treaty. The most egregious example was that of Burundi. Although the country's elephant population had long consisted of a single surviving specimen, it exported 1,300 tons of ivory from 1965 to 1986 under licenses that claimed the tusks came from domestically culled elephants.

The frequency with which illegal African shipments managed to piggyback onto legal ones meant not only that many export statistics were suspect but that they were highly unreliable as indications of impact on elephant populations. Nairobi was Africa's ivory capital in the early 1970s, later followed by Bangui in the Central African Republic, and then Khartoum. "In all instances," Parker and Martin observed in a joint report, "the ivory capital of the moment has attracted substantial quantities of ivory from beyond its own borders."

What's more, the system of CITES export permits required for elephant ivory did not include worked ivory, as it seemed too difficult to monitor carvings. This glaring omission created a huge loophole that was easily exploited by traders who were past masters at forging documents and disguising shipments. As Meredith explains,

> This meant that all that ivory traders had to do to avoid controls on raw ivory was to convert it to "worked" ivory. In one case, Hong Kong traders sent 67 carvers and 150 laborers to Dubai in the United Arab Emirates to set up two carving factories. They purchased poached ivory at a reduced price, had it carved in Dubai sufficiently to pass as worked ivory, imported it legally to Hong Kong and sold it at a much higher price on the world market.

The figures available from importing countries were not always easy to interpret either. Japan was Hong Kong's largest customer for raw ivory, but some of Hong Kong's imports were from Japan, even though they had originated in Hong Kong. "Such flow and counter-flow," Parker and Martin wrote, "is very much a feature of ivory trading." Even taking this into account, the combined totals of imports of raw ivory for Hong Kong and Japan together averaged 730 tons annually from 1979 to 1982. In 1983 and 1984, Japan itself imported 475 tons annually. The country was thought to account for 40 percent of all worked ivory produced. In fact, 25 percent of the world's consumption of raw ivory was going into *hanko*—signature seals—making them the late twentieth century's equivalent of piano keys a century before: a single use that sucked in an unreal amount of ivory.

FOR THOSE DEEPLY concerned about the level of elephant poaching, one ivory statistic in particular stood out as a grim warning that some populations were indeed in crisis: the average weight of tusks being traded. From twenty-one pounds per tusk in 1979, the figure had fallen to a new low in the mid-1980s—11.4 pounds. This could mean only that there were fewer bulls left carrying large ivory, and that breeding-age females and even juveniles were being targeted. With so few mature males, some females were now coming in estrus without being detected by a male, and with so many females being shot a high proportion of dependent calves were being orphaned; chances of survival for those are low to nil. Some populations, in other words, were being killed off faster than they could reproduce.

As evidence of the ivory trade's entanglement with intensified poaching mounted in the late 1980s, the increasingly bitter debate over the best way to curb the elephant killings reached far beyond the confines of scientific journals, game departments, newsletters of international wildlife organizations, and environmental magazines. It caught the public's attention and ended up transforming the conservation world. Up until this time, the outlook of mainstream conservation organizations in Europe and the United States, such as the World Wildlife Fund (WWF) and the African Wildlife Foundation (AWF), had been aligned with many of the sustainable use policies of southern African countries, such as Zimbabwe and South Africa, which could point to their successes in keeping poaching down and their healthy elephant populations, so numerous they were being culled, creating much-needed revenue. These conservation groups normally took their cues on policy from elephant researchers, many of whom at the time thought that the answer to out-of-control poaching was better regulation of ivory. Pilgram and Western expressed this view in 1986.

> Serious overhunting, while providing short-term profits for a few, will harm the majority of those involved in the ivory trade in the long term. Ivory-producing nations will lose an important source of foreign exchange, traders will find themselves handling less product, and carvers will suffer a reduction in the raw material available for their craft.

They concluded that "it is possible to develop simple regulations for the ivory trade which would result in better management of African elephants." Cynthia Moss, who had become widely known through her work with elephants in Amboseli, conceded in 1988 that it was "unrealistic" to expect a moratorium on trade. But she was convinced that three-fourths of the ivory currently traded came from poached elephants. Sympathetic to the notion that if enough consumers were repulsed by ivory its price would fall and poaching might fade, Moss urged "a worldwide campaign to reduce the demand for ivory."

As Bonner lays out in detail, that was exactly what happened. Hoping to mobilize public opinion in advance of the October 1989 CITES conference in Switzerland, Moss, Poole, and Douglas-Hamilton took their anti-ivory message to the media and conservation groups. The AWF held a press conference at the National Zoo in Washington, D.C., in February of 1988 to draw attention to the plight of the African elephant and was receptive to the "don't buy ivory" message—so much so that it launched a campaign around that theme in early 1989. But AWF and other conservation organizations soon found themselves boxed in by their own pro-elephant efforts. Their members expected them to take action to stop the slaughter of Africa's elephants. But an awareness campaign has its own requirements: for the message to be effective it has to be simple and attention-grabbing. Arresting advertisements, like the one that proclaimed "Dressed to Kill" over a picture of a woman wearing an ivory necklace, got the point across.

Lost in this emotional appeal was any sense of the complexities of African conservation. The sobering policies of sustainable use that both the WWF and the AWF had long backed, policies that could require difficult choices (i.e., shooting problem animals and culling programs), seemed to fly in the face of the sentiments that were being stirred up. Animal rights groups—some of which sprang into existence during this cause célèbre—launched their own efforts to stop the "elephant holocaust" and reduced the public message to gruesome pictures of slain elephants headlined "AFRICAN CHAINSAW MASSACRE." To conservationists, biologists, and, let us not forget, rural Africans who have to live with these creatures, there was a lot more to elephants than what was suggested by bumper sticker slogans. But having started down that trail, conservation groups found it hard to stop. The simpler—and more gut-wrenching—the message, the more money it raised. Any heart-tugging ad based on the wonder of elephants (especially baby elephants) was hugely effective in raising funds and swelling membership. The AWF and the WWF (in the United States) felt it prudent at the time to keep quiet about the value of sustainable use policies, a move that later made their positions on rural African communities benefiting from wildlife appear contradictory to some of their members.

"At the beginning of 1989, not one African country was in favor of a ban on ivory trading," Bonner wrote. "Nor had a single Western country called for one. Nor even had any of the major conservation organizations." But within months the anti-ivory juggernaut had gone global. There were similar campaigns in the UK and France and other European countries. The anti-ivory message attracted movie stars (Jimmy Stewart, Brigitte Bardot) as spokespeople and was covered endlessly in newspapers and magazines, and on radio and television, where undercover exposés featuring footage of poached ivory being lightly carved in Dubai and then shipped on legally to Hong Kong horrified audiences. The public quickly became convinced that worldwide lust for this beautiful material was threatening to extinguish the living source of it. For the first time in history, ivory started to look stained, tainted, suspect. For many it became something that was questionable to wear, use, and even possess. Images and slogans were swamping studies and analyses and driving the politics that—before the year was out—would bring to a halt a trade whose beginnings went back to prehistory.

BACK IN 1977 U.S. Congressman Anthony Beilenson introduced the Elephant Protection Bill (HR 10083), which, as he described it, would "ban all imports of ivory into the U.S." Two years later, it was passed by the House of Representatives but the Senate did not consider the measure. The California congressman had to wait until 1987, when mounting concern over the elephant had marshaled enough support for him to try reintroducing the bill. This time it passed both houses and was signed into law by President Ronald Reagan in October of 1988. The African Elephant Conservation Act banned ivory imports from any country that was failing in its anti-poaching efforts, as well as imports from ivory-carving countries (such as Hong Kong), unless they agreed not to import ivory from African countries that failed to meet the criteria imposed. It also provided anti-poaching grants.

If similar legislation had been in effect in every ivory-importing country, would it have provided a means to crack down comprehensively on poaching and ivory smuggling in Africa, while still allowing countries that managed their elephant populations effectively to benefit from them as a valuable resource? Without stringent enforcement, probably not. A global effort to reduce poaching by creating a single legal trade channel with strict licensing, transparent sales, and registration of legal stocks—in effect setting up a tightly controlled ivory cartel linked to elephant conservation—might have had a better chance of snuffing out any means of marketing poached ivory. But there was little interest now in exploring avenues other than criminalizing parts of the trade.

On June 4, 1989, President George H. W. Bush ordered a ban on all imports of African ivory into the United States—the first such action by an ivory-importing country. A week later the European Community took similar steps; by the end of the month the IUCN (World Conservation Union), WWF, and AWF had come out in favor of an ivory ban, and

Canada, Switzerland, Hong Kong, and Australia had also banned imports. Japan followed suit three months later.

The international ivory market's entanglement with criminal smuggling had made it easy to vilify not only the trade but sustainable utilization policies in Africa, as if poaching and culling were no different. In the public mind, elephants were being slaughtered, and this was all that counted. The global outcry over the grim statistics—elephant numbers had been halved in ten years to 650,000; there were now only 5,300 elephants left in Tsavo; etc.—reached new heights. Searing images of poachers' killing fields blotted out any pictures that might have suggested that not all of Africa's wilds looked that way.

There was one more indelible image to come: the internationally televised bonfire of elephant tusks that Kenya's president Daniel arap Moi ignited on July 18, 1989. The dramatic burning of a twenty-foot-tall stack of some two thousand tusks, heaped in a clearing overlooking the Athi Plains in Nairobi National Park, was intended to underscore his country's commitment to bringing an end to poaching and the trade in illegal ivory. The brainchild of paleontologist Richard Leakey, who just months before had been put in charge of revitalizing and rooting out corruption in Kenya's Wildlife Service, the event was seen by a worldwide audience and the image of the towering orange blaze and billowing black smoke set against the empty blue African sky appeared in newspapers and magazines throughout the world. Iain Douglas-Hamilton, who was there, described it as "idealistic, imaginative and moral." Pro–ivory ban forces were equally ecstatic, but many others were less thrilled, finding it a questionable publicity stunt that cost Kenya $3 million, the value of the stockpile of ivory destroyed—an act of wanton destruction, they said, in a poor country whose government officials had openly colluded with poachers and ivory smugglers.

It is not easy to get rid of ivory. In fact, it took sixty tons of firewood and a hundred and forty gallons of gasoline to start the pyre.

WITH ALL THAT had transpired in the months leading up to the Seventh Meeting of the Conference of the Parties to CITES that opened on

October 9, 1989, in Lausanne, Switzerland, one might have imagined that bringing the ivory trade to a halt was a foregone conclusion. Yet it was not all that easy for the ninety-one countries in attendance to make this happen. Two weeks of contentious debate took place; anti-ivory forces argued for listing the African elephant in Appendix I, which would have stopped the trade in tusks entirely. But some African countries balked at being steamrollered. They worried that, even if their elephant populations remained stable or managed to recover, it would prove politically impossible ever to "downlist" them to Appendix II. Mushanana Nchunga, the principal wildlife biologist in Botswana's Department of Wildlife, described the pro-ban attitude at the 1989 CITES meeting. "The issue had become a hot news item for the international press and a good piece of propaganda for some NGOs. Those of us who belonged to the group which did not agree with the proposed elephant [ivory] ban were made to feel that we were the rebels and therefore unpopular."

Various compromises were offered. Representatives of WWF and IUCN proposed that elephants in Zimbabwe, South Africa, and Botswana remain on the Appendix II list (which would have allowed trade in their tusks under CITES permits) if that was linked with a two-year moratorium on ivory trading. Finally, on a vote of 76 for, 11 against, and 4 abstentions, the African elephant was put into Appendix I, with the proviso that a mechanism remain whereby countries with well-managed populations could apply to CITES to have their elephants downlisted; if the case was proved they would be allowed to resume trade in ivory. Delegates stood, clapped, cheered, and whistled. International trade in ivory had been banned.

A historic shift took place with that act. Global commerce in a substance known and valued for millennia was halted. From now on, ivory would be seen as part of the elephants' story, and not the other way around, as had always been the case before.

In the aftermath of the decision the ivory market collapsed as ivory prices plummeted. Best of all, elephant poaching in Africa declined impressively. The ivory ban was a huge success—or so it first appeared.

8

THE IVORY BAN

I made a few wrong turns on the back roads in the open bush before the signs on the stone cairns started matching up with the directions I'd marked on my crumpled map. As a result, I was a bit late for my meeting with Karen van Rooyen in Skukuza, the main tourist camp and administrative hub of Kruger, South Africa's flagship national park. She was talking on her cell phone as I drove through the open metal gate past security men into the bare sun-bright courtyard between a set of nondescript buildings tucked away among garages and warehouses. A sandy-haired young woman in crisp khakis, van Rooyen had recently been brought into the park's conservation services to manage its wildlife products processing plant and to create some order in the ivory vaults.

Van Rooyen led me over to a low, red-roofed concrete building whose thick beige walls were pierced along one long side with a small pair of barred windows. We entered through a set of metal doors into a slab-floored storage room full of hides. I needed a moment for my eyes to adjust from the glare outside before taking in the huge stacks of mud-colored, stiff, wrinkled buffalo and elephant hides; a few lion skins; and cardboard boxes of hippo and warthog tusks taped together in different-sized bunches. There was a heap of elephant ears, as crinkled as giant potato chips, a pile of elephant tails with their impressive sprouts of stiff hair, like long-handled whisk brooms, and what looked like a tired length of fire hose. "Elephant penis," she said matter-of-factly. All the hides were collected from carcasses brought in by the field rangers, she told me, salted, and stored. Some came from animals that had died of natural causes, the rest from problem animals that had to be shot or, in the case of buffalo, from animals culled as part of research into the outbreak of the bovine tuberculosis that had been affecting them. The collection is constantly growing, and van Rooyen was helping to organize these largely leather goods for eventual sale to the hide industry or, for that matter, to local traditional healers. The park would seek CITES permission to sell the elephant products, with the funds earmarked for conservation projects.

Something else piles up from Kruger's twelve thousand–strong elephant population; it's kept in the adjoining space, behind a concrete wall with a single, massive, bolted red steel door with a huge padlock. Van Rooyen unlocked this last of a series of barriers to the vault within. "I'm sure you've seen this sort of thing before," she said as the door swung open, groaning on its metal hinges. A tilted rectangle of sunlight swept across the floor-to-ceiling stacks of curved elephant tusks lining the walls. I had, certainly, but not on this scale; I was startled by the sight of so many tons of ivory in clusters and piles and heaps, from little spikes and flutes to tusks that looked as big as alpenhorns.

Van Rooyen told me that the stout log racks, built so that different-size tusks could be sorted on them, finally cracked and collapsed under the growing weight and had to be rebuilt. Raw ivory is very hard to stack. There's no way tusks really fit well together, so that even if they are laid as neatly as possible they still resist organization. I fingered some of the thin edges of the open ends of the bigger tusks—the "bamboo" end, as Moore had referred to it—and trailed my hand down their rounded forms. I could see the lip lines, a faint discoloration marking the extent to which the tusks were buried in the head. Some of the tusks were weathered— dried and cracked from exposure—before they were recovered; others were pitiably small tapers—juvenile tusks.

Much of this was found ivory—removed from dead elephants. But it's not necessary to kill elephants to get their ivory, as many people today seem to assume. You can simply wait for them to die of natural causes. In days past, a large portion of Kruger's stockpile would have been a by-product of culling operations, but those were stopped in 1994. Then, too, there's always some ivory that's been taken from problem elephants shot because they'd flattened locals or threatened tourists, as well as some seized from poachers, although Kruger, as one of the continent's best-managed parks, has relatively little of that.

I was admiring some of the impressive sweeps of ivory from older tuskers on the shelves when I spotted two startlingly huge moon crescents of ivory on the lowest level of the back racks. I got down on my knees to try to fit my fingers around the fattest of these nine-foot-long ivories, but I could see it would take almost three hand spans to encircle it. "Those are Mandleve's tusks," van Rooyen said, admiring them alongside me. One of the park's more famous denizens, this great bull left behind the heaviest ivory ever recorded in Kruger: the right tusk weighs 162 pounds, the left tusk 152 pounds. Mandleve (Tsonga for "ears") had a substantial notch missing from one ear, although that hardly would have been his most notable feature. A local Skukuza resident, he was frequently escorted by four young bulls who helped him push over and plow up greenery. In his old age he liked to rest his heavy tusks on riverbanks or the fork of a tree; he died of natural causes in 1993 at the presumed age of fifty-six. Van Rooyen said they hadn't gotten around to sending up his tusks to the Elephant Hall at Letaba camp, where I was headed the next day.

As she locked the door van Rooyen told me I'd actually seen only half of their ivory cache—there was another vault as well, tucked away nearby. It too was overflowing with ivory. Nobody had totaled the amount recently, but Kruger's current cache had to be close to fifty tons. It wasn't possible to put a precise value on these tusks without a legal market for them, but without doubt I had just been looking at several million dollars' worth. Thieves tried to crack into it once but were foiled; extra security has since been added.

Kruger is not the only park with stockpiles of ivory recovered from elephants. In fact, one to five tons of ivory a year pile up in warehouses of the parks departments of a dozen African countries; Zimbabwe alone adds ten. There is little agreement about what should be done with this ivory fortune. But as long as there are elephants this mountain of tusks will continue to grow.

HAILED AS A great achievement by many, the ivory ban began to appear as a less than perfect solution to the problems it was intended to address not long after it took effect on January 18, 1990. True, poaching fell dramatically from the levels that had so alarmed conservationists. Richard Leakey, Kenya's wildlife director, was able to say that the country had moved from losing three elephants a day—more than a thousand each year—in its national parks to "sporadic and infrequent" elephant losses, forty-six in all of 1990. Ivory was bringing poachers a little over $1 a pound instead of the $32 a pound it had earned at its peak. Abandoned ivory caches found in Kenya and Tanzania led some to think that the old networks of corrupt ministers, diplomats, customs officials, and game wardens paid off by Hong Kong ivory kingpins had collapsed.

But poaching didn't disappear. It wasn't just that word hadn't filtered down to the man behind the gun. There were still unregulated markets, some operating openly in Africa. For Leakey, that meant it was not enough to make buying ivory "social anathema" in Europe and North America. His solution was brutally simple: "The only way to permanently stop poaching is to destroy the ivory market." Drying up all the value inherent in ivory by making it impossible to sell might be one way to make it pointless to poach. Whether that made sense, or could actually be achieved, was another matter.

Some researchers, including several participants in the Ivory Trade Review Group, the international panel of experts whose recommendation that the elephant be given an Appendix I listing under CITES helped bring about the ivory ban, were now having second thoughts. In 1990 economist Edward Barbier and three other authors, all former members of the group, argued that "the ivory trade ban must be considered an interim measure, not a solution." While conceding that previous attempts at monitoring and regulating the ivory trade had failed, and that it "has been doing the elephant great harm in the vast majority of the African range states," they pointed out that "in a small minority of states, the trade has been rendering the elephant important benefits. Thus, the crucial causal factor in the elephant's decline has not been the ivory trade *per se*, but rather the failure of some states to utilize it constructively."

This wasn't a point of view that enjoyed much support in Europe and North America, where most of the public was breathing a collective sigh of relief at the imposition of the ivory ban. Still, some dissident opinions surfaced over concerns that the ban could have the opposite effect from the one intended. "Without ways to make money from their ele-phants," an article in *The Economist* worried in 1991, "many African countries will see little reason to preserve them. For Kenya, the huge tak-ings from tourism may be incentive enough. In other countries, the ele-phant's main chance of survival will lie, counter-intuitively, in the value of its tusks." The magazine suggested looking into a "toughly controlled trading system to market a limited quantity of sustainably harvested ivory."

In the 1990s researchers analyzed the mechanisms of the ban as well, even working out economic models for poaching to study how its in-centives were shaped by ivory prices and law enforcement deterrence. One such study used mathematical models, which took into account probabilities of output of tusks, detection and conviction, variable costs (salaries to gang members, costs of fines and bail), fixed costs (equipment such as modern arms and training), and a host of other factors, including the probable supply of ivory from legal and illegal sources reaching over-seas consumer markets. It concluded that withholding legal production of ivory from overseas markets would only drive up illegal prices and en-courage poaching, "highlighting the need for CITES to consider more carefully the interactions between trade bans and illegal trade in endan-gered species in cases where enforcement of bans is imperfect." But these academic studies, thought-provoking as they were, received little media at-tention.

By 1994 nine African states were holding at least one hundred tons of stockpiled ivory, an amount that probably totaled two-thirds of the world ivory trade in 1988. Before the ban, the ivory trade had been worth something like $50 million a year to the African continent, perhaps dou-ble that if you added up all those involved in it, including indigenous carvers who made all the curios sold to tourists as well as more creditable sculpture. There was no effort to compensate states for lost revenues that could have gone to defray costly antipoaching efforts and game manage-ment or to support rural communities affected adversely by wildlife.

The unspoken issue lurking just under the surface of any discussion of the ban's effectiveness was that Africans and their interests were still be-ing ignored. In the 1930s the colonial view was that the "natives" couldn't be trusted not to wipe out the game. By the 1990s African countries were in charge of their own destinies, but they were still being instructed by

Europe and North America on how they should manage wildlife, especially their elephants. A lot of conservation on the continent had become
a not so subtle form of intellectual colonialism. The enterprise of inter-
vening "on behalf of nature" was couched in the language of assistance,
help, advice, and support but mostly for narrowly conceived wildlife interests. In contrast with the overexploited environments that the European
and North American public associates with its own countries (or at least
parts of them), the "animal Eden" that Africa conjures up inspires the desire to ensure that Africans don't follow the rape-of-the-land environmental
despoliation policies that are now cause for regret in the first world.

It is difficult to imagine, though, how struggling African nations
are supposed to keep vast swaths of their landmass pristine while simultaneously meeting their development goals. Africans can hardly be
blamed if they bitterly conclude that the only way they can satisfy the
developed world's more extreme conservation interests is to remain in a
permanent state of picturesque underdevelopment. No one in Washington or London would ever state the issue so starkly, but Africans, especially rural Africans, were still being urged to make choices that put
animals before people, or at least put them on an equal footing, which
is almost equally offensive. This arrogant approach was evident in the
imposition of the ivory ban, in which the "global concerns" of individuals and groups from first world countries trumped sub-Saharan perceptions. Somehow the idea that national sovereignty gives Africans the
right to be in charge of their own wildlife (something European and
North American countries take for granted as the basis of their own
wildlife policies) got lost in all the grand talk of saving the continent's
wildlife heritage (especially elephants) for future generations. In formu-
lating the ban without in-depth consultation with African governments
or local wildlife organizations, Africans, as one observer put it, were
"once again relegated to reactive positions, labeled as progressive if
agreeing with outside perceptions or cast as despoilers when presenting
their own views."

In 1991 Zimbabwe, Namibia, Botswana, and South Africa applied
for CITES permission to downlist their elephants to Appendix II, which
would have allowed them to reopen trade in ivory. A reported upsurge in
smuggling in anticipation of the possible resumption of trade in ivory

underscored the contention by advocates of the ban that a legal ivory trade would simply provide a cover for illegal trade based on poaching. At the March 1992 CITES meeting in Kyoto, the debate on this application featured much sermonizing and self-righteous proclamations, including a passionate statement on "the moral imperative for banning the ivory trade," from, of all countries, Burundi, which had previously operated as an ivory smuggler's El Dorado.

CITES was fast becoming a public relations forum, an opportunity for governments to be seen as doing something positive for the environment. Under press scrutiny, member states were especially mindful of their constituents. Rich countries—and their powerful lobbyists—held the most sway at these meetings. "It is the Western European and North American publics that stump up the money for wildlife lobbyists, and it is therefore, naturally, the rich man's philosophy of wildlife management that prevails," wrote David Harland. Because debates were pitched to appeal to the lobbyists' constituencies, complicated solutions were quickly dropped in favor of simpler ones—"ones that will have appeal at the bumper-sticker level," as Harland put it. "It is very much easier to say 'Save the Elephant: Ban the Ivory Trade' than it is to say 'Save the Elephant: Support a Programme to Make Elephant Habitat Viable Against Human Encroachment.'"

Zimbabwe, feeling that the fate of its elephants was being determined by Europeans and North Americans with scant regard for how southern Africans might view things, submitted a proposal to put the North Sea herring on Appendix I as an endangered species, which would have necessitated halting all trade in the tasty little fish (having made their point, they later withdrew it). But in the face of the objections of many African countries—including those struggling with poaching—who had joined the opposition to any downlisting of the elephant, the southern African countries were forced to drop their downlist proposal. At the 1994 CITES meeting, South Africa and Sudan proposed downlisting their populations. Sudan had insufficient justification, and South Africa abandoned its proposal when it was clear there was no support.

In 1997, at a CITES meeting in Harare, Zimbabwe, the first crack appeared in the ban: Botswana, Namibia, and Zimbabwe were successful in getting approval to downlist their elephant populations, with trade in

ivory limited to a tightly controlled, onetime sale from government stockpiles to Japan. The three countries earned a total of some $5 million.

ON A STEAMY hot July day in 1999, a freighter docked in Tokyo Bay with a
shipment of some fifty tons of ivory, consisting of 5,446 elephant tusks
from Botswana, Namibia, and Zimbabwe. This otherwise uneventful
landing of goods marked the first time in a decade that there had been
any legal international commerce in ivory.

Japanese ivory traders had been anxiously awaiting the shipment,
whose arrival held out the hope that their country's long ivory-carving
tradition—and their businesses—might have a future. Sales of ivory had
dropped 60 percent after the ban, despite the stockpiles on hand.

Japan's ivory trade, like that of every other country, had operated
without any specific regulations for all its prior history. Although the
country became a signatory to CITES in 1973, it took seven years before
it ratified the convention, out of concern to protect industries that utilized wildlife products. Even afterward, its adherence was less than enthusiastic. As in other ivory-carving cultures, traders had been conditioned
to see cherished carving material when they looked at creamy tusks. They
had known for centuries, of course, that ivory came from elephants, but
looking at it for hints of its origin, or at the long, strange zigzag trek it
might have taken to reach dealers' storerooms, was a new and alien way
for them to size up the raw material. Almost overnight ivory had taken
on a new set of meanings and the tusks themselves became forensic evidence.

At first, some Japanese traders thought these new ideas and pressure
for change were fashionable concerns that would fade away or bureaucratic impediments that could be safely ignored. In 1983 and 1984 one
trader was still importing ivory from Burma, despite the fact that the endangered Asian elephant was listed in Appendix I, which meant all commercial trade in Asian ivory was prohibited. Japan was also importing
huge quantities of ivory from Burundi, although the CITES secretariat in
Switzerland had specially requested that member states not do so, given

that all the ivory the elephant-empty country was exporting as its own was ipso facto poached. Under pressure, the country's major ivory trade groups—both the Tokyo and the Osaka ivory arts and crafts associations— had promised in mid-1984 to police their members better, but the two groups couldn't agree on import guidelines.

Mounting criticism of Japan's ivory trade practices inspired the formation of a new group, the Zôgei Bukai (Ivory Importers' Group), which brought together twenty-five ivory-importing companies, plus trade associations. Collectively, the members accounted for 98 percent of all Japanese ivory imports. They began implementing, initially on a voluntary basis, more stringent guidelines on ivory imports. Imports fell from the all-time high of 475 tons in the mid-1980s to 106 tons in 1988. Japan's ivory industry may have been late in taking seriously the worldwide concern over the decline of Africa's elephant herds, but it was now in full compliance with CITES and, at the same time, anxious to keep its ivory business alive. In the two weeks before the country's June 19, 1989, ban on ivory imports from non-African states, a flurry of shipments totaling twenty-nine tons arrived from reexporting entrepôts like Hong Kong. Following the lead of other industrialized nations, it halted the importation of all ivory several months later.

Hoping for an accommodation that would allow a limited international flow of ivory, Japan pushed for a split listing at the CITES meeting that October, which would put the African elephant population on the Appendix I listing—except for those in the southern tier. Japan's position was openly regarded with suspicion by some other delegations (and at home by its own small but vocal animal protection lobby), who wondered if its desire to gain support for a "sustainable use" elephant policy was part of an effort to build a case for its widely unpopular whaling policy. Caught between wanting to "avoid Japan's isolation in the international community," as one Japanese official put it, and wanting to yet remain sensitive to its domestic ivory industry, Japan abstained on the final vote to put the African elephant on Appendix I.

Japan's support for the southern African position did not go unnoticed. Japan is the largest consumer of wildlife products in the world; its participation in CITES is vital to that convention's success. What adds significance to the country's unique position is that although Japan is a major industrialized power—the second largest economy in the world—its support for the "sustainable use" point of view rather than the openly preservationist stance taken by most first world countries made it a natural ally of many of the African elephant's range states. As Kumi Furuyashiki details,

> When Namibian President Sam Nujoma visited Tokyo in October 1996 and appealed to then Prime Minister of Japan Ryutaro Hashimoto to support Namibia's proposal of downlisting the African elephant submitted to CITES together with Botswana and Zimbabwe for consideration at COP10 in the following year, and to allow export of ivory to Japan, Hashimoto announced Japan's support, on the ground that "Namibia's proposal is consistent with the principle" of "harmony between conservation and use" in dealing with wildlife.

Out of consideration for the "feelings of opposing countries" Japan declined to copropose the downlisting. Still, when Botswana, Namibia, and Zimbabwe proposed downlisting their elephants at the Tenth Conference of the Parties to CITES in 1997, it was hardly surprising that Japan was selected as the sole importer of their ivory. Not only was Japan a traditional ivory market; it could consume all the ivory products it produced within its own borders. Besides, high labor costs made it uneconomical to export worked ivory, even if it were allowed. In addition, Japan was able to put a number of regulations in place to ensure that the ivory industry would be tightly controlled. The country's traders, well aware that such changes, however burdensome, would be necessary, gave the system their full commitment. In mid-1995 the domestic ivory trade control system was begun. It required registration of every ivory trader, all tusks, cut pieces, even waste. In March of 1999 even more control procedures were introduced for production of *hanko* (name seals), the primary use for ivory in Japan. These required retailers to keep a record of *hanko* sales, purchasers, the size of *hanko*, remaining stocks, and the like. In practice, this meant that 80 percent of retail sales of ivory would be recorded and checked by the government.

Given the level of scrutiny Japan was willing to allow over its ivory industry, and the fact that reexporting ivory was prohibited, there was little more that could be asked. Some in the anti–ivory trade camp argued that not all the conditions for the shipment were properly fulfilled, and that this partial lifting of the ivory ban had led to an upsurge in poaching, but these objections failed to scuttle the sale.

BEFORE THE IVORY ban, upwards of thirty thousand Japanese made their living from ivory, including traders, traditional carvers, and shopkeepers selling *hanko*. In the Tokyo and Osaka ivory trades, names such as Kitagawa and Takaichi dominated, bringing in half the country's imports between them. From traders, the ivory spread out through a series of factories, workshops, and individual craftspeople. Japan's ivory industry was big business, exceeding, as Esmond Martin pointed out, the gross national product of some African countries. Those directly involved in the ivory industry earned more than $40 million annually; the retail value of finished ivory products was something like $250 million annually.

And what were the uses, other than *hanko*, to which all this ivory was being put? Small amounts went into the making of ivory components (and plectra) for traditional Japanese musical instruments such as the samisen, the koto, and the *biwa*. Ivory chopsticks, once a fashionable wedding present, but now less popular, were still produced at rate of four thousand pairs a month in the early 1980s. The craze for polished tusks, which took hold in the early 1970s when ivory looked as good as gold as a hedge against inflation, absorbed large quantities of ivory (one Toyota executive amassed a collection of a hundred such tusks, which he kept under the floors of his house in Nagoya). That fad soon faded when Japan experienced a recession. Ivory jewelry, lids for tea containers, even ear picks were still produced in quantity in the pre-ban days, and although much diminished, artistic traditions of ivory carving that dated back to the golden age of the netsuke masters persisted.

One noted figure was the Tokyo-based netsuke carver Masatoshi (Nakamura Tokisada). Esteemed for his birds, fish, mermaids, even blades of grass created from ivory, he had trained as an apprentice for seven years with his father, Ittensai Kuya. Kuya himself carved *bijin* (beautiful women) in ivory as well as netsuke and once crafted a cane with an ivory dragon handle for William Sebald, the American ambassador to Japan after World War II. Previous generations of the family had specialized in ivory *okimono*—finely carved ornaments. In the postwar period ivory was difficult to come by. Masatoshi searched shops and dealers for scraps and tusk remnants and sometimes used billiard balls or samisen plectra for his netsuke. Elephant ivory—*zôge*—was his favorite material, especially Asian ivory ("pinkish in color, small, even, and fine grained, oily, lustrous, and live"). But even for a master who bought only the "desirable parts of a desirable tusk"—notably the *marusaki,* or tip—some of the best African tusks could equal the Asian in quality. The important thing was to find the material "responsive." Then, he wrote, "my knives seemed to sing and move along of their own accord."

This exquisitely attuned sensitivity to ivory's material properties extended even to the polishing of the netsuke, a time-consuming process, each stage of which removed the marks of the previous abrasive. Any traces left by sandpaper and emery paper were expunged by several hours of rubbing with the soaked leaves of the *muku* tree. To reach difficult areas, such as recessed details, Masatoshi sharpened a willow-wood chopstick; no other wood would do, as its uniformity (even the annual rings are no harder than the material between) and its resiliency made it perfect for the job. Still, he confessed, "my use of a willow chopstick is a violation of my father's strict practice. He cut his own branch from a willow tree and shaped it himself into the sharp pointed sliver he wanted for his polishing." Various powders, including burned stag antler, came next, but if Masatoshi was pleased with his netsuke, he liked to finish polishing the smooth little ivory with his bare hands ("I feel as though I were caressing one of my children").

While the wondrously refined work of a handful of master craftsmen like Masatoshi was still sought by connoisseurs, the preponderance of ivory carving in Japan had fallen into repetitive forms of domestic and tourist bric-a-brac churned out by small factories of workers using drills to speed up what was left of a craft that once used some two hundred traditional hand tools.

In the early 1980s the manufacture of *hanko* absorbed just over half of ivory imports. Over the next two decades the percentage would grow to three-quarters of the quantity of ivory brought into the country. What accounted for this growth? Name seals are a traditional item of prestige and authority in East Asia. Originally the use of these circular or square ink stamps was limited to the aristocratic classes, but in the Edo period the use of *hanko* to prove identity became more common. By the Meiji period (1867–1912) laws requiring people to use *hanko* to mark official documents made them ubiquitous. The act of stamping such papers with personal seals typically dipped in a red ink paste authorized them; *hanko* were essential for cashing checks, concluding business correspondence, contracting to buy a car or home, or, for that matter, finalizing a marriage. Until the late 1990s, when the increasing use of credit cards requiring hand signatures for transactions became common, it was almost impossible to conduct business without the use of a *hanko*.

There are ten main types of *hanko*, three for individuals and seven for businesses. Martin estimated there might have been seventy million to one hundred million such seals in circulation in the early 1980s. The *jitsuin*, or personal seal, is used for legal transactions and is unique, registered with the government, and thus an important possession. In many ways, ivory is the ideal material for a *hanko*, as it can be finely carved, takes the ink well, and will last a lifetime. It's also nice to touch and hold and its color has special appeal. Prior to the 1950s ivory was too expensive for most Japanese, who made do with wood, horn, or crystal. When ivory *hanko* first became popular, only the face of the seal with its characters was carved of ivory; the handle was typically boxwood or buffalo horn. By the 1960s most Japanese could afford a solid ivory *hanko*; twenty years later one would have cost about $90, which included the carving of several characters, a case, and a small ink pad.

The manufacture of *hanko* became largely mechanized, much like that of piano key veneers (which the Japanese produced in quantity for piano makers Yamaha and Kawai). In small, cramped factories, where a three-month supply of tusks would share space with what looked like woodworking benches covered with ivory dust, a dozen or so workers could turn out a surprising number. In 1980, Martin visited factories in Osaka that employed only nine workers but managed to produce sixteen hundred *hanko* a day. These seals, cylindrical in shape and about two inches long and half an inch wide, are easily machined and the process is, in fact, reminiscent of piano key production. After tusks are cut into drums of suitable length, a worker marks a cluster of circles of various diameters in red ink on the face of a particular slice: smaller circles for *hanko* using two characters, larger ones for *hanko* of up to four characters. Great care is taken to maximize the number of *hanko* that can be cut. Small round pegs corresponding to the drawn circles are then cut out of the ivory drum on an electric band saw. Each one is then clamped in a vise, rounded on a belt sander, and buffed with emery paper. Further steps involve cutting them to precise length, preparing the face for the cutting of the characters, and polishing them overall with *boshu* sand. At that point all those short sticks of ivory are much like one another, until a buyer purchases one at a shop and supplies a drawing of his or her personal "chop." The shop then forwards this to a specialist, often a family-owned business in Rokugocho—famous as "*hanko* town"—in Yamanashi Prefecture. Carving characters on *hanko* is an exacting art. The head of the seal is cleaned with fine sandpaper, painted with red ink, and positioned in a vise, at which point a master craftsperson paints the individual characters on the red face in black. A carver carefully outlines the characters with a tiny electric drill, then examines the result under a magnifying glass; any last touches required are done with hand tools.

But ivory *hanko*, like ivory piano keys, are no longer what they were. Two million ivory *hanko* were made in 1980; almost a million in 1988. Their popularity was falling. Two years after the "onetime" ivory shipment arrived in Tokyo, only a little over a hundred thousand *hanko* had been produced—some still made entirely by hand by a few stubborn traditional craftsmen. Ivory use was dropping in Japan.

JAPAN'S IVORY TRADE regulations were complex and burdensome, even for retailers, but as critics of the country's ivory policies, such as the Japan Wildlife Conservation Society, made clear, they still had loopholes that could be exploited. The JWCS and others pointed to a 2000 incident in which a *hanko* manufacturer (and board member of the Tokyo Ivory Arts and Crafts Association) was arrested trying to collect half a ton of raw ivory smuggled in cut pieces from Singapore to Kobe. It was mixed in with a shipment of chopsticks. Critics weren't placated by the fact that the enforcement system worked well enough to catch the miscreant, but based on its findings in 2006 the CITES secretariat was satisfied that all that could be expected in terms of control was in place and recommended that "Japan should be, once again, designated as a trading partner."

Despite the arrival of the fifty-ton "experimental" CITES-approved ivory shipment from Africa in 1999, the hope that there might be future ones, and the existence of stocks that would keep many manufacturers going for quite some time, there was deep pessimism in the trade about the future of the ivory industry in Japan. It wasn't just the uncertainties of whether ivory would continue to be available; it was the public attitude toward it. That ivory might appear to younger Japanese as old-fashioned could be successfully countered by some stylish new use or novel jewelry design, but its increasingly negative image as a material associated, fairly or not, with the despoliation of nature had deeply affected the trade, and substitutes such as hippo teeth or mammoth ivory, along with synthetics, found little acceptance. By 2002 the retail value of ivory items produced in Japan had declined 90 percent since the imposition of the ivory ban. Little wonder that in his survey from the same year Martin found far fewer people working in the ivory industry, from traders to artisans, and an absence of apprentices. Without a steady supply—and, what's more, a change in the public attitude—Japan's ivory industry looked as though it might become a relic of the past.

THERE WAS ANOTHER ivory-consuming country waiting in the wings, one that would be more than willing to take Japan's place as the final destination for all the tusks that Africa could spare, and then some: China.

In some ways, the country was an unlikely candidate. Since the imposition of the ivory ban China has been implicated in the importation and sale of illegal stocks and accused of reviving elephant poaching to feed its newly awakened appetite for ivory. In monitoring raw ivory and ivory

product seizures, CITES found that China was "the single most important influence on the increasing trend in illegal trade in ivory since
1995." Some of this suspect ivory was hand-carried to the People's Republic: Chinese contract workers sent to work on large-scale building projects
in Africa where ivory regulations are poorly enforced regularly returned
home with illicit ivory. In Sudan, where up to five thousand Chinese
work in the construction, oil, and mining industries, the price of ivory
ominously doubled, a tip-off that local authorities were turning a blind
eye to the flourishing open ivory markets in Khartoum and Omduman
and the poaching that was supplying them.

Following the imposition of the ivory ban China initially did nothing about its own domestic trade in ivory. Then, in the early 1990s, the
government decided that all trade in ivory should cease. Since the trade
was conducted largely by government-run enterprises, and imports were
also under government control, one might have thought this sweeping
measure would have spelled the end to the several-millennium-old industry. Curiously, a few privately run factories and workshops continued to
manufacture ivory items and some retailers sold carvings openly—even
though all of them were ostensibly illegal—showing that the government
was putting few resources into enforcement.

In the early 2000s China reviewed its regulations. Encouraged by
the one-off sale to Japan, and recognizing that traditional carving skills
were being lost, the government decided to reopen its domestic ivory industry under strict controls, at the same time cracking down on illegal activities. As CITES reported, China clearly hoped to "eventually become
a legal importer of ivory from legitimate African sources and stockpiles."
The country began imposing its own elaborate ivory laws, registering pro-
cessors and retailers and their stockpiles, even tracking individual ivory
pieces that sold for more than 500 yuan (about $65)—dragging violators
to court, X-raying imports, and taking draconian measures with smugglers, who now faced penalties, long imprisonment, even the death sen-
tence for certain offenses, all in an effort to demonstrate the effectiveness
of its new ivory regime.

China pushed to qualify as an appropriate buyer of tusks. By one
measure alone China would be ideal. Although the country can find eager buyers for its ivory product exports, it has no need to do so. China's

sheer size—one-fifth of the world's population—guarantees that its own domestic market for ivory would be in no danger of reaching saturation in the foreseeable future. Its new wealth is impressive. In 2006 China had three hundred thousand millionaires, its four hundred wealthiest citizens had fortunes of $60 million or more, and the country boasted seven billionaires. Ivory, a historic marker of prestige and a symbol of wealth, is now within reach of many Chinese. Besides, along with all the traditional Chinese uses for the material, there are some tempting new ones. The *Guangzhou Daily* reported in 2006 that for a mere 180,000 yuan ($22,500) one could purchase an ornately carved ivory-cased mobile phone. Two of the first six made had already been sold.

The steps that the People's Republic took to regulate its ivory trade created something of a Chinese puzzle for the member states of CITES. Given China's recent history, they seemed unlikely to rush to approve it as a suitable market, even though the secretariat did. On the other hand, they did not want to wait too long to respond to China's new effort to regulate one of its most ancient trades. In its 2005 report to the secretariat, the CITES investigative team admits that it "was very aware that the long-term success of what has been established in China, and the enthusiasm and compliance that is being shown by the accredited traders, depends upon fresh stocks of legal ivory becoming available. If they do not, the system is likely to collapse and it is hard to imagine that illicit trade would not then gain ground."

In July, 2008, the Standing Committee of CITES agreed to designate China as an approved ivory buyer, along with Japan.

"WITH OUR LIMITED resources, we typically target more commercial operations," Edward Grace said, swiveling in his chair and reaching with a long arm to pull down an annual report. "We go after smugglers, someone who's trying to bring it in as something else, the galleries who know it's illegal and are selling it to someone who also knows this." The "it" was ivory, and Grace, senior special agent of the U.S. Fish and Wildlife Service, Division of Law Enforcement, is part of a cadre of agents who keep track of anything suspicious about ivory's comings and goings in the country.

His small office overlooking Fairfax Drive in a high-rise building in Arlington, Virginia, a subway stop from Washington, D.C., had the expected crowded desk, computer, files, and bookshelves. But there was a neatness to the paper piles that suggested someone who's often on the road. He'd helped crack smuggling operations that had brought in tons of endangered sturgeon roe and overseen investigations that led to the conviction of a New York retailer selling chimpanzee skulls, gorilla paw ashtrays, and other grisly items from endangered primates. But ivory remains a primary concern of his, and his casework on it has taken him as far as Kenya.

I had been asking him about what sorts of efforts his department was making to keep ivory from entering the country in the post-ban era. Grace gave me a basic overview of current U.S. regulations: no ivory, raw or worked, can be brought into the country, or reexported, unless it's a bona fide antique. "If it's over a hundred years old," he pointed out, "that's different."

There's actually a substantial U.S. trade in older ivories. Between 1997 and 2001, for example, worked ivory worth an average of $164.8 million a year was imported, over thirty thousand items, typically carvings, although ivory pieces, jewelry, and piano keys were brought in as well. Some ivory art, valued at $1 million or more, was destined for museums or private collections. The majority came from Britain; other exporters included France, Canada, and Japan. Ivory art is a specialized area of the international art market—just a few galleries, auction houses, antiques dealers, and Internet sites do most of the business, and there are reexports of these art ivories as well.

There are no more legal imports of raw (unprocessed) ivory into the United States, with one exception, Grace explained: tusks considered a personal "sport-hunted trophy" from an approved list of African range states (those with well-managed herds). However, these tusks, of which around three hundred per year are brought in, can't be sold; essentially, they must remain in noncommercial limbo. No raw ivory, including sport-hunted trophies, may be reexported. There are further refinements. Intrastate sale of ivory is allowed if the ivory is legally imported or acquired, but twenty-three states have laws that can complicate such transactions—at one point, California did not allow ivory to be brought into the state for commercial purposes. Interstate sale of ivory is also generally permitted, although for complicated reasons Asian ivory is subject to tighter restrictions on interstate (and intrastate) sales. The federal government doesn't attempt to monitor every domestic ivory purchase, although Grace's department will aggressively investigate individuals it suspects of dealing in illegal ivory. In short, domestic trade in ivory isn't closely monitored, as evidence, in 2004, that illicit ivory was being purchased from China over the Internet as "antiques" by credulous buyers clearly showed. Even though they should, "people don't ask questions," said Grace, shaking his head.

What is being policed with some effectiveness are the borders. The size and wealth of the American market make it a major destination for illicit ivory. In the period 1989 through 2001, the United States reported five times as many seizures of illegal ivory as did any other country. Much of the confiscated ivory is brought in by tourists who are not aware (though many surely are) of the law, and there is serious smuggling as well. Grace led the efforts to break up a smuggling ring that resulted in two of the largest ivory seizures in recent years, with a value of some $350,000. On September 17, 2000, fifty-three-year-old Oumar Keita, of Abidjan, Ivory Coast, arrived at JFK in New York on a KLM flight with a substantial amount of luggage, including fifty-seven ivory carvings that had been crudely covered with a mixture of sand and paper pulp to mimic stone sculptures. This stratagem had been used nine months before, but unsuccessfully, by another Ivory Coast denizen, Bayo Namory, who was caught and sent to prison. Agents found prison letters from Namory in Keita's luggage, along with business cards of African art dealers in New York. The second smuggling attempt didn't work either. Keita, too, was convicted and sent to prison.

Hiding costly material under a cheaper covering that could later be removed is an age-old smugglers' trick, and hardly confined to ivory. Ivory forgery itself, a distinct subspecialty of art forgers, has been around since ancient times. In the post-ban era, however, there are new variants in the venerable game of trying to pass off something newly created as something old and valuable. There is money to be made if a new carving can pass muster as an official "antique," no matter how crude. If such a ruse can get the new material safely into a country's internal market, it can always be recarved.

AS I WAS leaving his office, Ed Grace gave me a stack of documents on U.S. wildlife laws that deal with ivory—the major ones include the Lacey Act, the Endangered Species Act, CITES, the Marine Mammal Protection Act, and the African Elephant Conservation Act. Where these overlap, the stricter legislation prevails. Later, as I looked through them, I found complex provisions that deal with noncommercial use of pre–CITES ivory, the movement of personal and household effects, and the like, but no mechanism that directly regulates the internal, domestic trade in ivory. That is understandable: it would be exceedingly difficult to monitor.

By the time of the buildup to the ivory ban in the late 1980s, the United States accounted for only about 10 percent of world imports of ivory—and a lot of that consisted of trinkets from Hong Kong. But tons and tons of ivory were already in the country. The United States, like many first world nations, has huge amounts left from all the commerce that took place in the centuries before international trade in elephants' teeth was halted. The vast majority of such ivory is worked and has about as much documentation as one would normally have for furniture, tableware, musical instruments, figurines, or any other collectibles or baubles— in other words, almost none. And while little American ivory carving is being done, except for turning chunks of pre-ban raw ivory into knife handles, gun grips, and inlays for pool cues, a substantial number of ivory figures, jewelry, piano keys, and the like are bought and sold domestically, legally and openly. You can purchase museum-quality netsuke, lovely ivory jewelry like Elsa Peretti's Bone bracelet designed for Tiffany in the mid-1970s, antique pianos with ivory keys, nineteenth-century scrimshaw, narwhal tusk walking sticks, tasteless tourist trinkets, and a thousand other ivory items from galleries, dealers, shops, flea markets, estate sales, auctions, the Internet, or private individuals.

There are the same open domestic markets in Britain and the rest of Europe, where the total amount of ivory in each country could easily exceed that of the United States, given their long histories of ivory importation. Martin and Stiles found that the vast majority of ivory on sale in Europe in 2004 consisted of antique pieces; only in Germany and France are there any carvers left, creating new work from old and legal stockpiles. Their survey showed 8,325 ivory items for sale in 776 retail outlets in London alone. While virtually all of it was pre-ban material, some wasn't. Scotland Yard's wildlife crime unit conducted raids on three central London antiques dealers suspected of involvement in selling illicit ivory that had come from Africa by way of Asia. From there it was smuggled into the UK, where either reputable dealers were duped into purchasing ivory they believed to be genuinely antique or corrupt ones were willing accomplices in the deception. England and the United States are hardly the only markets smugglers target. According to one analysis, between 1995 and 2002 "shipments of illegal ivory in various quantities were intercepted and seized from more than 80 countries spread across every continent except Antarctica."

The impact of all this on elephants? It's difficult to determine the numbers of elephants that might be poached to supply the illegal trade, but three researchers—Nigel Hunter, then of CITES's MIKE (Monitoring the Illegal Killing of Elephants) program; Esmond Martin; and Tom Milliken of TRAFFIC, the joint WWF/IUCN wildlife trade monitoring network—studied the question in their 2004 paper. Using estimates of the numbers of carvers in various markets and the amount of ivory they use allowed these researchers to estimate ivory consumption in twenty-five countries around the world. They were surprised to find that "unregulated ivory markets in Africa appear to consume a higher volume of ivory than those in Asia"—an indication, it would seem, of how little control many African countries have of their own internal ivory trade.

Hunter, Martin, and Milliken concluded that some 4,800 to 12,250 elephants are killed each year to supply Africa and Asia—and beyond. "Significant quantities of carved ivory" from these two continents, they noted, "are being purchased for selling commercially elsewhere in the world." Where are these elephants coming from? Evidence points to the Congo Basin in Central Africa, where successive conflicts in the Democratic

Republic of the Congo have taken the lives of some five million people since 1998, creating one of Africa's worst humanitarian crises, a gaping wound that is far from healing. The animal toll in the war-torn Congo is clearly the collateral damage of its immense human tragedy.

THE DIFFICULTY OF distinguishing between objects made from pre-ban and post-ban ivories creates one sort of enforcement problem. Another is the difficulty of trying to determine the source of illegal ivory seized—a method for doing this would, obviously, vastly aid in cracking down on poaching. In the early 1990s researchers looked into trace element analysis of tusks to see if there was some way to discover their origin. Ivory from grass-eating elephants is higher in carbon-13 than ivory of elephants that consume shrubs, but analyzing isotopes of carbon and other elements in teeth to look for a diet "signature" that could be associated with a given geographic area proved futile. With habitat change, elephants shift their sources of food and thus show striking differences in carbon isotope ratios from individual to individual, even in the same herd.

But DNA analysis may offer the best chance of finding a "fingerprint" that would make it possible to examine raw (or worked) ivory and determine where it came from. Biologist Samuel Wasser at the University of Washington, Seattle, developed a technique in 2003 with two colleagues to drill out core samples from tusks for analysis, and found that they contained intact DNA—as good as that from skin or blood samples. Elephant populations have characteristic DNA profiles, so Wasser collected DNA gathered from four hundred elephants at twenty-eight sites across Africa. Fortunately, dung samples provided animal DNA as readily as tissue samples (elephants' high-fiber diet ensures that lots of cells are sloughed off from their intestines), making the information a lot easier to collect. "Using DNA," Wasser claimed, "it is possible to determine, with near 100 percent accuracy, whether an individual sample originated from a savanna or a forest elephant." Other researchers think that's an exaggeration, as hybridization between the two species can muddle the genetic picture. Still, Wasser hopes to create a reference map of African elephant habitats that could locate the origin of a tusk to within three hundred to six hundred miles.

The method was put to the test on tusks seized in Singapore in June 2002. The shipment, consisting of a twenty-foot container packed with six and a half tons of tusks in Malawi, had been shipped to Singapore via South Africa. After successfully extracting DNA from a sample of thirty-seven tusks, Wasser and his team went on to rule out forest elephants and conclude that the 532 tusks did not come from multiple locales, as originally suspected, but most likely originated from a narrow band of southern Africa, centered on Zambia—a claim that understandably rattled the wildlife service there.

Judging from the press reaction to Wasser's findings, the promise of this method led many to overlook its shortcomings. It needed far, far more precision before it could become a powerful antipoaching enforcement tool. And it was cumbersome—nothing that would lend itself to an instrument that customs officers at ports of entry could casually use on a tusk, the way a store clerk might swipe a bar code on a cereal box to get a price. It involved destructive sampling: the use of a 16-mm drill bit to remove a chunk of dentin the size of a pencil eraser—hardly appropriate for art objects, but feasible for raw ivory shipments. In addition, it cost $100 or so a test. Still, that might be a small price to pay in the quest to pinpoint elephant poaching.

WITH ELEPHANT IVORY in short supply after the trade ban, other animal populations have been tapped to yield what they can in carvable dentin.

This is where the hippopotamus reenters the picture. Although there are distinct size limitations to its canines and incisors and the thick enamel is a chore to remove, it nevertheless provides a source of carvable ivory suitable for jewelry, small figurines, knife handles, etc.; by itself, the tusk has trophy value. The species was listed on CITES Appendix II in 1995, so the international trade in hippo products is still legal, albeit more closely monitored. Gross exports of hippo ivory, raw and worked, fell after the listing but substantial amounts are imported into a number of countries. From 1995 to 2002 more than one and a half tons of hippo ivory was brought into the United States, far more by weight than the elephant ivory cleared for importation in the same period. Most of it originates in Tanzania, Zimbabwe, South Africa, and Uganda, but the vast majority of hippo ivory carvings that arrive in the United States have taken a detour to Hong Kong to be processed.

Prior to its listing on Appendix II, the total African hippo population was estimated at around 157,000 animals. International monitoring after the listing detected little to indicate that trade levels had a significant effect on populations, but in late 2006 came news that hippos in Virunga National Park in the Democratic Republic of the Congo's eastern border were being routinely slaughtered. Out of what was once one of Africa's largest hippo populations (estimated at more than 22,000 in the mid-1980s), there were thought to be only 315 animals left. Congolese rebel groups (of which there are at least three) in the highly insecure region are responsible for the depredation. In that desperate corner of the world, the slaughter may be driven more by the bushmeat trade than by the hope of selling some teeth.

The tusks and teeth of marine animals, such as sperm whales, narwhals, and walruses, constitute minor fractions of the remaining nonelephant trade in ivory and are listed as Appendix I, II, and III, respectively, as well as being subject to other legislation (such as the Marine Mammal Protection Act in the United States), which further restricts their trade. Commerce is completely unrestricted, however, when it comes to the teeth of the long-gone mammoth, whose often spectacular tusks are being dug up at a rate that alarms paleontologists. They would much prefer that these be carefully unearthed in the course of scientific research rather than grubbed up and sold as a guilt-free alternative to elephant ivory. It's not just that all the information about the location where they were found is lost; as Ross MacPhee told me, "It's also the tusks themselves that contain a great deal of information on the individual animal."

The urge to uncover this buried treasure is understandable. A year and a half after the ivory ban went into effect, mammoth ivory was going for $300 a pound, triple what elephant ivory fetched just before trade in it came to a halt. No wonder the Russians are mining their mammoth remains. By some estimates, ten million mammoths are buried in the

Siberian permafrost, and it's anyone's guess how many there might be in Alaska and Canada. With increased Arctic thawing brought on by global warming, it's becoming easier to find these great looping teeth. A Yakut can make $25 to $50 a pound by turning in the tusks he finds to the regional depository, perhaps more if the official channels are bypassed. A single small, striking blue-streaked mammoth tusk from Siberia's Taimyr peninsula went for £6,000 at a Sotheby's sale in 2006.

As an alternative to elephant ivory as carving material, however, mammoth ivory has received mixed reviews. German carvers in Erbach have cautiously adapted to it, deciding to play up the unusual coloration given to it by long burial in the earth, but it's widely disdained in Japan. There, carvers complain that mammoth ivory cracks, that the colors are unattractive, and that it smells "dirty" when it's worked. On the other hand it's become widely used in China (from 1994 to 2001 Hong Kong imported seventy-seven tons of it for reexport to the People's Republic). Mammoth ivory jewelry is even something of a fad in the United States, where its impressive age and odd coloration make it the perfect attention-getting material for provocative nasal, navel, and nipple piercings.

Other than pig tusks, there are no other ivories that could supply the market, although in 2002 bioengineered teeth were successfully grown in rat hosts, holding out the possibility that artificial ivory might be able to be grown in vitro. Somehow, the prospect of mass-producing dentin that way, even if it could be turned out in any size and quantity, like a kitchen-countertop composite, does not sound as if it would satisfy the age-old desire for ivory.

IT IS NOT complimentary to our vaunted civilization and technical knowledge," E. D. Moore reflected, "that our chemists and inventors cannot—though often they have tried—give us some material that in beauty and in touch will prove a satisfactory alternate for the jewels of the noble elephant." He concluded, with deep misgivings for the future of the elephant, that there was no such substitute. He was right, of course, but why is this?

In the nineteenth century there were many uses of ivory in which it functioned as the plastic of its age. Eventually, plastic proved to be a more than adequate substitute for some uses, and could even be superior: billiard balls are a perfect example. But whenever ivory is used *because* it is ivory, then there is no possible stand-in. Some ivory-ban advocates seem strangely confused about its appeal. "Ivory, after all, has little intrinsic worth. Much of its allure comes from the subliminal power of the elephant, which turns even the gaudiest bauble worn around the neck into an amulet, and a carved figure into a household god," wrote one journalist. "But without the elephant's magic, the market withers."

That view is flatly contradicted by history. Ivory was in demand for its luminous loveliness and ability to embody artistic vision even in cultures (like that of the Greeks) unsure of the creature it came from. India revered both the substance and the animal that provided it; China, Japan, Europe, and North America simply revered the substance. Even when the elephant was known, and a potent symbol to boot, the desire for ivory wasn't driven by interest in the elephant. Ivory itself, save in some African contexts, is rarely regarded as a talisman of the elephant. Undeniably, however, part of ivory's appeal is that it is a natural material. What draws people to ivory, as opposed to celluloid, alabrite, and the various resin compounds concocted to imitate it, is similar to what draws them to fine wood rather than to plastic. The material is individual, the genuine article, wrested from nature.

Pianists, understandably, were often conflicted about the ivory ban. Quite apart from ivory's aesthetic appeal on the keyboard, the reason to have it there was for its touch. Most pianists were convinced that it enhanced their ability to play the instrument. Mid-twentieth-century performers from Arthur Rubinstein to Liberace remained skittish about plastic — sweaty fingers could hydroplane on such keys. In the 1980s Gary Graffman was said to have "a deep fear of ivory deprivation." To provide for these purists, firms like Bösendorfer in Austria sold 150 pianos with ivory keyboards a year in the United States in the decade before the ban. Steinway quietly sold such pianos as well, but it was becoming politically incorrect to do so. The firm stopped using ivory in 1982.

Synthetic polymers had been in widespread use on keyboards since the 1950s but found few fans among serious pianists. In the 1980s Yamaha developed Ivorite, made from casein (milk protein) and an inorganic hardening compound, which was trumpeted as having both the moisture-absorbing quality of ivory and greater durability. Unfortunately some of the first keyboards cracked and yellowed, requiring refitting with a reformulated veneer. Clearly there was room for improvement. Steinway helped fund a $232,000 study at Rensselaer Polytechnic Institute in Troy, New York, in the late 1980s to develop a superior synthetic for keyboard covers. In 1993 the project's team created (and patented) an unusual polymer—RPIvory—that more closely duplicated the microscopically random peaks and valleys on the surface of ivory that allow pianists' fingers to stick or slip at will. Some pianists weren't able to notice any difference between playing on the new substance and playing on ivory. "But," Mischa Dichter admitted after choosing a Steinway grand with the new keys, "I'm relatively insensitive in that respect."

In the post-ban era, a pianist attempting a border crossing with a favorite ivory-keyed instrument could be in for a discordant shock. The Israeli-American concert pianist Ophra Yerushalmi found that out in January 1993. Like Liszt, who also played one, she fell for the tone of an Érard piano, a 1920 rosewood grand she came across in Paris the year before. Yerushalmi purchased the instrument and shipped it air freight to New York with its CITES form describing its ivory keys. But because it wasn't a century old it was refused customs clearance at JFK Airport. The law was clear; the Fish and Wildlife Service was firm: the piano had to be returned to France or have its ivory keys stripped. Distraught, yet unable to part with it, Yerushalmi brought her own piano restorers to perform the required maiming at the Air France warehouse. In advance of dismantling the piano and softening the ivory veneers with a steam iron, she insisted on giving a short Chopin recital to a dozen warehousemen, who paused to listen before the chisels were brought out.

I CAME ACROSS elephants soon after leaving the ivory vault at Kruger. Scores of them were crossing the shallow Sabie River that paralleled the route I was taking to Oliphants camp, some six hours north in the park. I pulled to the side of the road and watched through binoculars from my idling rental car as they emerged on the opposite bank, their dark wet legs and bellies giving them a two-toned appearance as they strode into the bush. I rolled back onto the blacktop. Aware that the speed limit in the park is a modest 30 miles per hour, I was conscious of the long trip ahead of me. It's difficult not to creep above that rate of progress on what look like unobstructed straightaways through open scrubland, but after having a couple of giraffes materialize seemingly out of nowhere to stand in the road I was more careful to check the speedometer.

My destination the next day was the Elephant Hall at Letaba, an hour or so farther on from Oliphants, which gave me an excuse to indulge in travel snobbery, the kind that those familiar with a landscape affect in the presence of gawking tourists. The scattered cars, vans, and occasional buses that shared the park's road system with me invariably stopped whenever they spotted a vehicle pulled over, taking it as a signal that there was some animal life within camera range, although sometimes it was just someone hoping to get a signal on a cell phone. Having been in several very off-the-beaten-track regions in Africa, I was sure I wouldn't see anything I hadn't already seen before and just kept driving. But soon enough I found it irresistible to stop to admire and sketch an impressive list of critters: impala, zebra, wildebeest, waterbuck, baboons, hippos, warthogs, monitor lizards, a tortoise. I watched black-feathered, hulking southern ground hornbills march around my car when I stopped to photograph a pair of mid-sized elephants in a marshy spot under a bridge, enjoying their midday salad bowl. Of course, I was experiencing only a very thin slice of Kruger's biodiversity, which extends over seventeen ecological zones that are home to 146 animal species and some five hundred of birds.

Although a lot of Kruger is a vast reservoir of bush, a fair portion of it is accessible to the public. You can't get out of your car and wander around on your own, obviously, but you can go on guided walks and game drives and stay in a wide range of accommodations. You can rough it in bush camps and fire up your own *braai*, or watch wildlife at a waterhole from the vantage point of your hot tub in an ultra-luxe lodge. Oliphants, a main rest camp perched on a hill several hundred feet above the river of the same name, was comfortably between, with a restaurant, petrol station, electricity in the huts, and, best of all, marvelous views of the slow, twisting river below in which hippos wallowed and burped as raptors wheeled in the sky above. It was Africa, all right, and I got to thinking it was probably wild enough for most of the million-plus visitors that come to the park each year. They're warned about snakes, bats, scorpions, spiders, and thieving baboons, but the deadliest creature they are likely to encounter is the malaria-carrying anopheles mosquito. That's a fair trade-off, considering the array of game that can be seen from the safety of a vehicle.

Early the next morning I was half a mile from the turnoff to Letaba when I glanced over at the acacia trees lining the road and thought I saw an elephant. I stopped and backed up slowly and, yes, there was big bull right behind a screen of trees, ripping off branches to chew. Several cars whizzed by as I came up alongside him. Other cars slowed and paused for a couple of snapshots but quickly tired of watching him shove sticks in his mouth. He moved closer to the road where there was less of a screen of trees. The bull was now in profile, and I took an entire roll of photographs.

Some animals are easy bystanders to all that goes on around them, fitting more or less seamlessly (or sneakily) into human settlements, such as pigeons in a town square or squirrels in a city park, rats in alleys, deer in suburban backyards. But elephants, unless persecuted, are used to doing whatever they want to do. This one was immensely indifferent to me. In the shell of a car I was familiar enough. *Homo vehicularis* is no threat to a park elephant but is sometimes an annoyance that requires scaring off. He munched on sloppily, dropping half-masticated branches from the front end while the back end dropped a volley of melon-sized turds that split and steamed as they plopped on the ground. Having moved his bowels satisfactorily, he shifted his hindquarters, swelling his penis into a piebald yardarm that descended until it almost reached the ground. He ripped off more leafy branches, constricted his trunk to turn them into a bouquet, and wedged them in his jaws. His penis slowly retracted as he angled closer to the road.

I clicked off another half dozen photos, thrilled at how his steady, shambling gait was bringing him nearer, filling my viewfinder until there was nothing but his forehead. . . . I started the car and rolled forward submissively on the shoulder of the road, not wanting to test his temperament with a rental car. He passed behind me and I could see he was carrying big ivory, especially the right tusk—thick, curved, long. I snapped a three-quarter shot just as a little *bakkie* scooted by, its startled driver swerving at the sight. The tusker never broke stride but crossed the road to the acacias on the other side, then was swallowed up silently by the bush.

I remembered a story someone had told me years back about how visitors to Kruger in a new Mercedes didn't move their car when a big bull strode toward them from behind, thinking he'd move around them. He did, but as he came around the front he decided to let them know what he thought of having his path blocked and promptly sat on the hood, crushing the front end of the car. The terrified occupants sprang from the vehicle like pips shooting from squished fruit. After a few minutes I drove slowly into Letaba.

In the thatched-roof exhibit space of the rest camp's Elephant Hall was the array I'd come to see: "The Magnificent Seven"—the mounted ivories of Kruger's biggest tuskers. About thirty years ago, Kruger's chief warden hatched the idea of gaining attention for the park's conservation successes by identifying seven bulls carrying one hundred pounds or more of ivory per side and borrowed the title of the 1960 Hollywood movie as their collective name. It was a public relations coup, and as each of the original group died its tusks were collected for exhibit. I wandered around marveling at each display, a few with full head mounts, a couple with skulls, but most with just photographs and stories of the old boys and of course their unreal ivories.

Some tusks were mirror images of each other, others more mismatched, but every one was impressively thick, long, and heavy—except for João, whose tusks, sadly, were broken off and never found. Most have local names: Mafuyane, Shingwedzi, Dzombo, Shawu, Ndlulamithi, Kambaku. All died of natural causes in their fifties and sixties, except for Dzombo, who was gunned down in 1985 by a Mozambique poacher who sneaked into the park but was surprised by rangers before he could make off with his ill-gotten booty. Since then, their ranks have been supplemented by the likes of Pelwana, Nhalangulene, and, of course, Mandleve, whose stupendous tusks I'd handled in the vault. It's an educational and scientific exhibit, certainly, but also a shrine to some of the most glorious tusks in nature.

Not many visitors lingered long in the hall. Understandably, most wanted to get out on the network of roads and possibly photograph one of the park's living legends, such as Duke, Sikele, Mashagadzi, and a dozen other up-and-coming fellows already carrying suitable names along with their big teeth. Should they live out their days in peace, they too might someday join their brothers in this elephant Valhalla.

The park's less impressive elephants, though, may face a different future.

"COULD BE AN eighty-pounder," Ian Whyte said. He pushed his glasses up his nose and studied the photo I'd taken of the bull I came across at Letaba the year before. "I'd say about forty-five years old. Give him another ten years and he'll need a name." He pushed it back to me across his desk.

Ian Whyte, who joined the park's staff in 1970, is Kruger's elephant man. The genial, beefy senior scientist and research manager of large herbivores had been flying transects for an animal census when I visited the ivory vault in 2005. I returned to talk with him to better understand the "southern African point of view" that had emerged in the ivory trade debates. I knew that when it began as the Sabie Game Reserve in 1898 Kruger had no elephants (all of them having been shot out by early settlers), but that the species had quickly reestablished itself. And I knew that Whyte's latest census had put its elephant population at 12,467, about four thousand more than the park is thought to be able to support without damage to its environment. But were there no alternatives to culling elephants? If those who say that soon enough most of Africa's elephants will end up in national parks are right, then I wanted to know what was likely to be in store for them in a well-run one.

We met in his paper-stuffed office in one of the modest staff buildings in Skukuza. When it was announced in 2005 that Kruger might be considering reviving the culling programs of the past, Whyte found himself in the spotlight, not a position he particularly enjoys. The South African press scrutiny was intense and the country's parks system had to reassure an entire range of conservation and wildlife groups, both domestic and international, that it would study the highly charged issue long and hard before taking any steps. Whyte apologized for fielding an inquiry on the culling issue from the *Washington Post* during our talk. "I'm becoming a full-time PR manager," he sighed. While he was on the phone I looked at a letter pinned on the bulletin board. Sent by a class of German schoolchildren in Frankfurt, it was decorated with hearts but bluntly compared culling to "mass murder," and asked why elephants have to be shot just because they eat trees and bushes and "affect the park a little."

I asked if the recent vast increase in the park's size could absorb the presumed excess of elephants. (In 2002 Kruger formally merged with Limpopo National Park in Mozambique and Gonarezhou in Zimbabwe. Kruger, itself a 7,700-square-mile chunk of land in the northeast corner of South Africa, and was now dropping the fences between it and the two neighboring parks, effectively doubling its area.) Whyte showed me the map of what's now collectively called the Greater Limpopo Transfrontier Park, one of several similar projects aimed at locking up great swaths of land for wildlife across Africa.

"To me those are some of the most positive initiatives in conservation that have come up in a very long time," Whyte said. But parks, he explained, no matter how big, are still islands in the middle of human settlement. "And these areas," he said, moving a stubby finger around the map, "are going to become more isolated from the rest of human development around it." Now that the fences were coming down, I imagined the elephants of Kruger spreading out into the less densely occupied parks next to it and, perhaps, delaying any population crisis.

When I shared this with him, Whyte shook his head and took me over to another wall, which was covered with maps decorated with scores of colored dots. Each color, he explained, represented a radio-collared elephant, some of which have been broadcasting their whereabouts since 1989.

"You can see that this elephant doesn't go far. And its home range has been much the same for seventeen years." The other colors of dot clusters didn't look much larger, including one around Oliphants.

Don't elephants migrate?

"There's no scientific basis, or even anecdotal basis, that supports that. It's all in people's heads. 'Open up the fences,' people say, 'and allow the traditional migration of elephants . . .' What traditional migration? We know absolutely nothing about 'traditional migrations.' It's rot."

I looked dubious.

"Elephants in Kruger live in these home ranges and, look, we do nothing to keep them there. They stay there by themselves; that's where they want to be. They know where water is in the droughts, and where to find food in a drought. They are not going to go to an area that they don't know. They stay where they're happy, like people in an area who know where to buy milk and where the supermarket is."

But what about elephant behavior in Namibia and Botswana?

"Certainly in the more arid regions," Whyte conceded, "studies show that the home ranges tend to be much, much larger"—elephants have to wander a lot farther afield to get what they need.

"The point is if you open up the fence between Kruger and Mozambique, who's going to go over there? It's not these elephants," he said, pointing to the recorded perambulations of the homebodies. "They don't even know there's a fence there. They've never been there."

Whyte added that the park did move twenty-five elephants to Mozambique in a pilot project. "They all came back to Kruger!" he said, looking over his glasses at me. "Still, they are moving across, but as if they are exploring." He flatly dismissed the idea that elephants in an area of abundant food and water would be drawn to a different area with harsher conditions where they would conveniently die, thereby cutting back their population.

"You know, elephants are not stupid," he said, ignoring his lit-up phone. "We expect that they will move into Mozambique, but it will be a slow process, and where there's only seasonal water elephants will not be able to establish themselves permanently."

And the argument that Kruger has too many artificial water holes, which are distorting the environment in their own way, boosting animal populations? Kruger was full of riverbeds, Whyte told me, many of them dry seasonally, but water was not a limiting factor in Kruger. "Animals don't die of thirst in Kruger," he said, adding that the trend was now to close the water holes that previously had been bored around the park.

In another office, Whyte showed me the vegetation of the park from a different point of view: photographs of horizons of the same locales taken years apart. The older ones showed lush panoramas, with tall knob thorn and fever trees used by raptors and storks; the newer ones showed the same landscapes progressively thinned out and sometimes reduced to shrub. "Elephant damage in Kruger is not drastic, but it's insidious," he said. "Elephants start to push over trees, they eat the leaves, the bark, the roots—they just keep going." Because they can make use of practically anything in the vegetable kingdom, by the time they start to die there's hardly anything left.

Whyte took me back into his office to look at a few graphs on his computer. The elephant population in Kruger is growing at about 6 percent a year—doubling every ten to twelve years. He clicked on more graphs. In Kruger, some sixteen thousand elephants have been taken out of the park over its history, either culled or translocated—more than its current population. I wondered out loud what the current population would be had nothing ever been done, and in answer he clicked on a graph that showed that if no culling had been done from 1966 on, Kruger would now have perhaps eighty thousand elephants, the equivalent of Zimbabwe's entire elephant population, squeezed into the park. There was another that showed that if no action was taken from now on, the park would have thirty-four thousand elephants by 2020, about what Kenya has now, quite enough to start a Tsavo-like situation in which the elephants would start eating themselves out of house and home.

Then what curbs could there be on population growth? I mentioned translocation.

"We'd have to move seven hundred fifty elephants a year just to stabilize the population. Unfortunately, we can't even give them away." And translocation is wildly expensive, as much as $8,000 per animal. You need a veterinarian and team, crews, trucks, hoists, helicopters, even air freight, depending on how far you have to take them. The park might find funding to airlift elephants to some area where they needed to be reestablished in a onetime operation, but finding the revenue necessary to translocate animals on a year in, year out basis, ad infinitum, was another matter.

Birth control?

"We've been accused by certain animal rights groups of ignoring contraception. On the contrary, we encouraged this research," Whyte said. "In fact the basic research that's done on it has been done at Kruger."

Whyte made it clear that some form of contraception or sterilization can be done for small populations—say, twenty elephants in a pocket park. Beyond that the problems with this approach become all too evident. Take the bull, for example. You'd think performing a vasectomy might not be all that difficult on a male elephant but, no, his cantaloupe-sized testes are under a foot or more of skin, muscle, and fat, tucked up right against his kidneys, necessitating major abdominal surgery. Even ignoring the huge expense of an operation that involves darting the animal, using a crane truck to put him a sling, employing a full medical team, and undertaking a two-hour procedure, if it's successful it won't guarantee that females won't get impregnated by an unsterilized bull. In short, Whyte said, "vasectomies just delay pregnancy"—they don't prevent it.

With female elephants contraception is equally complicated. There are implants that will ensure a constant release of estrogen into the cow's system, preventing estrus. But estrogen is metabolized by the cow and passed out in her urine. It's detectable to bulls, who read as a signal that she's in estrus. The bull chases her but she won't be receptive. So she often runs away to avoid harassment and gets separated from her family, even her calf. The approach was abandoned. "We just felt it was unethical," Whyte said.

He clicked on another diagram showing the normal social structure of a family group, where all the females stick together, led by a matriarch. If some form of birth control is imposed such that the females have fewer calves, instead of, say, a normal clan of eighteen, you could end up with only half a dozen individuals, and then it's not the same social system.

"Normally, you've got all these older females," Whyte said, "Some of them already adult with their own calves—there's lot of supervision here. If something goes wrong with this little calf, all of these females would rush in and help. Even the younger ones, ten years old, get terribly excited about what happens to each other. The other advantage is there's a learning process that these young females go through in a group like this. If you reduce the numbers, you've changed the whole fundamental system. There are gaps, opportunities lost. Is this fair to elephants?"

He pushed back in his chair. "None of it's easy."

There was more to using birth control than just going around zapping female elephants. To get the doses right, scientists would have to know which one was getting what, which meant they'd have to put a radio collar on each one in order to find them and give them the right boosters. To stabilize their numbers, about 70 percent of all breeding females have to be under treatment; this works out to 40 percent of the population . . .

"That's the point," Whyte said. "It's just not possible in a population the size of Kruger's. We'd be talking five thousand elephants." I also wondered how attractive all those elephants wearing collars would look to tourists.

"Now, here's an important point. You can't reduce a population by contraception," Whyte said. "If you sterilize every other animal in a population, you still have to wait for them to start dying to bring the numbers down." Then there's the political dimension.

"It would be extraordinarily expensive to do contraception in Kruger. We've got great numbers of rural people living on our boundaries. And we'd have to try and explain to these people that we're going to be spending millions of rand on stopping the elephant population from breeding, when they look at that population and see protein. They'd much rather we use the money on schools and hospitals, and, if there are too many elephants, well, they see them as an edible resource."

I felt the logical noose tightening.

In the end there won't be enough land, translocation would always be strictly short-term, and birth control disturbs herd structure and dynamics. One can squirm about the alternatives, but what's left? Doing nothing? About 1.3 million tourists visit annually, a big money earner for the parks system. Would they keep coming to Kruger if—

"If you don't manage the elephants and other species start to fail and the tall trees get knocked over? Look, people do come to Kruger to look at *trees*. They'll ask what the heck is going on here, why are you allowing this? That's one of the things that concerns us. Tourism is our economic base. We are responsible to tourists, to South Africa, to the world in general. And we have a legal mandate to support biodiversity."

That left culling.

He sighed. "It's a dilemma. Do we manage for elephants or do we manage for biodiversity? There is no right or wrong answer. You just have to manage according to the objectives you have, that reflect your public. Your national values."

That's not an answer some would want to hear. Whyte was blunt.

"I'm of the opinion that a lot of these animal welfare groups, animal rights groups, are fundamentally dishonest. We've had these guys come to Kruger and sit down and we run through a presentation of the issues we've been talking about and explain the situation, but they just carry on saying the same things. Let's face it, there's something about elephants that drives people to put their hands in their pockets."

Culling is not a prospect Whyte looks forward to; he knows what it's like. He once wrote of the special empathy that intensifies the longer one is exposed to elephants, admitting that such powerful emotions "are not comfortable bedfellows with the concepts of killing these wonderful animals."

"I'm horrified at the idea that you should go out and kill whales or seals just because you can," Whyte said. "But this . . ." He looked at the pinup photos of elephants around his office. "This to me is an ecological issue. It's about retaining certain species in the system."

In early 2006, the South African environment ministry decided to put off any decision on culling, based on the findings of a panel of experts that it wasn't clear whether or not the elephant population was too large. Was it a matter of postponing the inevitable? All I knew was that any future culling operation, whatever else it would accomplish, would add to Kruger's already bulging ivory vaults. Trophy hunters might fantasize about how they'd love to help out by relieving a few old long-in-the-tooth bulls of their twin "burdens," but those tuskers are exactly the ones tourists love to see. They wouldn't be shot, Whyte assured me.

One of the ironies of culling is that it, unlike any of the alternative means of elephant population control, can pay for itself and more, covering the costs of killing some and helping to fund the conservation of the rest. That is, as long as you can sell the products. The hides are very valuable. There's the meat, even elephant hair bracelets, and of course the ivory—if you have a market for it.

IN EARLY 2008, the South African government announced that it would lift its long-standing moratorium on elephant culling as a means of dealing with the species' growing numbers. According to Environmental Affairs and Tourism Minister Marthinus Van Schalkwyk, shooting elephants would be considered an "option of last resort." Ian Whyte described the decision as a "tough call" when I reached him by phone to discuss it. But he felt the right decision had been made. Whyte, who'd retired the year before, said he was pleased to be "out of all the politics"—and relieved he wouldn't have be involved in any future culling program that might be necessary.

IN LATE 2002 CITES had narrowly approved a proposal to permit another "onetime" sale of ivory, a total of sixty tons from stockpiles in Botswana, Namibia, and South Africa, possibly as early as 2004. There were lots of "ifs" attached to the decision. Only raw ivory from government-owned stocks could be sold, and then only to trading partners verified by the secretariat to have controls sufficient to ensure that no ivory would be reexported, and proceeds from the sale had to be used for elephant and community conservation in the elephant range. Furthermore, MIKE (Monitoring the Illegal Killing of Elephants) had to supply baseline information on elephant population numbers and poaching activity. Instances of noncompliance or discovery of detrimental impacts on elephants would be enough to put a stop to the plan. Ban advocates were sure that taking this action would cause an upsurge in poaching, but proponents argued that as a one-off sale, rather than a reopening of trade, it was unlikely to stimulate more poaching than usual. Both China and Japan had applied to be assessed as prospective importing countries, but by late 2006 only Japan was recommended as a trading partner. Approval of the sale itself would be considered at the next meeting of the standing committee of CITES in 2007.

9

ELEPHANT DREAMS, ELEPHANT REALITIES

Like the rest of the crowd standing in the hot midday sun, I was impatient to see the baby elephants. Having arrived in Kenya on a holiday weekend, I had some unscheduled time on my hands. So I took a taxi from my hotel to the David Sheldrick Wildlife Trust in a corner of Nairobi National Park, where Daphne Sheldrick runs an elephant and rhino orphanage. She was out of town, but the star attractions, all ten of them, would be coming out any minute, or so we were told.

We were a mixed group, from toddlers to elderly in age, and ethnically quite varied (Asian, Indian, European, African), and mostly tourists, I guessed. Although there were no animals in view, we pushed pointlessly on the thin rope that had been strung across the red-earthed clearing to create a stage in the open bush. A keeper clad in a dark green jumpsuit walked out from the buildings behind us with the opening act, a small, chest-high rhino, who had to be kept on course by having one of her ears strenuously twisted, without apparent effect. Already the size of a cow, she had a small mind of her own and drank formula greedily from a half-gallon plastic jug. She was led off to be hosed down.

A warthog group came into view before trotting back into the bush, but like squirrels on the grounds of a zoo they aroused little interest. They were interlopers who didn't fit the program. Then the baby "ellies" trotted over a knoll, ears flapping and trunks swinging. At eight months to two years in age, some were under waist-high to the keepers walking with them. Great cries of delight rose up from the crowd; children were hoisted onto shoulders; cameras clicked; everyone jostled for a better view of the parade.

"They're so *cute!*" shrieked a little girl, holding her turbaned father's hand and jumping up and down in excitement as the little elephants were led along the rope. The children all put out their hands and waved, then pulled their hands back as soon as an elephant got close enough that we could see its thick eyelashes. I managed to lean out and trail a few fingers on one little fellow's leathery rump. From its infancy an elephant comes equipped with skin as wrinkly as a crumpled map. It occurred to me that part of a baby elephant's appeal must lie in the contrast between its cuddly, miniature stature and the rumpled hide in which it's enveloped—skin that on a full–grown elephant seems to embody every mark of time, making the creature look wondrously old, observant, and patient.

These roly-poly tykes were a noisy bunch, squealing, bumping, and pushing, and when their keepers brought out bottles of formula it was obvious that the smallest ellies, who had yet to figure out what to do with their wiggly trunks, weren't as adept as the older ones in curling them out of the way to help get the bottle in their mouths.

There was a well-practiced monologue from one of the staff about the work of the orphanage, the rescue and rehabilitation of elephant and rhino orphans that have been lost, abandoned after a poacher's attack on their mother, or, in one case, had fallen into a mine shaft. Where possible, all are returned to wild herds, including those in Tsavo, and among its other activities the trust has a program to rid Kenya's parks of cruel snares. (Later, I saw the orphans' accommodations, individual wooden stalls with open slats so that they can stick out their trunks for attention, with clean, sweet-smelling straw, water, and fresh leaves for the older ones. The staff even sleeps with the youngest so they don't get lonely. Not a bad little dormitory, I thought. I'd stayed in worse hikers' huts.)

We were all duly impressed by this and then treated to the sight of the little ellies taking a mud bath. It helps protect their skin from insects and sun and explained their terra-cotta complexion. Keepers sloshed out buckets of water into a depression in the red earth to make a shallow pond, and the small fry jumped in, legs kicking, flopping, rolling, and squishing around in it until they were glistening. They ended up in a kind of piglet pile, and the littlest one let out a tremendous trumpet, unrolling his trunk like a New Year's Eve party favor, a very impressive performance for such a small fellow. A few came over to the crowd and slung their trunks around, spattering us with mud flecks, which nobody seemed to mind. I felt euphoric.

Then it hit me. I had been transported back to *The Saggy Baggy Elephant*, one of my favorite books when I was a child. Published in 1947 and reprinted endlessly, the story was charming enough—a little elephant can't figure out why he has such loose-fitting skin until he finds other elephants that look just like him—but it was the illustrations by Gustaf Tenggren that seized my imagination, especially the one that showed the rotund rascal floating belly up in a pond, the very picture of joy, splashing and spraying a jet of water from his marvelous trunk. How I loved that little guy; I practically wanted to be an elephant—well, at least while I was reading the book. Anthropomorphized images like that, wrapped around the core of feeling that all humans have, in one way or another, about animals, are now a large part of what fuels whatever caring we have for wildlife in the modern world. In an age when fewer and fewer of us live in direct contact with nature, such images may form our only bridge to it.

But caring for elephants and what happens to them has to take place in the real world we share with them. I'd seen the elephant reality in South Africa. What was it like in Kenya? And how did ivory fit into it?

IT WAS TIME to see Ian Parker. The former game warden and ivory expert's name kept popping up in my reading and research. Many sharply disagree with his controversial conclusions, most of which run counter to much current thinking in conservation circles. I wanted to hear his thoughts on elephants and ivory.

Parker lives in Langata, on the edge of Karen, both wealthy and primarily white suburbs of Nairobi known for large fenced properties with high hedges and steel gates. His compound is one of the more modest ones, with a simple brick-trimmed stucco farmhouse. Short, slight, white-haired, and balding, he met me at the door wearing a cardigan—it was cool that morning—and we sat in the living room with its copper-hooded fireplace, a large airy space hung with bird prints above shelves of books. His wife, Chris, brought out coffee.

"I've never been pro or anti ivory trade," he said, almost as soon as I mentioned the *I*–word. "I'm an observer. Although," he added, "destroying a perfectly legitimate trade seems pointless."

"Conservation" was the next word he seized on.

"You will not understand much about the ivory ban unless you have a firm grip on what conservation is about. As a psychological phenomenon, it's a faith. Conservationists turn to science to justify their faith. If the facts don't suit their faith, they're ignored."

Clearly, he was just warming to his subject.

"I'm not an 'ist' and I don't buy any 'isms.' If a person says they are an 'ist' they are saying 'I think this way.' One must always be able to say, 'Damn, I was wrong.' If you've dispensed with your ability to throw out a packet of ideas, you've announced you're no longer open-minded."

Parker spoke with deep conviction, often interweaving his ideas with philosophical speculation, but at the same time he rather enjoyed spicing his remarks with provocative one-liners like, "Conservationists aren't really interested in elephants." I also detected the exasperated air of someone who knows he's on to something but has trouble getting taken seriously for his against-the-grain views.

"Conservation is really about being conservative about nature," Parker said as he leaned back in his chair and rubbed his head. "The idea behind conservation was no more or less than common sense. What we have today is 'conservationism.'" He postulated that with the decline of religion people have turned to beliefs about nature as replacement and as a consequence are more interested in their "way" than the actual survival of species.

Parker became involved with ivory in a circuitous fashion. His grandparents came to Kenya in 1903. Born in Malawi, he started out as a game warden in Kenya in the 1950s. He was one of fourteen wardens for the entire country.

"I was twenty years old in 1956 and, with nine African scouts, in charge of twelve thousand square miles, essentially the southeast Kenya coast. Absurd to think we really had an effect. There were probably a million people in the area." Dealing with crop-raiding elephants as well as coping with poaching, Parker explained, was just part of the job.

"You could hunt ivory legally in Kenya until 1956. Sportsmen could sell tusks. But natural mortality was always the major source of ivory."

Even the elephant-hunting Waliangulu admitted to him that most of their ivory was "pickup" ivory. "They were looking for ivory all the time," he said. "Even the women and children." Ivory in the open might last only a year, he said, but under the right conditions it could last decades that way.

In 1965 Parker founded a Kenya-based wildlife consultancy with his wife and friends, doing everything from crocodile control to ornithological surveys in countries such as Uganda, Rwanda, Kenya, Tanzania, and Zimbabwe. He worked on several elephant culling operations, eventually figuring out how to do it in order to minimize disturbance to the population. By then it was accepted that it was less traumatic to remove entire family groups from the population than random individuals. Parker had it down to a science: his team could take out fifteen animals in forty-two seconds, from the first to the last shot. It could be done on foot, but helicopters were far more effective in herding family groups toward roads for disposal of the carcasses; he used to fly the helicopter, swinging the tail around so that the rotors would add to the thundering, alarming sound, keeping the animals off-balance, and then using their known social behavior—shooting the matriarch first to take advantage of the fact that other elephants would stay rather than abandon her—to get the operation over with as soon as possible. It was unpleasant work, he said. "It doesn't matter to an elephant whether he's shot by a game warden with compassion or by a complete barbarian—it's death."

Parker's firm conducted substantial culls in Uganda, Rwanda, Zimbabwe, and elsewhere. In many cases the tusks were theirs—"we ended up handling, and eventually selling, substantial amounts of ivory." That, in fact, was how he made his "great discovery." No elephant researcher knew anything about the ivory trade, but customs departments, he realized, "had always kept track of it." He pulled out a copy of the voluminous report he prepared in 1979 for the U.S. Fish and Wildlife Service and thumbed through it, pausing to look at its tables and lists over his half-glasses. "Beautiful records . . . there was everything that was happening to elephants."

What, in his view, had brought about the dropping elephant numbers that had so alarmed everyone in the 1980s?

"Local hunting, game departments, poachers, and habitat loss—all those factors." I asked about the last, habitat loss.

"In Kenya in 1925 humans were islands in a sea of elephants. In

1975 elephants were islands in a sea of humans." To drive home the importance of habitat loss, he flipped through his text and showed me graphs and maps of giraffe populations compared with human populations, decades apart. As human numbers soared and spread, giraffe numbers sank and retreated to undeveloped spaces. His point? "You don't have to have a valuable trophy to show these declines." Ergo, elephants would have been fading out even without the demand for their tusks.

I mentioned the particular allure of ivory. He smiled. "I've watched millionaire ivory dealers shed their jackets to handle their biggest tusks like they were embracing a woman's body."

What did this mean historically? Parker took the long view.

"Where there is a demand for a product, it will be met," he said, then embarked on the following train of thought. For the past five hundred years, about two hundred tons of ivory, on average, left Africa each year. "Even if only five percent of all those tons remain," he suggested, "that's five thousand tons. Five million kilos! If the price of raw ivory is two hundred dollars per kilo . . ." I did the numbers: a billion dollars, and that's just for its raw value, but almost all of it would be worked into objects, jewelry, art.

He let the implication of the staggering added value hang in the air.

"Think of the total value in worked ivory in Europe alone—there are huge quantities in France. You can't just declare it's illegal. Can't just confiscate it without compensation. It's too expensive."

While I was absorbing this he came up with another implication.

"What would happen if elephants went extinct? Ivory prices would skyrocket. Ban it—and it drives prices up. Prohibition didn't touch the demand—it increased the criminality. Knock the legitimate trade out and you lose control, you don't know what's happening."

Parker offered another thought experiment.

"Kenya has thirty thousand elephants. Ten percent die, let's say. Half will leave tusks. That's fifteen thousand times two apiece that end up lying in the dirt—and let's say they last three years. That's nine thousand tusks on the ground. People herding their goats and cattle will pick it up. Say five kilos each. That's forty-five tons of pickup ivory. It's not all handed into the Kenya Wildlife Service. Where is the rest? The 'ivory trade' is alive and well, otherwise we'd be stumbling over ivory in Africa. No trade ban has ever worked."

Where does that leave conservation?

"The megafauna on this planet is said to have disappeared when man appeared. There's some correlation, certainly. Why did megafauna survive in Africa? Man evolved with it here—nature has a way to keep man in balance on this continent." When Europeans came back to the mother continent as colonizers, he mused, the megafauna started collapsing. "We're developing the megafauna away."

Before World War I there was often game in the streets of Nairobi; lions frequently interrupted local horse races. The process of pushing back the wilderness from human settlement was, obviously, still going on. Most conservationists see this in terms of disappearing species, but Parker flipped it the other way and considered how it looked to the rural Africans who still frequently encounter large and often dangerous animals. If they weren't there, he pointed out, "schoolkids could come home without being killed." And old men could come stumbling back to their villages at night "pissed as newts without getting nailed." He fixed his pale blue eyes on me. "Would you say it's right that Africans should have to take those risks?"

Parker got up and went to find something in his office and came back out with *Elephant Bill*, by Lieutenant Colonel J. H. Williams, an account of working with elephants in the teak forests of Burma. "I was in culling, so I'm thought not to have any feelings," Parker said. "Actually, I believe elephants are highly intelligent." He showed me the touching passage where Williams witnessed a mother elephant struggling to save her three-month-old calf after they had both been swept down a rain-swollen river and separated. Catching up with her progeny,

> she pinned the calf with her head and trunk against the rocky bank. Then with a really gigantic effort she picked it up in her trunk and reared up until she was half standing on her hind legs so as to be able to place it on a narrow shelf of rock five feet above the flood level. Having accomplished this, she fell back into the raging torrent and she herself went away like a cork.

Half an hour later, while he was peering at the terrified calf shivering on a piece of ledge, Williams heard "the grandest sounds of a mother's love I can remember . . . a defiant roar, but to her calf it was music." Having

climbed out on the opposite side of the river downstream, the female returned and rumbled reassurance until the river fell during the night and
then recovered her calf.

I handed the book back. He wasn't uncaring about elephants,
Parker told me. "I just believe in controlling my sentiments. Elephants
are declining. Distressing as that is, there's no reason to dump logic."

Birds twittered in the trees outside as he walked me to my taxi. We
ended up talking about how following research wherever it leads sometimes took you into unexpected corners of thought.

"Ivory is a skylight into your mind," he said.

I told him I'd already discovered that.

RIDING IN A taxi just behind a couple of exhaust-emitting *matatus*,
Nairobi's minivan equivalents of New York's gypsy cabs, wasn't as alarming as it was on my last trip, when people were still allowed to hang precariously on the sides of the racing vehicles. But I was happy the same
bone-jarring potholes remained on the thoroughfares—they helped to
slow the frantic bumper-car traffic. As we headed toward Wilson Airport,
my thoughts seemed as rattled as my ride. By now the outlines of ivory's
impact on human history were plain to me, but what the future of ivory
might be, and its role in elephant conservation, was anything but. I scrib-
bled a few phrases in a notebook, trying to come to terms with the contradictory ideas I'd gathered and a welter of confused feelings.

Outside Africa, vast numbers of people regard elephants as threatened
by loss of habitat and, especially, poaching. Elephants would be fine, many
say, if they were just left alone. That attitude has become conventional wisdom, underscored by television documentaries, Web sites, and media reports on the fascinating lives of these remarkable and beleaguered giants.
The problem is not that this view is somehow wrong; it's that it leaves so
much out of the picture. Such as? The often ignored and sometimes deadly
impact of elephants on the lives of people who live next to them.

As Joseph, my driver, artfully skirted the snarl of a minor two-car col-
lision next to a mosque whose minaret blasted taped exhortations to the

faithful, I looked out the passenger window, eyes smarting from the pollution, at the crowd of humanity spilling over the sidewalks, walking, talking, buying, selling, and, above all, waiting. The poorest of Nairobi's citizens are beset with problems, but elephants aren't among them. In fact the only pachyderms they're likely to encounter are on the labels of Tusker, the ubiquitous Kenyan lager.

That's not the case with their rural cousins. Among a number of things that stuck in my mind from interviewing Ian Parker was his reminder of the real dangers Africans faced from the largest land animal. "School Closed After Invasion by Elephants" is not a headline one sees in many of the world's newspapers, but it appeared in Nairobi's *Daily Nation* in 2003. I'd been collecting a number of such stories which are so frequent in various African papers they rarely make the front page: "Elephant Kills Woman," "Jumbos Wreak Havoc in Ganze," "Elephant Victims Press Government for Compensation," "Panic as Elephants Impose Curfew on Villagers," "Elephant Kills Another Bobirwa Resident," etc. There were stories about a twenty-one-year-old woman farm worker carrying a baby who was chased until she tossed the child aside in desperation but was trampled anyway; about villagers forced to huddle in their huts after five-thirty in the evening for fear of marauding herds; about an old man crushed by an elephant that later went on to crash his funeral, scattering the mourners. One was particularly strange: walking to market, a woman and her two-year-old son were charged by a elephant and trampled to death, but the elephant stuck around long enough to bury their mangled bodies under leaves and twigs.

Another elephant seemed to have stepped out of the past. In Tanzania's Mbinga district, in the southwest corner of the country, elephants had largely given way to agriculture even before poachers wiped out the last herds in the 1980s, and that's why the morning arrival of a huge bull in the village of Ruhehe caused such a sensation. Crowds gathered and watched as the elephant began sampling the maize fields. He was pelted with stones, to no effect. One local, Lazaro Ndunguru, nineteen, boldly climbed a nearby tree and, when the elephant passed next to it, reached out and clubbed it on the head with a knob stick. Irritated, the bull yanked the youth from his perch with its trunk, smacked him like a rag doll against the tree, and stepped on his body, crushing him to death. The elephant strode off but returned over the next few days, destroying several acres of crops as he fed; he was finally shot by government game scouts. The recovered tusks weighed more than a hundred pounds apiece, a great rarity today.

These are all instances of what elephant researchers call HEC, the acronym for "human-elephant conflict," situations in which these substantial herbivores compete with farmers for food and water or otherwise endanger human lives and livelihoods. The voices of rural Africans in these reports struck a very different note from sentiments expressed by many of the field researchers, conservationists, and academics I'd been talking to. "We fear for our lives and our fruit trees," is a typical grievance, as is, "Elephants have left the park and are destroying our crops and plunging us further into poverty," or, "Because of elephants, we never rest. When the kids leave in the morning to go to school, we are not certain they will come back until we see them again." It's a drumbeat of horror stories, a steady pileup of sad statistics.

In developed countries, those whose view of African wildlife is gleaned from the popular media are likely to think of human-elephant conflict—if they think of it at all—almost entirely in terms of the pressure on the animal populations. One rarely, if ever, hears about the struggles of impoverished human communities trying to cope with a level of wildlife depredation that would never be tolerated in Europe or North America. Why, I wondered, do people there think such situations are acceptable in an African context? Is it just blinders, a type of elephant monomania, that leaves third world people out of the picture? I found it strange, until I caught myself falling into exactly the same overcompartmentalized thinking. I had to be honest: it was much more appealing to think about some grand old elephant matriarch and her latest adorable calf than some poor village woman who'd lost a schoolchild to a crop-raiding tusker.

Call it a clash of species. Elephants rarely attack unprovoked, but the instances seem to be growing as they become increasingly boxed in and stressed. They normally push back by seeking food and water where and how they can, the way Asia's dwindling population, a tenth the size of Africa's, now struggles in its fragmented habitats. It's obvious elephants don't mix with large-scale farming, housing developments, airports, hospitals,

highways. At some future point, when Africa is even more densely populated, the only place elephants will be found outside the confines of the continent's national parks and game reserves will be in the "buffer zones" of
thinly settled rural areas where people subsist on modest crops and herd
goats and cattle. Even in these regions, can elephants coexist with people
without constant conflict?

I was catching a flight to Laikipia, about a hundred miles north of
Nairobi, a farming and ranching district in central Kenya where cattle-
rearing landowners and locals try to tolerate wildlife. About six thousand
elephants, the largest population outside the country's national parks,
roam unfenced. When Joseph heard I was heading there, he told me that
he had grown up nearby, in the uplands of the Aberdares. As a boy, he used
to go with his friends at night through the forest to look at the lights in the
trees and watch the tourists at Treetops, the well-known resort that was established in the 1930s. He smiled when he remembered his adventures.

"But," he added somberly, "we were always worried about the elephants."

DURING THE FLIGHT up on a twin-engine prop plane I got a good look at
the vast shantytown that now spreads out like rust-colored spillage from
the city center of Nairobi. A century ago Kenya had a population of a million humans; it now has thirty-seven million. A century ago it had elephants that must have numbered in the hundreds of thousands; now there
are thirty thousand. Even so, the elephant population is on the rise again.

I hoped to find out more about what could be done for elephants.
Banning the ivory trade may have served to halt the poaching crisis, but
hadn't solved it—there was still plenty of poaching going on, particularly
in war-torn places such as the Democratic Republic of the Congo. I had
the idea that if some of the questions that swirl around elephant conservation could be answered, then it might be possible to consider—with
more objectivity—what should happen to all the ivory elephants continue to produce. I had seen the continent-wide future that might be
theirs in the microcosm of Kruger. What I wanted to know was what

would happen to all the elephants that are not park denizens yet, because most of them aren't.

Before leaving Nairobi I had a brief conversation with Leo Niskanen, the senior program officer at the IUCN's African elephant specialist group. "The simple way to put it," he said, "is that the human-elephant interface is increasing. It's never been bigger." He doodled on a pad on a table in his office, one big circle to represent a huge area like one of the new transfrontier megaparks and, next to it, an array of little circles. The same number of elephants in a giant area come in contact with people only at the edges. But put that number into dozens of little widely scattered pockets and you vastly increase the frequency with which they rub up against their human neighbors. Haphazard development and the frequent lack of national land use policy had created a mosaic of hot spots all across Africa.

On the flight, I pulled out some of the literature he'd given me to read. There were academic papers on defining the HEC issue, managing the landscape as well as community relations, detecting occurrences from remote stations, and the like. A lot of the research had an ivory tower air to it, too detached to come to terms with the underlying politics of a world where people and their livelihoods were getting trampled underfoot. Swelling populations of both elephants and humans, wildlife parks with insufficient habitat, and attractive crops being grown on the borders of these parks by communities that have sprung up next to the park boundaries are a volatile mix. The comic strip–style pamphlet prepared for small-scale farmers summed up the short list of solutions available to today's rural African: clear a zone around the crop, put up a sisal string fence with white, flapping material, and hang bells and bags of hot chilies (the fence can be greased with chili paste, too). Elephants can sometimes be warded off by rags dipped in engine oil and active beehives. If none of that works, there's beating on drums, shining spotlights, or putting chili dung bricks on small fires. If elephants persist in making a shambles of your *shamba*, there's always a banger stick, a homemade axlike contraption whacked on a rock to set off two boxes' worth of matchstick heads. It sounds like firing a rifle, which of course most Africans can no longer possess. In any case, they can do prison time for killing a problem animal themselves, although that doesn't always keep the Masai from lobbing spears at elephants to avenge cow killings.

In Kenya, the grieving relatives of someone killed by an elephant receive 30,000 shillings, about $400, but farmers receive nothing in compensation for lost crops or livestock. Little wonder that only 5 percent of Kenyans value having wildlife on their land. At the moment, locals in Laikipia were dealing with cattle rustlers ("13 Killed in Fresh Wave of Violence"), according to the lead story in the *Daily Nation* I'd brought with me. Apparently the raiders wanted to restock their herds after one of the worst droughts in memory, which left three and a half million people in the country in need of aid. In some areas, over half the livestock died.

With all this as a backdrop, the effort of the Laikipia Wildlife Forum sounded ambitious indeed. A nonprofit group of private and communal landowners, it works on ways to manage, conserve, and benefit from wildlife in the district, which straddles the equator in the Rift Valley Province. It's a harsh landscape. There are plains and grasslands, basalt outcroppings, low hills, and the dominating profile of Mount Kenya itself. It's occupied by a patchwork of ethnically diverse communities: Masai, Kikuyu, Europeans, Turkana, Samburu. There are giant cattle ranches and tiny garden plots, international businesses such as flower farms, and pastoralists who wander at will with their cattle and goats. Against the odds, wildlife is actually on the increase, although declining in the rest of the country.

THE LAIKIPIA WILDLIFE Forum's tiny suite of offices was situated in one of the two low buildings at Nanyuki's single-runway, one-windsock airport, making it easy for me to connect with Anthony King, the organization's new executive director, a trim, wiry man with a passion for wildlife policy. King's expertise is natural resource management, honed on projects from the Congo to Tasmania. As soon as I mentioned elephants, he launched into a discussion that told me he'd been over this ground before.

"Between 2002 and 2005 there were fifty-four elephants that had to be killed due to human-elephant conflict in the area, sixteen killed by poisoning—not a very nice way to kill an elephant—and thirty-eight killed by KWS in problem animal control," he told me. "Over the same period, nineteen people lost their lives, plus twenty-one seriously injured. Now this year alone, in the last couple of months, I know of three people who were killed by elephants, not in crop-growing areas but in pastoralist areas."

It was a top priority to lower these violent confrontations, King explained. "We're working on a strategy to develop an elephant fence to divide off land uses. Several hundred kilometers are in place, and we're trying to raise funds to add another hundred and fifty and close it off." When completed, the fence would function as a line dividing land use between ranching areas where wildlife can be tolerated and agricultural areas where it can't. He pulled out a large map and unfolded it on his desk.

"This dark line here is the fence—eight thousand volts. It requires lots of maintenance. This map shows the spread of cultivation, in wetter areas below the fence," King said. The fence would also enclose human-elephant conflict hot spots; once it was finished, the plan was to chase the elephants outside the fence with helicopters "We've had to put it up to protect lives and livelihoods."

Was this a long-term solution?

He shook his head. "We will be in a situation where there will be too many elephants. Because they are doing very well, there are almost six thousand at the moment. They move through here"—he swept his hand across the map—"and they are a demanding animal; they need a lot of greenery." As their numbers grow, "We are going to have a problem."

Part of it, King explained, were the traditional pastoralists—nomadic herders—in Laikipia. "It's a fallacy that pastoralists live in harmony with the land. They kill species that threaten them, predators and elephants, and they eat a number of species, bar the ones that are taboo. Competition between pastoralist communities and wildlife means that where they are, there are low wildlife densities. In ranching areas there is a much higher level of management of the land," King said. And landowners come under scrutiny. "As a single landowner, if you start to persecute wildlife, which is against the law, you're going to get in trouble at one point. But pastoralists don't seem to be under the same kind of examination. They are hard to police."

If ranchers and large landowners want to be tolerant of wildlife, the way many of them were in Laikipia, they have to be willing to carry the expense of whatever losses they incurred. Sometimes they end up carrying other people's costs as well.

"Last night we had a meeting. One landowner has twenty-five

hartebeest—an endangered species—and about twelve hundred head of other game. He's a horticulturalist, growing lettuce and peas and whatever for export to Europe. He's tolerating the game. And now he's stuck," King said. "He is surrounded by smallholders who are accusing him of 'harboring wildlife,' which are now eating their crops—and it's his fault! So now he has to pay to erect a game fence to keep the wildlife in his own land. It's a classic case."

Laikipia was a success story; its wildlife density is second only to the famed Masai Mara ecosystem, but it was an uphill battle. "Most of Kenya's wildlife is outside its parks and reserves. But the lack of an effective wildlife policy means that we are losing wildlife at such a fast rate that I fear we can't even draw the curve. We are going to lose our wildlife except for tiny pockets." I asked King to expand on that point.

"There's only one park in this country which can function without the space outside it, and that is Tsavo. It's almost an ecosystem unto itself. There is no other park or reserve in this country that can exist without buffer zones and corridors outside. Every time an animal steps outside that zone—as it may have to, to survive—it becomes a liability. It represents a cost to somebody. It's either competing for grazing; it's attacking people, breaking fences, water pipes, killing livestock—whatever it is, it becomes a problem.

"If you go into the north, where there are vast open spaces and nomadic cultures, there is no wildlife. I was just south of Lake Turkana this weekend, on Mount Kulal, and we did an eleven-hour hike up to the top, eight thousand feet high, in deep forest, dry bleak arid landscape, a lost world where you almost expected to see a dinosaur, and there's nothing— a few baboons. That's all we saw. What happened to the elephants? They were killed. The pastoralists speared them or shot them."

No one owns the wildlife in Kenya. In the abstract this policy sounds correct, until you realize that it means that no individual Kenyan has a stake in it. King, like so many others in Kenya, is pushing for a change in national policy that would expand the economic value of wildlife. "The wildlife policy we have has caused us to eliminate our wildlife because we can't live with it," he said. "The wildlife is in conflict with everything else we do to survive or scratch out a living."

His answer?

"You've got to look at your wildlife as a natural resource, and not get too sentimental about it. Because if it isn't a resource it has no value to local people."

AFTER TALKING WITH King I walked over to the adjoining airport building to wait for my ride. While searching in vain for a cup of coffee I met Tony Dyer, the last president of the East African Professional Hunter's Association, who was seeing some people off. I had taken him for an old settler, still clear-eyed and vigorous, a rancher perhaps; he wore a battered straw hat that cast speckles of light on his lined face. I found out he lived about thirty-two miles northeast of where we were.

"People like me, and my family who are involved in large-scale farming, but also in the tourist business, we've muddled along, we're survivors, in spite of everything," he said. "We ranch, but you might say we farm tourists. About thirty elephants on the farm, at times a hundred fifty to five hundred buffalo."

Dyer, who was born in Kenya in 1926, started in 1948 with Ker and Downey Safaris and later was a codirector of White Hunters (Africa) Ltd. He gave up professional hunting in 1961 but remained involved in the industry, becoming president of the East African Professional Hunter's Association in 1964. I asked him when the association, the continent's largest, had come to an end.

"Twenty-sixth of September, 1977," he said without skipping a beat. That same year the Kenya government banned all hunting, killing off the seventy-year traditional safari business "with the stroke of a pen," as Iain Douglas-Hamilton wrote. "For all those years it had been properly regulated until the corruption of the game department destroyed it." After that, during the decade of debate that led up to the ivory ban, the distinction between legal hunting and criminal poaching in Africa became so blurred that to this day a large segment of the public imagines there's no difference between the two.

With permission from the Kenya Wildlife Service, Dyer has dealt with his own problem elephants and buffalo, "fence breakers and man killers," he explained. "Five years ago, I calculated I had legitimately killed animals on the farm that could have been worth about fifty thousand dollars in government trophy license fees. Totally wasted."

Dyer remembered the old days when it was possible to take out a license for two elephants and sell the tusks. "Look, you didn't make big bucks, you might double the price of your license," he laughed. "The only ivory I ever sold, I seem to remember, was for thirty-five shillings a pound. But that was fifty-four years ago!"

MPALA RESEARCH CENTRE, about twenty miles northwest of Nanyuki in Laikipia, is in the middle of a forty-eight-thousand-acre wildlife conservancy so remote the British army sometimes uses it for commando training. But this largely flat landscape is accessible by African taxi. The paved road from Nanyuki with bicyclists carrying bags of twigs turned into a red earth track halfway there. We passed the odd herd of emaciated cattle, women carrying plastic water jugs on their heads, and a couple of giraffes by the roadside as we rattled along, stirring up clouds of dust in the middle of the vast, bone-dry scrubland that added another layer onto the gray-green vegetation. Views of distant, cloud-wrapped Mount Kenya dominated the horizon on my right and, finally, moved behind us.

My attention was drawn back to the road, now lined on both sides with a variety of fencing from cactus to barbed wire to expensive-looking metal, pierced every so often by an opening filled with short concrete stumps. I found out later that these are intended to let all manner of wildlife through except rhinos, which can't figure them out. I couldn't figure out the strangely tall gate we were approaching, essentially just two skinny posts on either side of the road connected by a thin cable, from which a series of wires dangled. "Elephants," my driver said as we passed under it. Of course: the wires were electrified.

Shortly after crossing the Ewaso Ny'iro River, we arrived at the cluster of modest thatched buildings that houses a rotating roster of wildlife researchers from all over the world who want to use the surrounding natural savanna habitat for their studies. It's no spa but comfortable enough. When the

buffet dinner is over in the communal dining hall and the generators have
been turned off, it's stone quiet and pitch black, save for the expected biodi-
verse orchestra of animal noises and the stunning star show above. I read the
page of advice and regulations in my hut by flashlight, noting the availability
of hot water, mealtimes, and the clear prohibition against hiking into the surrounding bush due to the presence of large and unpredictable fauna.

"READY FOR A walk?" Nick Georgiadis asked. I wanted to talk to the center's
director to get his perspective on elephants and ivory and was delighted not
to do it in his office. Georgiadis, who has collaborated on pioneering research on elephant genetics, has always had a keen interest in wildlife. In his
house at the center there was a wall of his trophies—the butterfly collection
he formed as a boy. Seeing that the stocky, curly-haired Kenyan-born biologist had armed himself with binoculars, I grabbed mine and we headed off
toward a high hill and a view overlooking the compound, plunging immediately into thick bush. We conversed as we worked our way up the rock-strewn
hillside, holding back nasty-looking thorn branches for each other.

Historically, on the African continent, "elephants were everywhere,"
Georgiadis told me, "except in the driest desert." It was also true that landscapes in Africa without human presence were exceptions. "Looking at elephants as a species, they are able to persist in a human-occupied landscape,
more than, say, zebras and giraffes, because they're smart, they learn, they
are extremely mobile, and they can crash through just about any fence or
physical barrier." We clambered uphill through some twisted trees.

"Those kinds of traits and abilities allow elephants to survive with a
surprising degree of development in a large landscape, where, if they
don't move, they die." And in Laikipia? I paused for a breath. Georgiadis
thought some of the area's elephants were using up to half the district as
their range, "which they need to do because it's so dry. They move huge
distances, and our duty here is try to maintain some landscape connectiv-
ity that will allow them to continue to do that in perpetuity."

Some minutes later we were sitting on a ledge. I took in the immense
vista and the strange, ancient rocky outcroppings in the near distance. For

Georgiadis, the goal was to determine "the minimum number and location, so to speak, of dark green patches on the landscape where the land use is primarily wildlife, and put that jigsaw puzzle together and figure out how people in and around them are going to profit sufficiently from that."

Profit? He was blunt about it as a motive and said there was no other way to add value to wildlife than through a person's livelihood. An abstract appeal to the importance of wildlife or how tourist dollars help the national economy was pointless. "It's no good appealing that way to a guy who's growing maize on a small plot," he said. "People have to get more out of a situation than they're losing. Wildlife in this environment can survive, prosper, and provide an income."

Other than tourism, how?

"At the moment, tourism is the only option here. I don't see elephant sport hunting coming back in Kenya, for the foreseeable future. I do see the possibility of sport hunting for other species," he said, adding, "I'm not a sport hunter. I long ago gave up trying to figure out why people who love wildlife so much would go out and blast it. There's no answer to that. But they are prepared to pay a lot of money for the privilege, and they do, and we can't afford, as a country, not to accept that money." Sport hunting, he pointed out, brings in a huge income from the "offtake" of relatively few animals.

"To my mind, this whole thing hinges on the Kenya government coming to grips with the reality that you can't have the wildlife in a natural environment if it's not paying for itself."

I wondered about the reaction of many animal welfare groups if Kenya lifted its prohibition on hunting.

"Those people who are against it, well, it's incumbent on them to come up with something else that would work instead. Everything's already been tried on the national level and it's failed because local people don't have a reason to hang on to that wildlife—and why the hell should they? They need the protein or whatever they can get out of it today."

Georgiadis had once referred to the list of ways to add economic value to wildlife as "lamentably short." I asked what he thought about allowing game ranching in Kenya. He was fine with that, but less keen on cropping for skins and meat, which provides the lowest returns for the highest offtakes. He also thought it too easy to abuse—"although there's always going to be some abuse," he admitted.

And resuming trade in ivory, if it were possible?

"People here are fearful that the whole thing could come full circle," he said, and, in the end, bring back uncontrollable poaching.

I scanned the distant horizon with my binocs. Mount Kenya had disappeared behind a bank of afternoon clouds. Except for the center below us, all that could be seen looked completely wild and desolate. I remarked that he probably didn't encourage many visitors to wander off on their own.

"Absolutely not. We don't allow it."

The sun was getting low in the sky, so I didn't disagree when he suggested it was time to be heading back. On the way down he explained that local communities who had a stake in wildlife—through tourism, hunting, game ranching, etc.—would have an obvious interest in policing themselves, in the same way they watched after their cattle effectively. Putting a value on wildlife was a way to meet conservation goals as well as help people's livelihoods. Anywhere you didn't do that, he said, "there will be no wildlife. That to me is a fundamental, self-evident truth." We got back to the center and made a plan to take a drive the next afternoon.

When I got back to my hut a pair of not very dangerous-looking dik-diks were waiting outside the door. No bigger than toy dogs on stilts, the miniature antelopes wiggled their mobile noses and snorted derisively before darting off. I organized the notes from my recent interviews, laying them out on the cot in my hut. Although everyone I talked to came at it from a different angle, the message was the same: elephant policy wasn't working in Kenya. Combining herds of the largest land animal with large numbers of humans made for a dangerous mix—anywhere. If elephants can't find enough food and water in parks and reserves, they raid the closest farms. That meant if there were going to be any elephants outside national parks, there needed to be more ways that rural people and their communities could benefit from them, instead of always losing by their presence.

"THAT'S A GREVY'S zebra over there," Georgiadis said, pointing out the window of his battered Land Rover. "Highly endangered. We've got three hundred of them in Mpala." I studied the narrow-striped equid through binoculars; it was one of a dozen species Georgiadis pointed out as we rolled slowly along a dry scrubby ridge north of the center. I noted the less common ones, hartebeest, jackal, reticulated giraffe. When we came across another vehicle and Georgiadis stopped to talk to the driver, I took the opportunity to make my notes a bit more legible.

"There's a dead elephant up ahead," he said quietly. "We'll take a look."

Ten minutes further into the bush we stopped and got out where other staff vehicles had already pulled over and followed their occupants around some acacias and broken trees until we saw the gray-brown carcass lying in the stunted grass in the fading light. It was a three-year-old male with pathetic little banana-sized tusks. Possibly just weaned, this youngster had clearly been in poor condition. He hadn't been there long, perhaps two days. Flies hummed all over him, but his eyes and his skin were intact; vultures and hyenas hadn't discovered him yet. Someone would contact KWS, which would send people out to recover the tiny ivories. Several of the onlookers pushed him over. He looked worse on the underside. Some decomposition had set in, although there was no real stench yet, just the persistent hum of flies as they roamed over the gas-bloated belly. This was a baby elephant I could touch all I wanted to, but the skin felt like cold bark. The long drought had been hard on wildlife.

Nature was doing its own culling.

THAT LAST NIGHT in Mpala I packed for a morning departure, then went to bed early, perhaps too early. I awoke some hours before dawn, unable to drift off again. As I turned and twisted on the narrow cot, careful not to bring down the mosquito netting draped around me, I thought of the parable of the blind men and the elephant: each one felt a part of it—the tail, the trunk, the great flanks, the tusks—but unable to grasp the whole, none could imagine how it all fit together. A herd of equally conflicting images paraded before me—places where elephant populations were being shot out, countries that had too many, struggling peoples and communities who had to live with elephants but didn't benefit from them . . .

and the gleam of raw ivory in a heap. I listened to the insects outside the hut, and doubtless inside too, and was reminded of the sound of the flies hovering over the dead little elephant, buzzing with the insistence of inescapable conclusions.

I'd come to a few of those. One was that there can be too many elephants for their own good. Take what was happening in Botswana's Chobe National Park. There are now so many elephants in the north of the country—130,000, almost a quarter of the continent's population—that lions were beginning to *eat* them. Not just small ones either, like the one I'd just seen, but fifteen-year-old elephants, big but weakened by the daily trek between food sources and the water that's available only along the rivers in the dry season; their numbers had stripped all vegetation on the riverbanks and the animals had to go farther and farther afield each day. Prides of lions ganged up on stragglers at night, not hesitating to claw down elephants they would never dare tackle in daylight, some clamping their trunks in their jaws, others chewing through the tough hide.

Perhaps this was the kind of species die-off, a natural reduction, that some speculate was common in precolonial Africa. But how much space remains for that to happen in today's crowded Africa? Only the largest national parks, or one of the new transfrontier megaparks, would be big enough to let elephants cycle through such ups and downs—a prospect many people today would find hard to watch unfold.

Such a hands-off policy would be hardly feasible for much-visited parks like Kruger, whose biodiversity would be at stake. Only a besotted elephant lover could say that every other creature, every tree on that impressive land ark, should be thrown overboard before a single elephant could. Still, many see culling as a monstrous act, an elephant pogrom, and believe that engaging in it somehow diminishes us. But humans have always lived at the expense of other species, and still do; only instead of knocking animals on their heads with rocks as we must have done in the Pleistocene, we are doing them in with pollution and habitat loss, global warming being just the latest weapon of mass habitat destruction. Because for increasing numbers of humans this all happens at arm's length, they are prone to laboring under the illusion that they themselves have never brought any harm to, or had any impact on, the natural world. Such people freely indulge their moral indignation at those who fish or shoot ducks or for that matter buy lamb chops when the real outrage is that we're making the planet less habitable for humans and wildlife alike.

Another inescapable conclusion is that there can be too many elephants for the good of the human communities that now surround them. Unless we are prepared to assert that elephants come first—or embrace another morally confused claim, that elephants are just as important as our own species—then we have to accept that they must be allowed to have value to people for whom they are little more than devastation on four legs. There was no simple answer to the vast patchwork of human-elephant conflict across Africa, I knew, because in each case it had to make sense to an individual community. If elephants were going to remain in unprotected areas, the whole panoply of possible utilization, from game viewing to elephant-back safaris and sport hunting—and, yes, even culling—might be necessary.

I stared into the dark. Somehow, I think I knew all along that I would end up knowing that it's not a contradiction to care about elephants and yet accept that in some places their numbers have to be reduced, and, yes, also accept that in other places, elephants have to "pay their way" in any manner they can—even with their ivory.

That didn't mean that a sense of wonder at them was misplaced. On the contrary, it's what tells us it is worth struggling with the difficult decisions that will have to be made if we are to succeed in creating a viable future for the species.

I was getting hopelessly tangled in the mosquito netting when I heard the *ruh-uh, ruh-uh, ruh-uh* call of a leopard close by. He kept it up. The rasping grunts cleared my brain and I finally dropped off.

EARLY THE NEXT morning at breakfast Georgiadis asked, "Did you hear that leopard? Damn thing woke me up. Couldn't get back to sleep." I drank another cup of coffee to dispel lingering grogginess while colorful starlings poked on the tables for crumbs. After packing, I came back to the dining porch to make a final sketch of Mount Kenya while waiting for my ride.

The tiny white glimmers visible on the mountain's sharp peak are what is left of its shrinking glaciers. The ice on the seventeen-thousand-foot-high extinct volcano, which once covered an area of two and a half square miles a hundred years ago, is down to less than half a square mile. The glacial rivers that flowed off the mountain will be dry in fifteen years, according to one UN study, creating a problem not only for the nomadic livestock but for the fragile hydropower-based electric grid that supplies Nairobi with electricity.

Mount Kenya's glaciers are in retreat; so are Africa's elephants. I recalled Isak Dinesen's image: "I had seen a herd of elephants traveling through dense native forest, pacing along as if they had an appointment at the end of the world." It might seem as if much of ivory's story involved constant warfare against elephants, from the ancient Egyptian hunting campaigns in Nubia through the nineteenth-century slaughter to the peak of poaching in the 1980s. But the way E. D. Moore thought the story would end—with the elephant's extermination—was by no means inevitable. Elephants will survive in the wild in good numbers, if we face the hard choices and take the necessary steps to give them that chance.

The ivory would continue to pile up. Was there some way it could help reconcile dreams for elephants with elephant realities?

WHEN I RETURNED to Nairobi I met with Esmond Bradley Martin at his house in the Nairobi suburb of Mbagathi. An American geographer, he has lived in Africa since the 1960s. Tall and lanky, with an impressive mop of white hair, he is one of those people who insist that visitors sign a guest book. This detail-mindedness has been put to great use in the steady stream of reports he has produced for over a decade, many in collaboration with other researchers, on ivory markets around the world from New York to Singapore.

Martin invited Nigel Hunter, the gravel-voiced, barrel-chested, then director of MIKE, CITES's elephant poaching monitoring program, to join us for tea. We sat in Martin's high-ceilinged living room with its pale green walls, antique furniture, and black-and-white photos of elephants.

We began talking about what might be done about all the stockpiles of ivory in Africa, and the desire of some countries to have a mechanism in place to resume a carefully regulated legal trade.

"It's a matter of political will," Martin explained. It was possible for African governments to put more pressure on CITES to allow such sales, but whether it would happen was anyone's guess.

What about the argument that the 1999 sale to Japan set off a round of poaching?

Martin shook his head. "Dan Stiles and I worked in Africa at the time of the sale, and in East Asia afterward, and then in South Asia, and we didn't see much of an effect at all. What we did see was that a few people, traders, in Africa got confused, and stayed in business because they thought the trade would reopen. Some customers thought that the sales meant you could now buy. But in Asia we saw almost no influence at all."

Still, there were African states where war and poaching seemed to go hand in hand. "If you have a breakdown in law and order, as in the Congo, poaching is going to continue, no matter what happens. Even if the price of ivory went down by half, the Congolese, the Angolans, the others, would still be poaching," Martin said.

Hunter described the flow of weapons in African states. "Where you get a breakdown in government, or poor government, corruption, civil strife, it's very easy to get AK-47s, and that makes it much easier to go after ivory," he said. "Everyone has an AK-47, true, but there's the opposite as well. Good old-fashioned homemade weapons are still being used. Can't blame poaching on the availability of modern weaponry. Wherever there's a demand, poachers will try anything. Not that they don't prefer something better than poisoned arrows."

I wondered if, in today's Africa, people shied away from ivory if they came across it. Martin thought it depended on whether they thought they'd be caught.

Hunter expanded on this. "In Kruger, there's good enforcement, but in Cameroon nobody would think twice about picking up an ivory [tusk] because they know exactly how to get rid of it. There's no wildlife person anywhere near them." He listed African countries where there were indications of ivory movement. "In moving the illegal stuff, there's less raw ivory being moved, and more carved ivory being moved. China is definitely the main market. When it comes to something like a necklace, the Chinese don't seem to mind whether it's carved in, say, Lagos.

"Look, ivory is a great, gorgeous material," Hunter added. "It's nice to wear if you're a lady, against your skin it feels nice, people buy it because they like it. The 'personal effects' market is underestimated."

We returned to the subject of the growing ivory stockpiles.

"What's going to happen in ten or twenty years?" Martin asked. "We're going to have huge quantities of ivory."

Hunter, who worked in Botswana's wildlife department, remembered when the country's ivory cache "was just a pile in a tin hut." He laughed. "I don't know why none of it walked."

Now it had swollen to forty tons or more.

Hunter broke the silence we'd fallen into. "The dream in the end, or the vision, has to be you're trying to make it legal. Ivory isn't going to disappear. So the more you muddle it up, the more the black market will try and operate." He put his cup back on the tea tray. "There's nothing like ivory, I agree with that. Historically, how did countries deal with illegality? Well, that's the reason we have hallmarks on gold and silver. That's how they managed to legalize a precious commodity, and now that culture is deeply embedded . . . and I think that's where we have to go."

And CITES's approach to the ivory issue?

"It's a good one; it's step by step. What people need is patience. I was director of wildlife in Botswana, so I know only too well the southern [African] viewpoint. Something worth waiting for is worth being patient for." It was important, he felt, to get scientific monitoring in place, so that there would be some means of telling if there is a relationship between the sale of ivory and poaching or not.

Hunter conceded there were difficulties with "the appendix approach" CITES used. If a species was put on it, he said, "then you breathe a sigh of relief, oh it's safe, everybody stops thinking about it, and the resources in many ways go down." After the ban, resources for elephant conservation went down in Africa "because everybody thought, we've put it on [Appendix I], we've done our bit." He wondered if it was the most productive way of all moving toward "what we all want: to have elephants but also to realize their value, in a sustainable manner. If elephants die, you're going to get ivory, whether you like it or not.

"What would be more encouraging is to say to countries—I don't think CITES will go this way, but it's a thought for you—if you can demonstrate that you have your elephants properly managed, under control, in other words, the illegal offtake is lower than natural replenishment, then the reward for you is that you can sell the ivory based on the biological quantification. If you've got ten thousand elephants, and you're managing them, and they're staying at ten or eleven thousand, you can calculate that you're going to get a natural supply of ivory of something like five tons per annum or whatever. But you can't get access to that market if you can't prove that you are managing your elephants in a sustainable manner."

So was it foolish to ignore the fact that sales of ivory could help fund elephant conservation?

Hunter nodded. "Every African country except Kenya has said that that is their aspiration. They will not burn their ivory. They see value in it."

ON THE WAY back to the United States I stopped in London and visited the Natural History Museum on Cromwell Road. The great Kilimanjaro tusks had been on public display up to 1973, at which time they were put into storage. Now they had gone back on public view, wedged in between displays of other gigantic natural history relics across the animal kingdom, all jumbled together in an updated version of a hall of wonders. As a crowd pleaser, the exhibit was a hit—it was packed with mums and dads and children from infants in strollers to preschoolers banging on fat buttons that lit up displays telling how many of them it would take to tip the scales with a dinosaur.

I found contemplating the tusks in that context a challenge. It was a bit like trying to imagine the former glory of an Egyptian obelisk long wrenched from its original setting and now standing in an urban traffic circle. These great yellowed sweeps of ivory appeared utterly detached from their moment in history as well as from the natural world.

As I walked back down the entrance steps of the museum it occurred to me that perhaps their disembodiment simply underscored the fact that so many of us have lost touch with the seductive sheen of the substance that first captured humans so long ago. The Kilimanjaro tusks were merely the most stupendous examples recorded of the "jewels of the elephant." But, then, even the smallest piece of ivory contains in its soft gleam and cool touch something of its nature and history. If we look hard we can, if we want, read triumphs and horrors in its milky mirror and feel the seductive power of the art that can be made from it.

The story of ivory has a number of turning points, but none more fundamental than the shift in thinking that turned elephants from being regarded as mere bearers of treasure to creatures we find more important than ivory itself.

Still, there is one more chapter that could be written. The stockpiles of tusks are here, and growing bigger. All that sleeping beauty remains unused, dormant; the ideas that might be expressed in the material and multiply its value remain unrealized. But ivory need not be the elephant's curse; ivory, we must remember, is the great gift that the elephant leaves behind at the end of its life. If we can return that undeserved favor by finding some way that ivory sales could help conserve rather than endanger the elephant, ensuring that both the animal and its treasure endure, then—only then—could we feel right about accepting it.

Epilogue: 2007

In June 2007, several thousand delegates from 171 member states and a small army of wildlife advocates and lobbyists, trailed by a phalanx of global journalists, converged for the Fourteenth Conference of the Parties of CITES. Every two or three years CITES holds this gargantuan event in some major urban center around the globe. This time it was at the World Forum Conference Centre in The Hague, Netherlands, whose four floors ("Oceans," "Continents," "Rivers," and "Mountains") featured geographically named meeting areas ("Yangtze" and "Kilimanjaro," and the like) and gave attendees plenty of room to mingle, negotiate, petition, and plead. The site had the decor of an up-to-date international airport terminal, and for nearly two weeks delegates flowed in and around the 430,000 square feet of the cavernous building while being lobbied to get on board one proposal or another.

At these CITES gatherings, countries that have newly signed on to the convention are welcomed into the fold (this year was Kyrgyzstan's turn), and individual delegations get down to the business of wrestling with proposals to amend the growing list of more than thirty thousand plants and animals whose commerce is now monitored internationally. As always, focus fell on the eight hundred–odd highly endangered species. International commercial trade in these is — with some exceptions — banned. At this meeting, depending on how the voting went, some trade in ivory could again be permitted. With scores of topics on the agenda, from the spiny dogfish and the slow loris to European eels and Guatemalan rosewood, no one wanted the tangled and contentious ivory issue to dominate discussions, but as usual at CITES meetings that issue was inevitably the elephant in the room no one could ignore. For CITES's own logo forms a stylized elephant silhouette out of the letters of its acronym, more evidence, if one needed it, of the deeply symbolic role the animal plays in conservation circles.

The African elephant, as no delegate needed to be reminded of, is both an emotional subject and a regulatory headache because of its so-called split listing. The elephant populations in most of the three dozen countries where the animal is found were listed in Appendix I, the category reserved for species threatened with extinction; this listing meant any cross-border commercial trade in elephant products (meat, hides, ivory, etc.) was strictly prohibited. The populations in a few southern African countries, however, were listed in Appendix II in recognition of their less threatened status, allowing for some controlled trade in their products, under certain conditions.

By now, this bifurcated approach to the African elephant had also become a fault line that split wildlife organizations into two uneasy camps and further divided African countries into two opposing blocs. A CITES press release issued before the conference attempted to characterize the difficulties delegates faced over ivory: "The long-running global debate over the African elephant has focused on benefits that income from ivory sales may bring to conservation and to local communities living side by side with these large and potentially dangerous animals versus concerns that such sales may encourage poaching. This year's proposals," it went on, "again reflect opposing views on how best to improve the conservation and sustainable use of the world's largest land animal."

The language showed a new emphasis on what CITES had long acknowledged: that the developing world is not only where much of the world's biodiversity is found but where wild flora and fauna are often central to local economies. In remarks at the opening ceremony Willem Wijnstekers, secretary-general of CITES, stated that decisions on whether to provide trade protection to a species "should take into account potential impacts on the livelihood of the poor." Given that a well-controlled animal trade can not only help needy communities but generate funds for conservation, CITES was not likely to support trade bans without solid evidence that commerce was detrimental to a species.

The yawning gulf that has always been evident between conservationists who want to strike a balance between concern for wildlife survival and addressing human needs and wildlife advocates drawn to preservation without reservation was now out in the open. Both sides arrived at the conference with their long-standing, differing attitudes toward wildlife intact and staked out their claims.

No one at the conference would dispute the fact that elephants are under siege in Central Africa, where war, corruption, and the crumbling infrastructure of national parks are clearly undermining conservation efforts. But there were sharp differences of opinion on whether trade in ivory was exacerbating that situation—or perhaps could help underfunded wildlife departments all over Africa.

Mainstream science-based conservation organizations at the conference, such as the World Conservation Union (IUCN), the World Wildlife Fund (WWF), and the African Wildlife Foundation (AWF), were solidly behind sustainable use. Philip Muruthi, of AWF's Nairobi office, came to the conference with the foundation's position statement. Although AWF had played a leading role in bringing about the 1989 ivory ban in the face of plummeting elephant populations, the organization supported "in principle the concept that when species are given value, such as through trade, the incentive for conserving them is increased."

Sue Mainka, the head of the IUCN delegation, made it clear that the international coalition of scientists was similarly aligned. "What we do not want is that banning or limiting trade in a species drives people further into poverty," she said. "What we do want is effective measures that discourage illegal trade in wildlife, while allowing sustainable use of healthy species populations that generates income and opportunities for local communities."

In line with their deeply held views, however, animal advocacy groups—the International Fund for Animal Welfare (IFAW), Born Free, and others with a fixed focus on strict preservation—are distinctly less sympathetic to development and poverty concerns in the elephant's range states. To them, any consumptive wildlife use is suspect, an approach that would lead only to increasing the multibillion-dollar worldwide trade in wildlife products. They painted any effort to lift the ivory ban as an ominous attempt to reopen trade before adequate policing can stanch the poaching that continues to threaten many of the African continent's most vulnerable elephant populations.

Not surprisingly, animal advocacy groups remain unmoved by the economic value that African nations see in their legitimate ivory stock-piles. Will Travers, head of the Born Free Foundation, believes that such stockpiles—not just in Africa but in every country—should be put "permanently beyond use" through destruction or burial. (Presumably he would not, like some latter-day Savonarola, advocate putting a torch to ivory art, but it's unclear what he'd like to see done with worked ivory in general.)

Back in 2002 Mavuso Msiamang, South Africa's national parks chief executive, had said, "If someone wants to buy our ivory and burn it, we will sell it," he said. "Because believe you me, we need the money." Pro-ban groups like Born Free, despite their deep pockets, have yet to pursue that possibility. Instead they've been pressuring African countries to destroy their own stocks on the theory that crippling legitimate commerce would help stop illegal trade. But would it?

The records of some twelve thousand seizures of illegal ivory by customs officers, police, and various authorities worldwide have been gathered over the past decade by TRAFFIC. The extensive database fails to show a correlation between CITES decisions on ivory sales and illegal trade—even after the 1997 one-off sale to Japan. This lack of hard data doesn't impress animal advocate groups, whose positions are, after all, based on conviction rather than on science. They claim that anecdotal evidence shows otherwise, and that an uptick in elephant poaching has always followed any suggestion of restoring legal trade in ivory.

African delegations were also split—in fact, deeply divided—over whether to vote to uphold the ivory ban or to lift it to some degree. Among them were a number of vocal sub-Saharan states that resented being lectured on what they should do with their ivory by lobbying groups from nations that had for centuries plundered Africa's ivory treasure and profited mightily from it. Southern African states in particular bristled at the implication that their interest in selling their ivory stockpiles to generate funds for elephant conservation implied they didn't care about their herds. Didn't the fact that they were awash with elephants show that their management policies were working and that their populations were healthy? For them, imposing the ivory ban amounted to punishing countries that had done right by their elephants in order to provide cover for the conservation failures of other states, especially those anxious to appease powerful animal advocacy groups. According to some delegates, those particular NGOs used carrot-and-stick methods to gain an undue influence on the wildlife policies of several African nations, Kenya in particular. "Kenya's the jewel in the animal rightists' crown," one conservationist told me privately. In his view, these groups would do whatever they could to keep that East African country from going "consumptive," offering funds in support of policies they approved of, while not hesitating to threaten tourist boycotts in retaliation for wildlife policies they disagreed with.

THE STAGE HAD been set for contentious ivory-and-elephant debates even before the conference opened on June 3. For months Kenya, supported by Mali, had been calling for a twenty-year moratorium on international trade in raw or worked ivory. Patrick Omondi, the head of species conservation and management at the Kenya Wildlife Service, saw the lengthy moratorium as necessary to let elephant populations recover and "to refine the mechanisms of law enforcement." He argued that "elephants are dramatically becoming depleted." That position seemed out of step with an earlier statement by KWS director Julius Kipng'etich announcing an experimental program of birth control to keep the country's "optimal" current population of elephants from increasing unduly. "We want to take measures now to avoid a crisis in the future," he told the *Standard* in Nairobi. Nonetheless, Kipng'etich said his country would firmly oppose any move to reopen the ivory trade. "We cannot control poaching," he said flatly.

In contrast, Edward Mbewe, a spokesperson for Zimbabwe's Parks and Wildlife Management Authority, said his country, like others with burgeoning elephant populations, wanted to see the focus on prevention of poaching rather than the prohibition of ivory trading. "We want communities to continue benefiting from wildlife in order to alleviate poverty," he said.

Botswana, with its bulging herds, came with related proposals, supported by Namibia, for annual ivory export quotas for future sales from southern African countries; in addition, it was proposing yet another one-off sale of forty tons from its own huge stockpile.

Gathering continent-wide support for a sweeping moratorium or the reopening of international trade on an annual basis looked increasingly unlikely. Debates became so heated they threatened to consume the conference. What kick-started them was the premeeting decision on June 2 by the CITES Standing Committee. Now that the required field data on elephant poaching and population levels had been gathered, and Japan had set sufficiently strong domestic ivory trade controls, the committee decided that the long-postponed implementation of the one-off sale of sixty tons from ivory stockpiles in South Africa, Botswana, and Namibia approved in 2002 could go forward. Susan Lieberman, WWF's Global Species Program director, agreed with the ivory sale to Japan, although she cautioned that it "should be closely monitored," as she put it, to ensure "early detection of potential problems or trends." She emphasized that enforcement—stopping poaching and illegal sales—should be the focus of CITES.

Animal welfare groups were aghast. "Pro-ivory traders were breaking open the champagne!" Travers wrote in disgust on his Born Free blog. Peter Pueschel of IFAW, which had sought to sway delegates with a prominent billboard outside the center featuring a fading elephant image against a bloodred sunset ("Will only words remain? Give them a break! Vote for the 20-year moratorium."), condemned the authorization of the sale, citing "all sorts of loopholes" in Japan's ivory controls. "This decision is a disgrace," he fumed.

These groups were also alarmed by the surprise last-minute effort by China at the Standing Committee meeting to be included in the one-off sale with Japan, which created an instant furor in the basement conference room. China pitched the advantages of its inclusion in economic terms: it would create healthy competition and increase profits to the ivory exporting countries. Since CITES was allowing one-off ivory sales to help raise funds for conservation, this was an attractive argument to some, but others felt China was not yet ready to effectively police its own black market. (The measure was narrowly voted down, but China would gain approval from the Standing Committee a year later.)

Over the course of the twelve-day conference that followed, Kenya and Mali, which had lined up nearly two dozen African countries for their push to get a twenty-year moratorium on ivory sales, saw support for this sweeping measure erode. Southern African states slammed their agenda as draconian and impugned Kenya's motives. Namibia's environment and tourism minister, Willem Konjore, pointed out that his country's elephant population had doubled in the past decade, and said, "Illegal killing has been so low as to be insignificant." The sale of elephant products would bring funds back into rural communities willing "to coexist and share resources with elephants," he said. Gerhard Verdoom, the executive director of Birdlife South Africa, went on the attack. Telling the media that Kenya's arguments were "rubbish," he asserted that "the elephants in South Africa, Botswana, and Namibia are well managed. There is minimal poaching. In East and West Africa there is a lot of poaching going on due to poor wildlife management," he said, pointedly adding that "we do not want to be punished for the wildlife mismanagement in Kenya."

After two weeks of exhausting and emotional negotiations, the German delegates, representing the European Union, met with the opposing groups. They hoped to merge the two proposals to avoid acrimonious arguments on the floor of the plenary session and the possibility of CITES having a political disaster on its hands should no consensus be reached. But bickering African delegations were still deadlocked. Kenya and Mali had offered to scale back their proposal for an ivory trade moratorium to twelve years and conceded that the latest one-off sale would be acceptable. South Africa countered by proposing, on top of the just-authorized sale, generous export permits—for itself, Botswana, Namibia, and Zimbabwe. The funds would be used for elephant conservation; a six-year trade ban would follow.

The AWF's position paper had put the matter succinctly: "The future of Africa's wildlife is ultimately in the hands of the people of Africa." Kenya Wildlife Services' Patrick Omondi conceded as much. "Africa is huge, and we all have different challenges," he said. "We really need a practical way out." Delegates headed into closed-door sessions with—for the first time—ministers from their respective countries, adding a political dimension to the negotiations and signaling their seriousness. In a final, agonizing effort, delegates from the elephant range states worked until four in the morning on June 14 to hammer out their first regional consensus on ivory.

Under a compromise presented by Zambia and Chad, South Africa,

Botswana, Namibia, and Zimbabwe would be permitted to make a single sale in addition to the one-off sale of sixty tons agreed upon in 2002, which had just been given the go-ahead. This additional sale would be limited to all stocks in government hands that had been registered and verified as of January 31, 2007. Each sale would consist of a single shipment to a permitted destination, and proceeds were to "be used exclusively for elephant conservation and community conservation and development programs within or adjacent to the elephant range." After the shipments were completed, no new proposals would be considered by CITES from these countries for a "resting period" of nine years. In the meantime, the CITES Standing Committee would work on "developing a new and more effective approach to taking future decisions on the international ivory trade."

There were grumblings over the inclusion of Zimbabwe, whose imploding state and rising poaching under the last stages of President Robert Mugabe's regime made it suspect to some delegations (the United States, for one). And there were complaints that Japan's domestic control over ivory was far from perfect; the seizure of a shipment of nearly three tons of illegal ivory in Osaka the year before was read by some as evidence of a brisk black market, though by others as evidence of effective law enforcement.

Overall, the decision was greeted with relief and cautious optimism. "Elephants get nine-year reprieve," was a typical media sentiment. Save the Elephants founder Iain Douglas-Hamilton said his group was "afraid the sale will stimulate a parallel surge of demand for illegal ivory but we are quite glad that Africa has actually come to a consensus. Once the ivory sale is over, at least there will be a nine-year period without it." Some animal campaigners were quick to denounce the deal. IFAW warned that it would "excite a demand that can never be supplied by legal sources."

Mainstream conservation groups were positive; the WWF called it a "milestone" consensus. African media rallied around the decision, pleased that the delegations had struck their own continent-wide compromise. Zimbabwe's Environment and Tourism minister announced that "this will allow human beings and elephants to coexist in Africa." Julius Kipng'etich, the KWS head, did an about-face and hailed the accord as "Africa's finest hour, a proud moment for the continent, its people and the elephant."

Additional political wrangling, bureaucratic snafus, and a growing number of empty seats left by delegates scrambling to catch early flights home on the last day of the conference meant that some important business was left hanging in the air—notably, how to shut down the illegal but flourishing domestic ivory markets in places such as the Democratic Republic of the Congo, Angola, Thailand, and China and tighten enforcement and border checks for illegal shipments.

And there were a lot of questions about the compromise. No one seemed to know just how many tons of ivory might be in government-held stocks over and above the sixty tons originally agreed to; early estimates ranged from a hundred fifty to two hundred tons more, but Esmond Bradley Martin thought the figure might be closer to hundred tons. He also noted that Japan had been using a modest ten tons a year from its own dwindling stocks—would it now be able to absorb upwards of a hundred tons in a single gulp? The Japanese ivory industry, like others worldwide, had never really recovered from the 1989 ban, and it was an open question whether that industry could spring to life to accommodate this unexpectedly large dump of ivory on the market. It was also unclear what price the Japanese would pay. There would be competition among the country's ivory dealers for the best lots, raising hopes that they might pay handsomely and underscore Japan's usefulness as a good conservation partner. South Africa announced it expected to earn $200 a kilo, which meant roughly $9 million from the 50 tons of stockpiled ivory in Kruger alone.

These issues, however, seemed minor in comparison to the unknowns that the inclusion of China brought to the impending transaction. The 2008 CITES decision to designate it as an importing country raised fresh concerns which the Convention's secretary-general sought to address. "The Secretariat will closely supervise this sale and evaluate its impact on elephant population levels throughout Africa," Willem Wijnstekers said. "We will continue monitoring the Chinese and Japanese domestic trade controls to ensure that unscrupulous traders do not take this opportunity to launder ivory from illegal origin."

DECISIONS TAKEN AT the 2007 CITES meeting tried to meld competing visions of how to ensure the survival of the African elephant in the wild.

Given the changing fortunes of the African elephant in the evolving landscape of the developing African continent, complex responses, like the one worked out in the Hague, look likely for years to come. The heart of the issue remains how to reconcile worldwide concern for the magnificent, beloved elephant with the rights of nations to benefit from their natural resources. For many people in countries that harbor elephant populations, it is self-evident that they must be allowed to gain from the gleaming ivory that inexorably accumulates within their borders, tusk by tusk.

It is possible — only possible, I admit — that the 2007 CITES meeting may prove to be a turning point in the troubled history of the ivory trade. But that can happen only if ivory exports, long stained with the slaughter of elephant herds and human misery, are treated strictly as a self-renewing resource that funds the effective conservation of the animal that has always been its greatest source. To achieve this requires vision, courage, regulation, and political will.

As long as there are elephants, there will be ivory. Now, surely, it is ivory's turn to help ensure that there will always be elephants.

NOTES

All reported dialogue is from my tapes or notes taken at the time. For the history herein I relied on a number of secondary sources in addition to the archival research and interviews I conducted. The texts I found most useful are cited below; referenced passages are identified by the page on which they appear and their key words.

PROLOGUE: 1898

1 *That much is certain*   This reimagining of the hunt that yielded the Kilimanjaro tusks is based on the most reliable accounts, primarily those found in W. D. M. Bell, *The Wanderings of an Elephant Hunter* (London: Neville Spearman & The Holland Press, 1958, reprint of 1923), pp. 38–39; George Frederick Kunz, *Ivory and the Elephant* (Garden City, N.Y.: Doubleday, Page, 1916), pp. 410–11; and E. D. Moore, *Ivory: Scourge of Africa* (New York and London: Harper and Brothers, 1931), pp. 216–18.

3 *worn smooth from ripping tree bark and gouging water holes*   Elephants use their tusks for digging, prying open trees, smashing bush, and lifting branches and trees; they are also important in display and can be formidable weapons. See Joyce Poole, *Elephants* (Stillwater, Minn.: Voyageur Press, 1997), p. 35.

1. MAMMOTH TEETH

Among recent texts on prehistory, Claudine Cohen's *The Fate of the Mammoth: Fossils, Myth, and History* (Chicago: University of Chicago Press, 2002; translated by William Rodarmor) and Richard Stone's *Mammoth: The Resurrection of an Ice Age Giant* (Cambridge, Mass.: Perseus, 2001) supplied much valuable material.

9 *According to paleoanthropologist Randall White*   My account of early ivory usage leans heavily on White's research; see his "Ivory Personal Ornaments of Aurignacian Age: Technological, Social and Symbolic Perspectives," in *Le Travail et L'Usage de L'Ivoire au Paléolithique Supérieur*, ed. J. Hahn et al. (Ravello: Centro Universitario Europeo Per I Beni Culturali, 1995), and "The Dawn of Adornment," *Natural History* (May 1993).

10 *oldest ivory find yet*   "Excavations at Vogelherd Cave in Southwestern Germany

Produce Spectacular New Artworks from the Ice Age," University of Tübingen press release, June 19, 2007.

11 *a clutch of similar small carved ivories*   N. J. Conard, "Palaeolithic Ivory Sculptures from Southwestern Germany and the Origins of Figurative Art," *Nature* 426 (2003), pp. 830–32.

11 *modern man . . . set out to colonize the world*   F. E. Grine et al., "Late Pleistocene Human Skull from Hofmeyr, South Africa, and Modern Human Origins," *Science* 13, no. 5809 (12 January 2007), pp. 226–29.

11 *pierced fox teeth*   *Proceedings of the National Academy of Sciences* 103: 12643–48 (2006).

13 *their nimbus of meaning*   R. Dale Guthrie makes a similar suggestion in his *The Nature of Paleolithic Art* (Chicago: University of Chicago Press, 2006), p. 371.

14 *carefully observed and delicately crafted*   Notably the splendid ivory horse from Vogelherd in south Germany shown in Alexander Marshack, *The Roots of Civilization* (New York: McGraw-Hill, 1972), pp. 250–51.

14 *so-called Venus figures*   Some two hundred have been unearthed. See Randall White, "The Women of Brassempouy: A Century of Research and Interpretation," *Journal of Archaeological Method and Theory* 13, no. 4 (December 2006). White suggests that "Brassempouy served as a kind of atelier for ivory-sculpting."

14 *La Poire*   In the collection of the Musée des Antiquités Nationales, Saint-Germain-en-Laye; shown in Massimo Carrà, *Ivories of the West* (London: Hamlyn, 1970; translation of 1966), plate 2.

15 *Whacking a fresh tusk*   Ivory is relatively soft, ranking up to only number 3 on Mohs' field scale of hardness, used by mineralogists—i.e., the hardness of calcite. But a fresh tusk, which is 30 percent collagen and 70 percent inorganic matter (mostly calcium and phosphate), also has a certain amount of elasticity and toughness, making it difficult to crack.

15 *more careful methods . . . were devised*   Jeffrey J. Saunders et al., "A Mammoth-Ivory Semifabricate from Blackwater Locality No. 1, New Mexico," *American Antiquity* 55, no. 1 (January 1990), pp. 112–19.

15 *Ivory is dentin*   More precisely, "Ivory is a mineralized collagenous matrix consisting mainly of calcium phosphate hydroxide $3Ca3\ (PO4)2 \bullet Ca(OH)2$. Depending on its age and state of preservation, ivory contains varying amounts of organic material, mainly the fibrous protein collagen, with small amounts of elastin, mucopolysaccharides and lipids." Terry Drayman Weisser, "A Method for Reinforcing Fragile Ivory," *Journal of the American Institute for Conservation* 17, no. 2, (1978), pp. 44–47.

15 *Teeth are not bones*   This overview follows Simon Hillson, *Teeth*, 2d edition (Cambridge: Cambridge University Press, 2005).

16 *The exceedingly compact, uniform structure of ivory*   See T. K. Penniman, *Pictures of Ivory and Other Animal Teeth, Bone and Antler* (Oxford: Pitt Rivers Museum, University of Oxford, 1952), p. 13.

16 *incisors grow some seven inches a year*   Poole, *Elephants*, p. 31.

17 *Norris and I were standing in the Childs Frick building*   November 14, 2006.

18 *All have disappeared*   See Jeheskel Shoshani and Daniel C. Fisher, "Extinction of the Elephant's 'Ancestors,'" in Shoshani, ed., *Elephants: Majestic Creatures of the Wild* (New York: Checkmark Books, 1992; revised edition, 2000), and Alfred L. Roca et al.,

"Genetic Evidence for Two Species of Elephant in Africa," *Science* 293 (August 24, 2001), pp. 1473–77. The woolly mammoth is now thought to be more closely related to Asian elephants than to African elephants. All three had a common ancestor up to 6 million years ago, when the African elephant split off into a separate species; less than half a million years later Asian elephants and mammoths diverged.

19 *Charles R. Knight*   Knight (1874–1953) was associated with the American Museum of Natural History for fifty years. He was the first artist to make a serious study of the appearance of extinct animals and painted the mural series "Life in the Ice Ages" between 1911 and 1921.

19 *slaying from a safer distance*   There is considerable debate over the issue of bow-and-arrow technology; some believe there is no clear evidence for its use prior to the Mesolithic era (12,000 to 3,200 BCE).

20 *drying up of their food supply alone can't account*   See Todd Surovell et al., "Global Archaeological Evidence for Proboscidean Overkill," *Proceedings of the National Academy of Sciences* 102, no. 17 (April 26, 2005), pp. 6231–36. The authors examined forty-one kill/scavenge sites on five continents and determined that woolly mammoths and elephants disappeared from the fossil record once a region became colonized by humans.

21 *"overkill" or "blitzkrieg"*   This hypothesis is associated with Paul Martin, who observed that late Pleistocene extinctions in the Americas largely affected megafauna, the presumed targets of human hunting. See P. S. Martin, ed., *Quaternary Extinctions* (Tucson: University of Arizona, 1984). R. Dale Guthrie argues that "hypotheses of a subtler human impact . . . are more consistent with the data," at least in Alaska. See his "New Carbon Dates Link Climatic Change with Human Colonization and Pleistocene Extinctions," *Nature* 441, May 11, 2006, pp. 207–9.

21 *Ross MacPhee . . . has his office*   January 24, 2005; and November 14, 2006.

22 *"losses of this kind"*   See MacPhee and Clare Flemming, "Requiem Aeternam: The Last Five Hundred Years of Mammalian Species Extinctions," in MacPhee, ed., *Extinctions in Near Time* (New York: Kluwer Academic/Plenum, 1999), pp. 333–71.

22 *"Musk oxen pulled through"*   Ross D. E. MacPhee et al., "Late Quaternary Loss of Genetic Diversity in Musk Ox (*Ovibos*)," *BMC Evolutionary Biology* 6, October 2005.

22 *On a 1998 expedition*   Clare Flemming, "Mammoth Prospecting," *Natural History* 107, no. 10, December 1998/January 1999, pp. 78–79. At first, it was reported that the Wrangel specimens all came from a "dwarfed" island population, but apparently this was more a case of large variability in body size. See Don Alan Hall, "Explaining Pleistocene Extinctions," *Mammoth Trumpet* 14, no. 1 (January 1999).

23 *our capacity for snuffing out entire species*   Some examples: about 1,700 years ago on Madagascar, Malaysian sailors did in pigmy hippos, various flightless birds, giant tortoises, and more; some 750 years ago, the ancestors of the modern Maori apparently knocked off all eleven species of the ostrich-like moa, a slow-breeding, flightless bird, in under than a century. See Richard Ellis, *No Turning Back* (New York: HarperCollins, 2004).

24 *the Schreger pattern*   Schreger lines are also known as the "lines of Retzius," after another scientist, but as the term "Schreger lines" "appears to be the earliest known and accepted scientific appellation for the probiscidean ivory pattern," it is widely used. See Edgard O'Neil Espinoza and Mary-Jacque Mann, "The History and Significance of the

Schreger Pattern in Proboscidean Ivory Characterization," *Journal of the American Institute for Conservation* 32, no. 3 (1993).

2. TRIBUTE AND TREASURE

Three authoritative works in particular were of much use: Anthony Cutler's *The Craft of Ivory: Sources, Techniques, and Uses in the Mediterranean World: A.D. 200–1400* (Washington, D.C.: Dumbarton Oaks Research Libarary and Collection, 1985); H. H. Scullard's *The Elephant in the Greek and Roman World* (Ithaca, N.Y.: Cornell University Press, 1974); and Olga Krzyszkowska's *Ivory and Related Materials: An Illustrated Guide* (London: Institute of Classical Studies, Bulletin Supplement 59, 1990).

25 *The exquisitely carved ivory neck rest* From Thebes, ca. 1325 BCE. Now in the Griffith Institute, Ashmolean Museum, Oxford, England.

25 *so-called concubine figures* Carrà (in *Ivories of the West*) calls them "concubines of death." For an indication of their variety, see Peter J. Ucko, "Anthropomorphic Ivory Figurines from Egypt," *Journal of the Royal Anthropological Institute of Great Britain and Ireland* 95, no. 2 (July–December, 1965), pp. 214–39.

26 *important sources of ivory* As hippo populations persisted for some time in the Middle East, notably in Syro-Palestine, the animals' teeth would remain an important source of ivory in the ancient world. See the wide-ranging study by Kathryn A. Lafrenz, "Tracing the Source of the Elephant and Hippopotamus Ivory from the 14th century B.C. Uluburn Shipwreck: The Archaeological, Historical and Isotopic Evidence," unpublished master's thesis, University of South Florida, 2003, pp. 29–31.

26 *different hieroglyphs* Martin Meredith, *Elephant Destiny: Biography of an Endangered Species in Africa* (New York: PublicAffairs, 2001), p. 7. The English word "ivory" comes (through Old French and Middle English) from the Latin word for ivory, *ebur*, which itself derives itself from the Egyptian hieroglyph "abu," used for elephant and ivory.

26 *As historian Edward A. Alpers puts it* Edward A. Alpers, "The Ivory Trade in Africa: An Historical Overview," in Doran H. Ross, *Elephant: The Animal and Its Ivory in African Culture* (Los Angeles: University of California, 1992), pp. 349–50. My account of early and later African ivory history is drawn largely from Alpers' concise summary.

27 *Thutmose III took time out to conduct a hunt* Scullard, *Elephant in the Greek and Roman World*, p. 27

29 *a commercial treaty with King Hiram* Derek Wilson and Peter Ayerst, *White Gold: The Story of African Ivory* (New York: Taplinger, 1976), p. 20. Tyre was the largest sea power in the Mediterranean at the time, with a number of trade links.

29 *"ivory, and apes, and peacocks"* King James translation. Tharshish (or Tarshish) is obscure; it may refer to the port of Tartessus in southern Spain, which had Phoenician trade links. The tiny ivory pomegranate thought to have topped a high priest's scepter in the temple in Jerusalem—the only original artifact from the site and the Israel Museum's most important item—was discovered in 2004 to be a fake.

30 *"Woe to them . . . that lie upon beds of ivory"* Amos, 6–4, 3–15

30 *thousands of ivory carvings* See the analysis in Richard D. Barnett, *Ancient Ivories in the Middle East* (Jerusalem: Qedem, Monographs of the Institute of Archaeology 14, 1982), pp. 50–52.

30 *In his memoirs*   Max Mallowan, *Mallowan's Memoirs* (New York: Dodd, Mead, 1977), p. 260.

31 *"I had my own favorite tools"* Agatha Christie, *An Autobiography* (New York: Dodd, Mead, 1977), p. 443.

31 *Mallowan reflected*   Mallowan, *Memoirs*, p. 270.

32 *a Cretan is shown with a tusk*   Cretans exported timber, and probably olive oil, and imported precious metals and ivory. See Krzyszkowska, *Ivory and Related Materials*, p. 19.

32 *free-form ivory acrobat*   Now in the archaeological museum, Iráklion (Candia). Plate 16 in Carrà, *Ivories of the West.*

33 *hippopotamus that once flourished*   Hippos might have reached certain islands in the late Pleistocene by swimming. See Wilhelm Schüle, "Mammals, Vegetation and the Initial Human Settlement of the Mediterranean Islands: A Palaeoecological Approach," *Journal of Biogeography* 20 (1993), 399–412.

33 *Both hippo ivory and elephant ivory were utilized*   See Krzyszkowska, "Aegean Ivory Carving: Towards an Evaluation of Late Bronze Age Workshop Material," in J. Lesley Fitton, ed., *Ivory in Greece and the Eastern Mediterranean from the Bronze Age to the Hellenistic Period* (London: British Museum Occasional Paper 85, 1992), p. 28.

33 *rip into the groins of hunters*   In Greek myth, Odysseus was gored in the thigh and Adonis gored in the groin by their respective boar quarry. The animal is associated with Artemis, the goddess of hunting, especially her violent side; out of vengeance she sent the monstrous Calydonian boar to a king who had failed to offer her the pick of his harvest. The future emperor Augustus thought he had plundered the tusks of the legendary boar from a temple near Tegea on the mainland of Greece in 31 BCE, but what he found was in all probability fossilized mammoth tusks. See Naomi J. Norman, "Asklepios and Hygieia and the Cult Statue at Tegea," *American Journal of Archaeology* 90, no. 4 (October 1986), pp. 425–30

34 *a distracting mosiac effect*   Alfred Maskell, however, thinks the height would have made the joins "imperceptible"; see his *Ivories* (Tokyo and Rutland, Vt.: Charles E. Tuttle, 1966; reprint of 1905), p. 478. Albizzati agrees (see his "Two Ivory Fragments of a Statue of Athena," *Journal of Hellenic Studies* 36 [1916], p. 398). But both these authors may be led to this opinion by having to account for Pheidia's effective use of the material while dismissing the possibility that larger sheets of ivory were used.

35 *some now forgotten method of peeling a tusk*   Kenneth Lapatin, "Pheidias elefantourgos," *American Journal of Archaeology* 101, no. 4 (October 1997), pp. 663–82. Kunz, *Ivory and the Elephant*, argues similarly, p. 23; see also Maskell, *Ivories*, on this subject, p. 477.

35 *"a tangle of bars and struts"* Quoted in Lapatin, "Pheidias elefantourgos," pp. 667–68.

36 *the full-scale use of elephants in battle*   See Scullard, *The Elephant in the Greek and Roman World*, chapter 3, for a detailed analysis of Alexander's use of elephants.

37 *the military historian Arrian*   Lucius Flavius Arrianus (ca. 95–175 CE) served under the Romans and wrote the *Anabasis of Alexander*; quoted in Karl Gröning, ed., *Elephants: A Cultural and Natural History* (Cologne: Könemann, 1998; English translation 1999), p. 201.

39 *"beasts fresh from the wild"* . . . *one scholar wrote*   Lionel Casson, "Ptolemy II and the Hunting of African Elephants," *Transactions of the American Philological*

Association 123 (1993), p. 254. The description of Ptolemy II's elephant program here largely follows Casson's account.

39 *"they immediately run away"* Quoted in Meredith, *Elephant Destiny*, p. 16. On the species of elephant used by the Ptolemies, see William Gowers, "African Elephants and Ancient Authors," *African Affairs* 47, no. 188 (July 1948), pp. 173–80.

40 *an elephant wearing a saddle blanket* Illustrated in Gröning, *Elephants*, p. 110.

41 *"Asia preferred its elephants alive and Africa, dead"* Robert Delort, *The Life and Lore of the Elephant* (London: Thames and Hudson, 1992; translation of 1990) p. 43.

41 *the death penalty for anyone killing an elephant* See Bist et al., "The Domesticated Asian Elephant in India," in Baker and Kashio, eds., *Giants on Our Hands: Proceedings of the International Workshop on the Domesticated Asian Elephant*, Bangkok, Thailand, February 5–10, 2001.

42 *one Indian ivory statuette* Mirella Levi D'Ancona, "An Indian Statuette from Pompeii," *Artibus Asiae* 13, no. 3 (1950), pp. 166–80.

42 *intricately carved ivory handle* Jessica Rawson, ed., *The British Museum Book of Chinese Art* (London: Thames and Hudson, 1992), fig. 133. See also Craig S. Korr, "A Note on the Geographical Distribution of Carved Ivory in the Late Second Millennium B.C.," *American Journal of Archaeology* 88, no. 3 (July 1984), 402–403.

42 *used for work and for war* Edward H. Schafer, "War Elephants in Ancient and Medieval China," *Oriens* 10, no. 2 (December 31, 1957), pp. 290–291.

42 *China's growing human population diminished the herds through habitat loss* "The retreat of the elephants maps *in reverse*, both in space and time, the growth of the Chinese farm economy"; Mark Elvin, *The Retreat of the Elephants: An Environmental History of China* (New Haven and London: Yale University Press, 2004), p. 17.

43 *second only to jade* Jade was so highly regarded it was imbued with moral qualities.

43 *an entire bed* Later poets such as Ku Hsiung (Gu Xiong) would employ the imagery of an ivory bed (literally, "elephant bed") as befitting "a royal or divine bedroom." See Suzanne Cahill, "Sex and the Supernatural in Medieval China: Cantos on the Transcendent Who Presides over the River," *Journal of the American Oriental Society* 105, no. 2 (April–January 1985), pp. 197–220.

43 *a Roman embassy to Emperor Huan* These Romans may have been adventurous merchants masquerading as ambassadors.

43 *Romans thought silk grew on trees* Silkworm culture remained a near monopoly of the Chinese until silkworm eggs were brought to Byzantium during the reign of Justinian, in 530 CE.

43 *Seneca . . . sniffed* *Declamations*, vol. 1.

44 *an ivory chair* It had the form of a curule chair, the traditional low-armed, backless, folding seat from which Roman authorities ruled.

44 *it was a fixture in triumphs* See Peter J. Holliday, "Roman Triumphal Painting: Its Function, Development, and Reception," *Art Bulletin* (March 1, 1997), pp. 130–47.

44 *Chariots, couches . . . and the useful* strigil During Constantine's reign there were said to be seventy ivory statues in Rome; Albizzati, "Two Ivory Fragments," p. 401. On use of ivory in furniture, see Dorothy Kent Hill, "Ivory Ornaments of Hellenistic Couches," *Hesperia* 32, no. 3 (July–September 1963), pp. 292–300.

44 "The flesh, or what so seems"   Book X, *Metamorphoses* (1 CE). English translation by Sir Samuel Garth, John Dryden, et al. (1713).

45 *Historian Anthony Cutler*   Cutler, *The Craft of Ivory*, p. 22. This section closely follows Cutler's detailed analysis of ivory trade routes and craft.

46 *the famous Symmachi panel*   At one point the panel came under suspicion as a forgery, but the evidence in support of its authenticity is clearly defensible. See Dale Kinney, "A Late Antique Ivory Plaque and Modern Response," *American Journal of Archaeology* 98, no. 3 (July 1994), pp. 457–80, with a postscript by Anthony Cutler.

46 *the tradition for Roman consuls*   The common iconography of sixth-century diptychs is discussed in Nancy Netzer, "Redating the Consular Ivory of Orestes," *Burlington Magazine* 125, no. 962 (May 1983), pp. 265–71. See also Kim Bowes, "Ivory Lists: Consular Diptychs, Christian Appropriation and Polemics of Time in Late Antiquity," *Art History* 24, no. 3 (June 2001), pp. 338–57.

46 *laws had to be passed*   In 384 CE; Cutler, *The Craft of Ivory*, p. 52. See also Alan Cameron, "A Note on Ivory Carving in Fourth Century Constantinople," *American Journal of Archaeology* 86, no. 1 (January 1982), pp. 126–29.

47 *"many an elephant go shorn of the glory of his tusks"*   Book III, *On the Consulship of Stilico*, from the 1922 Loeb Classical Library translation.

47 *Pliny the Elder contemplated the eradication*   Pliny devoted thirteen chapters of his *Historia Naturalis* to elephants. He claimed, in chapter 4 of Book 8 of that text, that "Large teeth, in fact, are now rarely found, except in India, the demands of luxury having exhausted all those in our part of the world."

48 *"showered curses on Pompey"*   Book 8, chapter 7, *Historia Naturalis*, translated by John Bostock and H. T. Riley, 1855.

48 *Cutler soberly concludes*   Cutler, *The Craft of Ivory*, p. 24.

3. THE MASTER CARVERS' MEDIUM

Archer St. Clair and Elizabeth Parker McLachlan, eds., *The Carver's Art: Medieval Sculpture in Ivory, Bone, and Horn* (New Brunswick, N.J.: Zimmerli Art Museum, Rutgers, 1989); Paul Williamson, *An Introduction to Medieval Ivory Carvings* (London: Her Majesty's Stationery Office, 1982); Abdul Sheriff, *Slaves, Spices and Ivory in Zanzibar* (London: James Currey et al., 1987); Edward Alpers, *Ivory and Slaves* (Berkeley and Los Angeles: University of California Press, 1975); and Klaus Maurice, *Sovereigns as Turners: Materials on a Machine Art by Princes*, translated by Dorothy Ann Schade (Zurich: Verlag Ineichen, 1985), were invaluable guides to this period.

49 *colorful, elaborate chart*   Reproduced in Oscar I. Norwich, *Maps of Southern Africa* (Johannesburg: AD. Donker [Pty] Ltd., 1993), pp. 44–45.

49 *Arab geographer al-Masudi*   Quoted in Sheriff, *Slaves, Spices and Ivory*, p. 78.

50 *"In the days of sati"*   Ibid. After the sixth century, India was not able to produce enough ivory from local sources for its own needs; demand for African ivory persisted into the the twentieth century. See also Alpers, *Ivory and Slaves*, pp. 86–87.

50 *Chinese officials . . . used ivory tablets*   Much the way consuls of Byzantium did; Cutler, *The Craft of Ivory*, p. 53, citing J. Needham, *Science and Civilization in*

China, IV.i (Cambridge University Press, 1959), p. 321. The evidence for use of ivory tablets in China is complex and not always clear (Mark Elvin, pers. comm.).

51 *"eight thousand pounds"*   Cutler, *The Craft of Ivory*, p. 51.

51 *and caskets to hold perfumes*   Mariam Rosser-Owen, "Ivories from Spain," in Tim Stanley et al., *Palace and Mosque* (London: Victoria and Albert Publications, 2004), pp. 80–81.

51 *A pyxis . . . shows a seated figure*   This container (Victoria and Albert: 368–1880) dates from 970; reproduced ibid., p. 80.

51 *an inscription on the lid*   Quoted ibid., p. 78. This pyxis (ca. 968) is reproduced in Francisco Prado-Vilar, "Circular Visions of Fertility and Punishment: Caliphal Ivory Caskets from Al-Andalus," *Muqarnas* XIV (1997), p. 22. Many of these Muslim ivories from Spain owe their survival to their being put to use as reliquaries in Spanish cathedrals, sometimes with their Arabic inscriptions erased.

52 *lingered on in the secular art*   The survival of classicism in Byzantine art has been evidenced by finds from twentieth-century excavations in Russia. See Robin Cormack et al., *The Road to Byzantium: Luxury Arts of Antiquity* (London: Fontanka, 2006).

53 *a demanding craft whose traditions and skills were centuries old*   Ivory workers in Constantinople had even been exempted by edict from civil obligations in order to perfect their craft. For more detail on methods, see Anthony Cutler, "The Making of the Justinian Diptychs," *Byzantion* 54 (1984), pp. 79 and 81.

54 *when there wasn't enough costlier ivory*   See the discussion in St. Clair and McLachlan, *The Carver's Art*, pp. 7–10.

54 *gyrfalcons and walrus ivory*   Jared Diamond, *Collapse: How Societies Choose to Fail or Survive* (London: Allen Lane, 2005), p. 241.

54 *walrus tusks provided . . . nearly all the ivory*   Williamson, *Introduction to Medieval Ivory Carvings*, p. 17.

55 *carved ivory plaques . . . now in the Louvre*   These elephant ivory plaques were used as book covers; MR 372–3 Louvre.

56 *The Lewis chessmen*   The tallest pieces are about four inches in height. Virtually all are made of walrus ivory, a few from whale teeth. The majority are now in the British Museum; the Hebrides were subject to Norway in the 1200s.

56 *"By turning to the art of the ivory carver"*   Williamson, *Introduction to Medieval Ivory Carving*, p. 5.

56 *"ivory was a synonym for the chastity"*   Aleksander Pluskowski, "Narwhals or Unicorns? Exotic Animals as Material Culture in Medieval Europe," *European Journal of Archaeology* vol. 7, no. 3 (2004), p. 305.

57 *"The richer the patron, the grander the object"*   Williamson, *Introduction to Medieval Ivory Carving*, p. 18.

57 *a kind of Gothic contrapposto*   This sinuous line or S-curve has also been called the "Gothic sway."

57 *Fancy ones were made of ivory*   See Richard H. Randall, "A Group of Gothic Ivory Boxes," *Burlington Magazine* 127, no. 990 (September 1985), pp. 577–81, 583.

57 *visual cat-and-mouse game*   All this implies self-conscious artistry. See C. Jean Campbell, "Courting, Harlotery and the Art of Gothic Ivory Carving," *Gesta* 34, no. 1 (1995), pp. 11–19.

58 *the tusk is a great curiosity of nature*   William I. Broad, "It's Sensitive. Really," *New York Times*, December 13, 2005. Some ten million nerve endings connect the outer surface of the tusk to its inner core, making the tusk a sensory organ whose purpose is not yet fully understood.

58 *doges of Venice and the Hapsburg emperors*   "Perhaps the most impressive object to incorporate narwhal tusks is the seventeenth-century royal throne of Denmark, now in Rosenborg Castle, Copenhagen." Arthur MacGregor, *Bone, Antler, Ivory and Horn* (London and Sydney: Croom Helm, 1985), p. 43.

59 *test the dishes he was served*   Pluskowski, "Narwhals or Unicorns?" p. 300. The duke's *Ainkhürnschwert* ("unicorn sword"), with its hilt of narwhal ivory, is in the Imperial Treasury in Vienna.

59 *a "fish's tooth 'three palms long' "*   Charles Nicholl, *Leonardo da Vinci: Flights of the Mind* (New York: Penguin, 2004) p. 326. "Fish-tooth" was a common term for walrus ivory. See Berthold Laufer, *Ivory in China* (Chicago: Field Museum of Natural History, 1925), pp. 48–49.

59 *"many I perceive suspect an Imposture"*   Chapter XXIII, "Of Unicorns Horn," *Pseudodoxia Epidemica* (1646; 6th edition, 1672).

60 *sent an African elephant to Henry III*   Phillip Drennon Thomas, "The Tower of London's Royal Menagerie," *History Today* 46 (August 1996).

60 *ears that unfolded like a lady's fan*   "De Elephanto," p. 410 in Conrad Gesner, *Historia animalium* (Zurich: Apvd Christ. Froschovervm, 1551–87).

61 *a dizzying geometric pattern of ebony and ivory zigzags*   Notably the 1623 guitar Sellas made for the grand duke of Tuscany's household, now in the Victoria and Albert museum (no. 7356–1861).

61 *Nuremberg . . . became famous . . . for its ivory sundials*   To mention just one: the portable diptych sundial (ca. 1598) by Hans Troschel the Elder in the Metropolitan Museum of Art (03.21.38).

61 *Ornate ivory flea traps*   The first such traps, they were the brainchild of Franz Ernst Brückmann, a German physician.

62 *"fingers white as ivory"*   Nicholl, *Leonardo da Vinci*, p. 111. Alas, the lower half of the portrait (now in the National Gallery of Art, Washington, D.C.), which presumably would have included the famous hands, was at some point chopped off.

62 *mammoth ivory . . . reached London by 1616*   Stone, *Mammoth*, p. 81.

63 *Emperor Kangxi . . . reminded his audience*   W. F. Mayers, "The Mammoth in Chinese Records," *China Review* VI (July 1877–June 1878), p. 274.

63 *evidence of unicorns*   Leibniz himself considered this idea. See the chapter "Leibniz's Unicorn" in Cohen, *The Fate of the Mammoth*, pp. 41–60.

64 *trade in tusks from the tundra*   Some sediments in Siberia may contain six hundred mammoth skeletons per square kilometer; see Stone, *Mammoth*, p. 69.

65 *The trade vastly increased*   Alpers, "The Ivory Trade in Africa," pp. 352–53.

65 *These riches — gold, ivory, and slaves — traded places in importance*   See Robert W. Harms, *River of Wealth, River of Sorrow: The Central Zaire Basin in the Era of the Slave and Ivory Trade, 1500–1891* (New Haven and London: Yale University Press, 1981), pp. 39–40.

65 *tusks . . . key to obtaining prized European imports*   Harvey M. Feinberg and

Marion Johnson, "The West African Ivory Trade During the Eighteenth Century: The '. . . and Ivory' Complex," *International Journal of African Historical Studies* 15, no. 3 (1982), pp. 435–53, 452.

66 *"more elephants in Guinea than . . . cattle in . . . Europe"*   Quoted in Meredith, *Elephant Destiny*, p. 55.

66 *"an urban, and even subtly racist myth"*   John A. Van Couvering, "Proboscideans, Hominids, and Prehistory," in Ross, *Elephant*, p. 75.

67 *The late-eighteenth-century Scottish explorer Mungo Park*   Mungo Park, *Travels in the Interior Districts of Africa* (London: Eland, 1983; reprint of 1816 edition), p. 237.

68 *Elephants and their ivory were of great importance in . . . African societies*   The richness of African ivory traditions is reviewed in considerable detail in Ross, *Elephant*.

68 *Among the African products that the Portuguese took back to Europe*   See Suzanne Preston Blier's study, "Imaging Otherness in Ivory: African Portrayals of the Portuguese ca. 1492," *Art Bulletin* 75, no. 3 (September, 1993), pp. 375–96.

69 *and took so much of it away in ivory and slaves*   In 1897 a British delegation was ambushed en route to the *oba's* palace; in retaliation, the British sent the *oba* into exile and burned the palaces but not before removing two thousand pieces of art, which can now be seen in many of the world's museums.

70 *"great quantities of English patterns"*   Quoted in John M. Driggers et al., "Treatment of an Ivory-Inlaid Anglo-Indian Desk Bookcase," p. 1. See http://aic.stanford.edu/sg/wag/1991/WAG_91_driggers.pdf.

70 *exquisitely carved solid ivory chair*   Given to Warren Hastings by Mani Begum of Murshidabad in the late eighteenth century; in the collection of the Victoria and Albert Museum.

70 *the leading producer of Christian art in ivory*   See *Power+Faith+Image: Philippine Art in Ivory from the 16th to the 19th Century*, catalogue of the 2005 exhibition, Ayala Museum, Makati City, Philippines.

70 *the seven extraordinary armadas*   Jonathan Mirsky, "China at Sea," *Times Literary Supplement*, January 24, 2007.

71 *crop-ravaging nuisances*   Up to the Ming period, however, some regarded them as useful in warfare; see Elvin's *The Pattern of the Chinese Past* (Stanford, Calif.: Stanford University Press, 1973), p. 93.

72 *The Pursuit of Pleasure in the Course of the Seasons*   See Efrat El-Hanany, "Sex in the Imperial Garden," *Apollo Magazine*, March 1, 2005.

72 *the Japanese were late to ivory*   See the detailed acount in Esmond Bradley Martin, *The Japanese Ivory Industry* (Tokyo: World Wildlife Fund–Japan, 1985).

74 *"such a length . . . of animated ivory!"*   John Cleland, *Memoirs of a Woman of Pleasure* (New York: G. P. Putnam's Sons, 1963 reprint), p. 85.

76 *a treaty*   The Treaty of Nerchinsk, 1690. The silks are now in the Palazzo Pitti. See Kirsten Aschengreen Piacenti, "Developments in the Textile Collections in Palazzo Pitti," *Burlington Magazine* 126, no. 975 (June 1984), p. 340.

77 *the later addition of the flywheel*   Joseph Conners, "Ars Tornandi: Baroque Architecture and the Lathe," *Journal of the Warbourg and Courtauld Institutes* 53 (1990), p. 218.

78 *lamented a diplomat*   Friedrich Carl Moser, 1751, quoted in Maurice, *Sovereigns as Turners*, p. 23–24.

78 *an enormous amount of ivory was brought into Europe*   In the late eighteenth century Tranquebar, a colony founded by the Danish East India Company, supplied the Danish court with ivory. In 1782 the director of the royal art cabinet wrote that "several thousand tusks, some weighing between 100 and 125 pounds, had come to Copenhagen in the past few years." These weights point to ivory of African origin.

79 *pièces excentriques*   Conners, "Ars Tornàdi," p. 223.

79 *Charles Plumier*   Plumier was also one of the greatest botanists of his time. He named the begonia, the magnolia, and the fuchia and made three expeditions to the Americas; he died while setting out on a fourth, in 1704; ibid., p. 225.

79 *the possibility of the modern factory was born*   "It is in the nature of things that only after the manufacture of commodities by machinery had attained a certain extent did the need to produce the machinery itself by machines make itself felt." Karl Marx, *Collected Works of Marx and Engels*, vol. 33, p. 390 (New York: International Publishers, 1991), p. 390.

4. PIANO KEYS AND BILLIARD BALLS

Much of the material in this chapter is drawn from company records and other materials on the Connecticut ivory industry held at the Connecticut River Museum in Essex and the nearby Ivoryton Library Association, as well as in the archives of the Smithsonian Institution's National Museum of American History in Washington, D.C. Two texts in particular helped flesh out the story: Robbi Storms and Don Malcarne, *Around Essex: Elephants and River Gods* (Charleston, S.C.: Arcadia Publishing, 2001); and Don Malcarne, Edith DeForest, and Robbi Storms, *Deep River and Ivoryton* (Charleston, S.C.: Arcadia Publishing, 2002).

83 *Pratt . . . was issued a U.S. patent*   Malcarne et al., *Deep River and Ivoryton*, pp. 47–49. The first British patent for a comb-cutting machine dates from about 1808. See Fiona St. Aubyn, ed., *Ivory: An International History and Illustrated Survey* (New York: Harry N. Abrams, 1987), p. 140.

84 *Although very difficult to burn*   Teeth are often the only recognizable remaining parts of a burned corpse, hence their importance for forensic investigations.

84 *a smell the workers described as "animal"*   That whiff—difficult to elicit but unmistakable—provides one of the tests for genuine ivory: heat a needle until red hot, then stick it into the base of, say, an ivory chess piece and it will barely penetrate; give it a quick sniff it and it says *tooth*. If it turns out to be a case of mistaken identity and the pawn is pure plastic, the synthetic will curdle and blacken around the needle point and reveal the deception by a telltale chemical stench.

84 *Ezra Williams had set up his own comb business*   George S. Roberts, *Historic Towns of the Connecticut River Valley* (Schenectady, N.Y.: Robson and Adee, ca. 1906), pp. 56–57.

84 *an increasingly steady stream of African tusks*   Storms and Malcarne, *Around Essex*, p. 22. Ivory was first brought into the United States in the eighteenth century, perhaps earlier, in the form of personal effects.

84 *the world's largest producers of ivory goods*   Pratt-Read Corporation Records, 1839–1990, Smithsonian Archives, AC NMAH 320 [296]. See the discussion in Malcarne et al., *Deep River and Ivoryton*, p. 47.

85 *Comstock "was a man of enlarged views"*   Beers, *History of Middlesex County*, 1885, p. 363.

86 *A photograph from that year*   Malcarne et al., *Deep River and Ivoryton*, pp. 28–29.

86 *scores of factory houses for workers*   Storms and Malcarne, *Around Essex*, pp. 56 and 69. Between 1871 and 1925 the company built 135 small houses for its workers.

86 *even the outhouses had ivory doorknobs*   Moore, *Ivory: Scourge*, p. 235.

87 *the colossi of the ivory-cutting industry worldwide*   The two firms ended up dwarfing ivory-cutting firms in New York and Buffalo; Wood and Brooks Company in the latter city had also specialized in ivory for piano keys.

87 *90 percent of the ivory imported into the United States*   Malcarne, "Ivoryton, Connecticut: The Ivory Industry and Voluntary and Involuntary Migration in the Late Nineteenth Century," *North American Archaeologist* 22, no. 3 (2001), p. 286.

87 *the handles of . . . corkscrews*   Bernard M. Watney and Homer D. Babbage, *Corkscrews for Collectors* (London and New York: Sotheby Park Bernet, 1981), pp. 24–25, 153.

88 *scrimshaw*   The practice is thought to have begun on whaling voyages in the Pacific in the 1820s. The smaller teeth of killer whales (orcas) also allow for modest scrimshaw.

88 *used to carve sacred figures in Fiji*   T. T. Barrow, "Human Figures in Wood and Ivory from Western Polynesia," *Man* 56 (December 1956), pp. 165–68; Aubrey L. Parke, "The Waimaro Carved Human Figures—Carvings from Cachalot Whale Teeth in Fiji," *Journal of Pacific History* (September 1997).

89 *Before being sent to the ivory-cutting department*   This description follows the outline of the process given in Edith DeForest's "Ivory Cutting Routine" and "Review of Ivory Shop Routine," unpublished mss. in the Ivoryton Library Association. The exact details of these procedures were considered trade secrets and handed down orally from worker to worker. See also Anne Farrow, "After Africa: The Transformation of a Tusk," *Hartford Courant*, Complicity: Northeast Magazine Special Issue, September 29, 2002, p. 64.

89 *"each workman actually fondles and caresses it."*   Quoted in Richard Conniff, "When the Music in Our Parlors Brought Death to Darkest Africa," *Audubon* (July 1987), p. 86.

89 *Ivory had become the plastic of its age*   The staggering variety of ivory goods produced is covered in detail in Benjamin Burack, *Ivory and Its Uses* (Rutland and Tokyo: Charles E. Tuttle, 1984).

90 *never been a significant tradition of hand-carved ivory*   Fine crafts firms such as Tiffany's and Gorham's employed descendants of European craftsmen for their necessary ivory work; St. Aubyn, *Ivory*, p. 312.

90 *These droll, tiny-footed odalisques*   Compare the coy figure shown in Kunz, *Ivory and the Elephant* (opposite p. 125), with the come-hither model in Gröning, *Elephants*, p. 381.

91 *ivory as an insulator of electrical current*   David H. Shayt, "The Material Culture of Ivory Outside Africa," in Ross, *Elephant*, p. 376.

91 *even a cosmetic ivory penis* George M. Gould, M.D., and Walter L. Pyle, M.D., *Anomolies and Curiosities of Medicine* (Philadelphia: W. B. Saunders, 1896), Chapter XIII, p. 681.

91 *nasal implants* B. Vilar-Sancho, "An Old Story: An Ivory Nasal Implant," *Aesthetic Plastic Surgery* 11, no. 3 (1987), pp. 157–61.

91 *an 1864 advertisement for ivory* Harvey and Ford, Dealers in Ivory, from an 1864 New York State Business Directory, p. 178; author's files.

91 *the elephant . . . in U.S. circuses of the period* See Shana Alexander, *The Astonishing Elephant* (New York: Random House, 2000), pp. 105–7, 111.

92 *"and trained to wipe its eyes on cue"* Ibid., pp. 117, 120–21.

92 *A sheet of ivory . . . fifty-two feet long* The figure of fifty-two feet was claimed in J. Pratt, *Centennial of Meriden* (Meriden, Conn., 1909). Pratt mentioned "scroll-cut ivory" in his specification for U.S. Patent No. 42,507 of April 26, 1864, which described his "improvement in ivory-covered books."

92 *A thin ivory plate . . . was an ideal "canvas"* Caroline Taylor, "Miniature American Portraits on Ivory Embody Feelings of Love, Loss and Separation," *Inside Smithsonian Research*, no. 7 (Winter 2005), p. 10.

93 *"tones of the ivory to represent the hue of the skin."* Kunz, *Ivory and the Elephant*, p. 85.

93 *ivory veneers made large sheets available* In the mid-nineteenth century, two kinds of ivory plates were available: small ones called "leaf" ivory showing "mackerel marks" if not cut close to the center of the tusk and "twist" ivory—"so called from its being cut by a saw working vertically, whilst the tooth or tusk is pressed hard against it at an acute angle; the result is, that by the tooth being made to revolve, a sheet of ivory is obtained, far larger than can be cut transversely from even the largest teeth, and possessing also the important advantage of having no grain or mackerel mark in it. But there is another side of the question; this ivory is so much more expensive than the other, that where only small pictures, say not more than 3¼ by 4½, are to be produced, few would incline to pay the price." Samuel Fry, "Printing on Ivory," *Photographic News* (London), April 12, 1861, p. 171.

93 *Page-sized sheets cut from tusk cylinders also had a tendency to curl* Kunz warns that "such ivory flattened never loses its tendency to regain its original shape, and in consequence can only be used when mounted solidly with moisture-proof glue or cement." *Ivory and the Elephant*, p. 88.

93 *Goya managed to compress onto small plaques of ivory* "Goya's Last Works," an exhibition at the Frick Museum, New York, February 22 to May 14, 2006; exhibition catalogue of the same name by Jonathan Brown and Susan Grace Galassi (New Haven: Yale University Press, 2006).

93 *Sarah Goodridge* See Chris Packard, "Self-Fashioning in Sarah Goodridge's Self-Portraits," *Common-Place* 4, no. 1 (October 2003).

93 *Her coolly confident* Self-Portrait 3¾ inches × 2⅝ inches (9.52 × 6.73 cm); collection Museum of Fine Arts, Boston (95.1424).

94 *"We are yours for the taking, in all our ivory loveliness"* John Updike, "The Revealed and the Concealed," in his *More Matter: Essays and Criticism* (New York: Knopf, 1999), p. 715.

94 *"like a sugar-drop at the back of his mouth"* Ibid., p. 716.

95 *some 70 percent . . . was bought for other markets*   J. R. McCulloch, Esq., *A Dictionary, Practical, Theoretical, and Historical, of Commerce and Commercial Navigation* (London: Longman, Green, Longman, and Roberts, new edition, 1859), pp. 785–86; Kunz, *Ivory and the Elephant*, p. 458. Some 4,900 tons of raw ivory entered the United States from 1884 through 1911: about 175 tons a year. But the United States reexported only a small amount of worked ivory.

95 *its own newly mechanized ivory industry*   By 1851 comb making was completely industrialized in Aberdeen, Scotland; one firm employed six hundred workers. St. Aubyn, *Ivory*, p. 140.

95 *"ivory generally retains its overall form and finish"*   Shayt, "Material Culture of Ivory," p. 373.

95 *twenty-six tons of better grade ivory in its vaults*   Kunz, *Ivory and the Elephant*, p. 413.

96 *Renoir's favorite formulation of the color*   Victoria Finlay, *Color: A Natural History of the Palette* (New York: Random House, 2004), p. 102.

96 *"I shall look upon it as an altar"*   From the letter of February 7, 1818, reproduced in http://www.uk-piano.org/broadwood/lvb_wood.html.

97 *"The Piano-Forte is a badge of gentility"*   Quoted in Gary J. Kornblith, "The Craftsman as Industrialist: Jonas Chickering and the Transformation of American Piano-Making," *Business History Review*, 69, no. 3 (Autumn 1985), p. 353; emphases in the original.

97 *"The piano in the parlor . . . helped create it"*   Conniff, "Music in Our Parlors," p. 85.

98 *"it is yielding to the touch, yet firm"*   Moore, *Ivory: Scourge*, p. 222.

98 *was only the first stage of the process*   See David H. Shayt, "Elephant Under Glass: The Piano Key Bleach House of Deep River, Connecticut," *Journal of the Society for Industrial Archaeology* 19, no. 1 (1993).

99 *It was critical to know that these pieces came from the same tusk*   "The matchers essentially sought to create within a single horizontal plane what had existed vertically and in circular form within the tusk." Ibid., p. 52.

100 *Billiards became one of the few important indoor sports*   Robert Friedel, *Pioneer Plastic: The Making and Selling of Celluloid* (Madison: University of Wisconsin Press, 1983), p. 34.

101 *billiards was available at fifty-seven licensed locations in Paris*   These historical details are drawn from *William Hendricks' History of Billiards* (Roxana, Ill.: self-published, 1974; revised 1977), p. iv. See also Mike Shamos, "Which Came First?" *Billiards Digest* (August 1999), pp. 141–44.

101 *with a key "that never left her possession"*   Quoted in Victor Stein and Paul Rubino, *The Billiard Encyclopedia: An Illustrated History of the Sport* (New York: Billiard Encyclopedia, 1994), p. 230.

101 *Phelan won . . . with a run of forty-six balls*   Rick Kogan, *Brunswick: The Story of an American Company from 1845 to 1985* (Skokie, Ill.: Brunswick Corporation, 1985), pp. 12–13.

102 *"The game of billiards has destroyed my naturally sweet disposition"*   From a speech, April 24, 1906. The house Twain built in Hartford, Connecticut, has a splendid billiards room and study on the third floor, where he wrote many of his best-known works.

102 *thirty billiard tables, four of which were reserved for ladies' use* Godfrey Harris, *The Fascination of Ivory: Its Place in Our World* (Los Angeles: Americas Group, 1991), p. 52.

102 *three million people in the United States played the game each day* "Wanted— Substitute for Ivory for Billiard Balls," *Illustrated World* XXXII, no. 6 (February 1920), p. 926. The Chicago publication states that there were 50,000 "rooms" (pool halls) with an average of half a dozen tables each, which would require 60,000 new balls a year.

102 *"ivory was not only preferred, but required"* Friedel, *Pioneer Plastic*, p. 34.

102 *George C. Britner . . . made the balls for a number of championship matches* J. G. Davis, "George C. Britner, Billiard Ball Maker," *Montgomery Advertiser*, December 1, 1911. Britner worked for Brunswick-Balke-Collender in Chicago from 1878 until his retirement. Comstock, Cheney supplied balls to Brunswick.

103 *Each cylinder of ivory was clamped and turned on a lathe* T. A. Marchmay, "Making Billiard Balls from Ivory," *Scientific American Monthly* (April 1921), pp. 316–68.

103 *a "good ball" would "pass muster"* Quoting Frank Buckland in Major W. Broadfoot et al., *Billiards* (London and Bombay: Longmans, Green, and Co., 1896), p. 90.

103 *the best a billiard ball maker could hope for* Compared with the two thousand or more piano keys one might get from a large tusk.

103 *"never-ending complaints of members on the subject of balls"* Broadfoot, *Billiards*, p. 88.

105 *"Hyatt set out on his experiments"* Friedel, *Pioneer Plastic*, pp. 29–30.

105 *which made everyone in the room draw his gun* Ibid., p. 35.

105 *"the click of them is dull and harsh"* Riso Levi, *Billiards for the Million* (Manchester: Riso Levi, 1920), p. 118.

105 *ivory was used for . . . billiards events until the 1990s* In 1991 the Conservatoire Internationale de Billard Artistique (CIBA) stopped requiring ivory balls. Shayt, "Material Culture," p. 381n.

105 *"a long-standing objective of nineteeth-century inventors"* Friedel, *Pioneer Plastic*, p. 29.

106 *"the destructive war, carried on of late against elephants"* Quoted ibid., pp. 30–31; the dealer was probably H. A. Meyer of Germany.

106 *"At first thought, some thin-skinned person"* Quoted in Elizabeth Holmes, "On the Tusks of a Dilemma," *Billiards Digest* (December 1990), p. 72.

5. "A TOOTH OF IVORY AND A SLAVE TO CARRY IT"

The Ernst D. Moore Collection 1888–1932 in the archives of the Smithsonian Institution's National Museum of American History in Washington, D.C., includes Moore's diary, business records, photographs, and other ivory-related material. Anne Farrow's chapter, "Plunder for Pianos," in Farrow, Joel Lang, and Jenifer Frank, *Complicity: How the North Promoted, Prolonged, and Profited from Slavery* (New York: Ballantine Books, 2005), is a concise summation of the human cost of Connecticut's ivory industry.

107 *"A Tooth of Ivory and a Slave to Carry It"* "It is the custom to buy a tooth of ivory and a slave with it to carry it to the sea shore," noted Michael W. Shepard, on a trading voyage to Zanzibar in 1844. Conniff, "Music in Our Parlors," p. 81.

107 *"Ivory first, child afterwards!"*   Alfred J. Swann, *Fighting the Slave-Hunters in Central Africa* (London: Seeley and Co., 1910), pp. 48–49; emphasis in the original.

107 *Swann was not a completely disinterested observer*   James B. Wolf, review of *Fighting the Slave-Hunters in Central Africa* by Alfred J. Swann, in *African Historical Studies* 3, no. 2 (1970), pp. 499–502.

108 *"The arrival of Tippoo, with tons and tons of ivory"*   Moore, *Ivory: Scourge*, pp. 116–17. Tippu Tip arrived in Zanzibar in 1882; he sold his ivory for £30,000.

109 *"Stories of adventures in Africa"*   "Bwana-Pembi—The Ivory Master," *Hartford Daily Courant*, September 21, 1930.

109 *the largest ivory importing firm in the United States*   Arnold, Cheney and Co., established in 1849, had its head office at 158 Water Street (and later 82–92 Beaver Street) in New York. Rufus Greene of Providence carried on East African trade in his own ships, in partnership with two brothers, W. S. and B. R. Arnold; Greene, Arnold and Co. would become Arnold, Hine and Co., and finally Arnold, Cheney.

109 *"I dare say I held in my own hands"*   Moore, *Ivory: Scourge*, p. xvi.

109 *I met Richard Moore*   October 24, 2004.

111 *"Worked hard today"*   Ernst Moore, diary, October 6, 1907.

111 *"pick up the threads of the local business"*   Letter of D.M. to E.D.M. ("Hans"), September 19, 1907.

111 *"I am in the midst of historical scenes"*   Moore, diary, November 5, 1907.

112 *"We get the stuff away tomorrow all right"*   Moore, diary, October 26/27, 1907.

112 *"throw that million dollars a year sales into the rear"*   J. Jones to G. L. Cheney, September 4, 1907; Cheney-Downing Collection Archive, Connecticut River Museum.

112 *"We ought to buy at least 20,000 lbs."*   Ibid., October 5, 1907.

113 *"Everybody seems to like it here"*   Moore, diary, December 17 to 20, 1908.

113 *"rubbing the varnish off the chairs at the Club"*   Moore, diary, April 7, 1908.

113 *"It has a more compact texture within the tusk"*   E. D. Moore, "Jewels of the Noble Elephant," *Asia* (November 1931), p. 720.

114 *"If I don't have a nightmare with a long prehensile nose tonight"*   Moore, diary, March 2, 1909.

114 *"the art of juggling prices, grades, and proportions"*   Moore, *Ivory: Scourge*, p. 238.

114 *had spies count the tusks*   Ibid., p. 239.

114 *"there was a trick to be uncovered"*   Ibid., p. 238.

114 *British East African government ivory auctions*   Moore, diary, May 26, 1909. An entry of August 18, 1909, reads, "Ivory auction on today. The way the BEA [British East African] Govt. corrals it is a caution. They simply take it from the native, whether he likes it or not, but soften the confiscation at the rate of four rupees a pound. I wish we could get it for that figure. 100% in ivory makes a nice little profit."

114 *An old photograph of one such auction*   Moore, *Ivory: Scourge*, p. 240.

115 *"We're the kingpin ivory wallahs in these parts"*   Moore, diary, January 28, 1909.

115 *"Our score is twenty or more"*   Ibid., August 27, 1909.

115 *he finds they've shipped 1,034 tusks of ivory*   Ibid., February 5, 1910.

115 *"if we paid more than Childs & Co. . . . were offering"* Arnold, Cheney to Moore, December 8, 1909.

116 *"I traded for ivory in Arabic"* "By E. D. Moore," untitled, undated autobiographical typescript, copy in author's files, p. 2.

116 *TR in jodhpurs, speaking with Moore* Smithsonian Archives, 89–4279.

116 *"shores are simply lined with the thickest . . . palms"* Moore, diary, February 18, 1909.

117 *"Gee whiz, but I am stuck on Zanzibar"* Ibid., February 20–24, 1909.

117 *Arab merchants shifted much of the ivory trading* Alpers, "The Ivory Trade," p. 356.

117 *ivory was for a time transported by camel caravan* Marion Johnson, "By Ship or Camel: The Struggle for the Cameroons Ivory Trade in the Nineteenth Century," *Journal of African History* 19, no. 4 (1978), p. 540.

118 *ivory trading links between the Lake Nyasa region . . . and Indian traders* Alpers, "The Ivory Trade," p. 354; see also his *Ivory and Slaves*, p. 104.

118 *East African coast . . . the focus of intensified European . . . demand* In the first two decades of the nineteenth century, some 70 percent of British ivory imports came from West Africa; by 1840 the percentage from that region had been cut in half.

118 *Ivory trading there was in full swing* R. W. Beachey, "The East African Ivory Trade in the Nineteenth Century," *Journal of African History* 8, no. 2 (1967), p. 270.

118 *"the El Dorado of ivory seekers"* H. M. Stanley, "Explorations in Central Africa," reprinted in the *Journal of the American Geographical Society of New York* 7 (1875), p. 274.

119 *This drew . . . men away from traditional labor* Alpers, "The Ivory Trade," p. 356.

119 *one Englishman wrote in his diary* "The Zanzibar Diary of John Studdy Leigh, Part II," edited by James S. Kirkman, *International Journal of African Historical Studies* 13, no. 3 (1980), entry for April 14, 1839.

119 *bestowed on the man who could carry the heaviest tusk* Moore, *Ivory: Scourge*, pp. 232–34

119 *"tsetse fly prevented the use of beasts of burden"* Sheriff, *Slaves, Spices and Ivory*, p. 104.

120 *"one caravan in the 1880s carrying 27,000 yards of* merikani" Beachey, "East African Ivory Trade," p. 273.

120 *"The intertwining of ivory porterage and slaving"* Alpers, "The Ivory Trade," p. 356.

121 *"some, to ingratiate themselves with the Arabs, became eager slave-hunters"* Quoted in Melvin E. Page, "The Manyema Hordes of Tippu Tip: A Case Study in Social Stratification and the Slave Trade in Eastern Africa," *International Journal of African Historical Studies* 7, no. 1 (1974), p. 72.

121 *One British observer wrote in his journal* Captain W. D. Stairs, quoted ibid., pp. 72–73.

121 *"These, in turn, make one of the strangers chief"* Quoted ibid., p. 73.

122 *"some one will eat up yours!"* Swann, *Fighting the Slave-Hunters*, pp. 174–75; emphasis in the original.

122 *could not have been ignorant of the use of slaves* "They, perhaps, wished to conveniently ignore what was happening, and/or considered it a 'business' decision." Malcarne, "Ivoryton, Connecticut: The Ivory Industry and Voluntary and Involuntary Migration in the Late Nineteeth Century," *North American Archaeologist* 22, no. 3 (2001), p. 288.

123 *"a fugitive slave was directed from New Haven"* See Conniff, "Music in Our Parlors," pp. 79–81.

123 *"Every tusk . . . has been steeped and dyed in blood"* H. M. Stanley, *In Darkest Africa* (New York: Charles Scribner's Sons, 1891), vol. I, p. 240.

123 *in 1823 the first U.S. ship landed in Zanzibar* Sheriff, *Slaves, Spices and Ivory*, p. 92.

124 *"George has never struck one himself"* Letter of August 4, 1853, quoted in Harriet Cheney Downing, "Tales of Zanzibar," unpublished ms. dated January 5, 1942, copy in author's files. Downing was Sarah Cheney's granddaughter.

124 *Sir Bartle Frere, who had been sent from London* Quoted in Sheriff, *Slaves, Spices and Ivory*, p. 205.

125 *his uncle . . . who knew Tippu Tip well* Moore, *Ivory: Scourge*, p. 145.

126 *German firms secured nearly a quarter of Zanzibar's foreign commerce* W. O. Henderson, "Germany's Trade with Her Colonies, 1884–1914," *Economic History Review* IX, no. I (November 1938).

126 *Stanley was reporting a phalanx of firms* H. M. Stanley, "Explorations in Central Africa," p. 214.

126 *orders for twelve thousand pounds of ivory a month* Norman Robert Bennett, "Americans in Zanzibar: 1865–1915," *Essex Institute Historical Collections* XCVII, no. 1 (January 1962), p. 48.

127 *a single huge shipment of 355 tusks* Ibid., p. 66. In 1896 Bombay imported more than six thousand tusks from Zanzibar, and sixteen hundred packets of small and broken tusks were exported to New York, London, and Hamburg; Beachey, "East African Ivory Trade," p. 288. Much ivory sent to India was reexported to London. See Sheriff, *Slaves, Spices and Ivory*, pp. 85–86.

127 *ten million pounds of raw ivory* Shayt, "Elephant Under Glass," p. 40.

128 *"light-blue hair lines run lengthwise in the tusk"* Moore, "Jewels," p. 720.

128 *"We got a little ivory from Champu Bhanjie"* Moore, diary, October 22, 1910.

129 *overtook Zanzibar in importance as an ivory market* Bennett, "Americans in Zanzibar," p. 61.

129 *daguerreotypes of Egyptian antiquities* Nicolas Monti, *Africa Then: Photographs 1840–1918* (New York: Alfred A. Knopf, 1987), p. 6.

130 *"two valuable bits of dentistry"* Moore, diary, December 28, 1908.

130 *"the greatest price . . . paid for the tusks of a single elephant"* Moore, *Ivory: Scourge*, p. 217.

130 *purchased by the Natural History Museum* Details of how the Kilimanjaro tusks ended up in this collection are given in J. E. Hill, "Record Ivory in the Collection of the British Museum (Natural History)," *Tanganyika Notes and Records*, no. 46 (January 1957). For their time in New York, see Kunz, *Ivory and the Elephant*, pp. 410–11. "Abnormal Elephant Tusk for British Museum," *PLA Monthly* (September 1933), p. 334, confirms their diminishing weights by noting that the museum had acquired a tusk weigh-

ing 214 pounds, which belonged with another of 224 pounds that had been in its possession since 1901.

131 *a striking image of an ivory slave coffle* The illustration is by George Giguéra; Smithsonian Archives, 89–20434.

131 *"we were perfectly content to take what we had"* Hartford Daily Courant, September 21, 1930.

132 *focuses blame squarely on the Swahili middle man* Moore, Ivory: Scourge, p. 247.

132 *"just for a couple of jaw ornaments"* Moore, diary, November 4, 1907.

133 *"bloodstains, dried tissue . . . could not be overlooked"* Moore, "Jewels," p. 719.

133 *"the teeth . . . they find in the woods"* Johnson, "By Ship or Camel," p. 540.

133 *Moore knew better* Moore, "Jewels," p. 719.

134 *thirty thousand African elephants had to have been killed* Moore, Ivory: Scourge, p. 215.

134 *nearly forty-four thousand African elephants were killed annually* See Esmond Bradley Martin's analysis, "The Great White Gold Rush," BBC History (August 2001), pp. 30–32.

134 *He admitted there was no substitute for it* Moore, Ivory: Scourge, p. 222.

135 *"from the viewpoint of an old ivory man"* "By E. D. Moore," typescript, p. 4.

6. IVORY HUNTERS

There is a substantial literature on ivory hunting. Key titles for this chapter include W. D. M. Bell's *The Wanderings of an Elephant Hunter*, cited previously; Richard Tjader, *The Big Game of Africa* (New York and London: D. Appleton and Company, 1910); H. C. Maydon (ed.), *Big Game Shooting in Africa* (London: Seeley, Service and Co., 1932); John Taylor, *Pondoro: Last of the Ivory Hunters* (New York: Simon and Schuster: 1955); J. A. Hunter, *Hunter* (New York: Harper and Brothers, 1952) and Hunter's *Hunter's Tracks* (New York: Appleton-Century-Crofts, 1957).

136 *"in time the space was clear of living elephant"* Bell, Elephant Hunter, p. 102–3.

137 *the first efforts to regulate hunting* See Beachey, "East African Ivory Trade," p. 285.

137 *"now they were forbidden to sell or deliver ivory"* Adam Hochschild, *King Leopold's Ghost* (Boston: Houghton Mifflin, 1998), p. 118.

137 *by backing "penniless adventurers"* Beachey, "East African Ivory Trade," p. 279.

138 *a white tusk had the significance of a death's-head* "This elusive quality it is, which causes the thought of whiteness, when divorced from more kindly associations, and coupled with any object terrible in itself, to heighten that terror to the furthest bounds." Herman Melville, chapter 42, "The Whiteness of the Whale," *Moby Dick* (1851).

138 *before the Sudanese could establish effective control* See W. Robert Foran, "Edwardian Ivory Poachers over the Nile," African Affairs 57, no. 227 (April 1958).

138 *"Ivory would be almost inexhaustible"* Quoted in Beachey, "East African Ivory Trade," pp. 281–82.

138 *top-grade ivory in New York had doubled in price from 1895 to 1905*   Friedel, *Pioneer Plastic*, p. 32. Similarly, prices in London reached $435 per cwt (112 pounds) for whole tusks in 1908; Kunz, *Ivory and the Elephant*, p. 443.

139 *Arthur H. Neumann, another fabled Victorian ivory hunter*   See Arthur H. Neumann, *Elephant-Hunting in East Equatorial Africa* (New York: St. Martin's Press, 1994; reprint of 1898).

140 *it was a high-risk business*   Foran, "Edwardian Ivory Poachers," p. 133.

140 *"sun and putrefaction"*   Bell, *Elephant Hunter*, p. 32.

141 *"like the blossoming of a great opalescent flower"*   John Alfred Jordan, *Elephants and Ivory* (New York: Rinehart, 1956), p. 41.

141 *a two-man saw to split the skull*   One might find strange things in an elephant skull, such as a coconut-sized ball of ivory—a deformed tusk; Jordan, *Elephants and Ivory*, p. 22. There are, very rarely, even four-tusked elephants. See Clare Flemming and Ross D. E. MacPhee, "Four-Tusker!" *Explorers Journal* 83, no. 4 (Winter 2005/2006), p. 48.

142 *"quite equal to any animal in creation"*   See Sir Samuel Baker, "Fifty Years of Rifles," in Kenneth Kemp (ed.), *Tales of the Big Game Hunters*, (London: The Sportsman's Press, 1986), pp. 178–79.

142 *Bell preferred to use a .275 Rigby*   Bell used solid rather than soft-nosed bullets to achieve the required penetration.

142 *Bell's reputation as a crack shot was never questioned*   "Those who have not had much experience elephant hunting cannot be expected to appreciate what an astounding feat it was to kill eight hundred elephant with a .275 (7-millimeter) rifle. I am thoroughly qualified to appreciate it at its true worth, and in view of it I class Bell as the greatest elephant hunter of all time." Taylor, *Pondoro*, p. 41.

143 *"So much for the elephant cemeteries"*   Bell, *Elephant Hunter*, p. 73.

144 *Legal ivory hunting on the grand scale*   In nine months in Lado Bell shot 210 elephants, yielding five tons of ivory. However, he returned to the Sudan in 1912 and in a single day managed to kill nine elephants, collecting 1,463 pounds of ivory worth £900. Meredith, *Elephant Destiny*, p. 106.

144 *"Where are my clothes, boy?"*   Tjader, *Big Game of Africa*, pp. 292–93, 324, 339.

145 *As the game warden of Kenya put it*   Captain A. T. A. Ritchie, "Epitome of Kenya Game Laws," in H. C. Maydon (ed.), *Big Game Shooting in Africa* (London: Seeley, Service and Co., 1932), p. 412.

145 *"I'd take any chance with you behind me, J.A."*   Bartle Bull, *Safari* (New York: Viking, 1988), p. 234.

146 *"I was enough of a Scotsman to like a bargain like that"*   Hunter, *Hunter*, p. 113.

146 *To him it became a familiar story*   Hunter, *Hunter's Tracks* pp. 3–4.

147 *When adult elephants go into* musth   See P. S. Easa, "Musth in Asian Elephants," in Shoshani, *Elephants*, pp. 85–86.

147 *trainers or bystanders . . . extinguished by male elephants in musth*   One particularly ghastly incident occurred on May 5, 1978, when an experienced trainer, Eloise Berchtold, performing with three Asian bulls from the Gatini Circus in Rock Forest, Quebec, tripped in front of Teak, one of the two males in musth. He gored and disemboweled her and hurled her body across the ring in front of horrified spectators. Gröning, *Elephants*, pp. 286–87.

148 *Tusko was eventually purchased*   George "Slim" Lewis and Byron Fish, *I Loved Rogues: The Life of an Elephant Tramp* (Seattle: Superior Publishing Co., 1978), pp. 120–21.

148 *as Robert Friedel explains*   Robert Friedel, "A Material World: An Exhibition at the National Museum of American History" Smithsonian Institution, 1988, p. 34.

149 *cheaper plastics wiped out the tagua trade*   Anne Underwood, "The Good Fake," *International Wildlife* 21, no. 4 (July/August 1991), p. 29.

149 *"Only a New Orleans pimp would carry a pearl-handled gun."*   Quoted in Massad Ayoob, "Handguns of the Generals," *Guns Magazine* (August 2003).

149 *"ivory when warmed by body heat"*   M. G. Shanahan, "Visualizing Africa in Nancy Cunard's Negro Anthology (1934)," *Journal of Colonialism and Colonial History* 6, no. 2 (Fall 2005).

149 *"The hollow of my hand was still ivory-full of Lolita"*   Alfred Appel Jr. (ed.), *The Annotated Lolita* (New York: Vintage, 1991), p. 67.

150 *"99 and 44/100% pure"*   In 1879, Procter & Gamble cofounder Harley Procter found the perfect name for the soap that his company had invented the year before when he heard a minister in church read from Psalms 45:8: "All thy garments smell of myrrh, and aloes, and cassia, out of ivory palaces, whereby they have made thee glad." Ivory's long association with purity, underscored in the twentieth century by the soap's success, has given it a distinctly unsensual overtone; there is even a Christian-oriented "Ivory Club Home Page" ("In Support of Teenage and Young Adult Celibacy and Virginity") on the Internet, at http://diskbooks.org/ivory.html.

151 *Pratt, Read of Deep River could boast sales*   Malcarne, *Legacies of White Gold*, program and guide, May 21, 2006, p. 15; author's files.

152 *the possibility of importing mammoth ivory*   For a description of efforts by UK firms to secure Soviet-era mammoth ivory, see Charlotte and Denis Plimmer, "White Treasure from the Dark Continent," *Saturday Evening Post*, November 24, 1951, p. 73.

152 *a fascinating account of guiding an Indian maharaja*   Hunter recounts the adventure in his *Hunter's Tracks*, pp. 208–40.

152 *the ruler of a southern Indian state*   Peter Beard mentions J. A. Hunter speaking of guiding the "ample Maharaja of Saguia," but that may have been a different client of Hunter's; see Beard's *The End of the Game* (San Francisco: Chronicle Books, revised edition, 1988), pp. 135–37.

7. RESEARCHERS AND POACHERS

This chapter draws on the writings of a number of elephant researchers, Iain Douglas-Hamilton, Cynthia Moss, and Katy Payne among them; Raymond Bonner's incisive *At the Hand of Man: Peril and Hope for Africa's Wildlife* (New York: Vintage, 1993); as well as the extensive media coverage on the anti-ivory campaigns leading up to the 1989 CITES ivory ban.

159 *Drummond fully expected the disappearance of the elephant*   Quoted in Moore, *Ivory: Scourge*, pp. 166–67.

159 *"the brutal hunting of natives"*   F. Bley, German administrator in Africa, 1899, quoted ibid., p. 168.

159 *clearing entire districts of the troublesome giants* Ibid., pp.168–69. Moore cites instances of elephant slaughter during the World War I British invasion of German East Africa (now Tanzania), including bombing by aircraft.

159 *ivory accounted for almost half of export earnings* Bonner, *At the Hand of Man*, p. 48.

160 *"any difficulties in the way of stock-breeding"* Quoted ibid., p. 42.

160 *"governments prohibited Africans from owning rifles"* Ibid.

161 *profiting from their demise where they were not wanted* Stuart A. Marks, "On Cake as Metaphor for Elephant Control: Sustainable Development in Northern Rhodesia During the 1930s," unpublished MS in author's files, p. 9.

161 *"the department earned £16,000 from the sale of ivory"* Bonner, *At the Hand of Man*, p. 50.

161 *ivory . . . reached $32 a pound less than ten years later* David Western, "An African Odyssey to Save the Elephant," *Discover* (October 1986), p. 60.

162 *"blasted out the bass line in a Bach chorale"* Katherine Payne, "Elephant Talk," *National Geographic* (August 1989), p. 266.

163 *"Half measures . . . could not be tolerated"* Marks, "On Cake as Metaphor," pp. 9–10.

163 *"until elephants were trained to read the GAME RESERVE notices"* Wilson and Ayerst, *White Gold*, p. 151.

164 *these efficiently laid out ancient elephant trails* Richard Despard Estes, *The Behavior Guide to African Animals* (Berkeley: University of California Press, 1991), p. 260. In fact, elephants avoid energy-wasteful hill climbing; Roxanne Khamsi, "Why Elephants Avoid the High Road," NewScientist.com., July 24, 2006.

164 *stress-related diseases of the cardiovascular system* Laws, epilogue in Beard, *End of the Game*, p. 274.

165 *Even the meat was sold* Some twenty-five thousand elephants were killed in Zimbabwe between 1981 and 1988, earning over $13 million, a significant sum in a country with seventeen thousand square miles of national park land to protect. Katy Payne, *Silent Thunder: In the Presence of Elephants* (New York: Penguin, 1998), p. 198.

167 *"between 2,000 and 3,000 nursing mother elephants died"* Boyce Rensberger, "The 'Elephant Slums' of Tsavo National Park" (1973). See http://www.aliciapatterson .org/APF001973/Rensberger/Rensberger03/Rensberger03.html.

167 *examining the skulls and ivory of their own species* K. McComb, L. Baker, and C. Moss, *Biology Letters* (Royal Society, 2006), pp. 2, 26–28.

167 *scientists wondered if what had happened was anything like a natural cycle* S. K. Eltringham, *Elephants* (Poole, Dorset: Blandford Press, 1982), pp. 157–60.

168 *"natural tragedy soon obscured by the mists of time"* Daphne Sheldrick, "The Elephant Debate," in The David Sheldrick Wildlife Trust newsletter (n.d., after 1992), author's files.

168 *"Mombasa is slowly taking over the role"* Quoted in Beachy, "East African Ivory Trade," p. 289. After World War II, Wilson and Ayerst point out, ivory auctions "came under the control of the Game Department and every tusk legally exported had to carry the Department's stamp." In addition, only licensed dealers could bid. *White Gold*, p. 156.

168 *Wilson and Ayerst wrote of their visit there* Wilson and Ayerst, *White Gold*, pp. 156–60.

169 *Hong Kong had some three thousand craftsmen*   Esmond Bradley Martin and Daniel Stiles, *The Ivory Markets of East Asia* (Nairobi and London: Save the Elephants, 2003), p. 40.

169 *forced Japanese traders to turn to African sources*   Martin, "The Great White Gold Rush," pp. 31–32. Sri Lanka's elephant population had been halved by 1914 for land clearances. In the mid-1800s, Martin explains, "a Major Rogers" did his bit by shooting "over 1,300 elephants."

170 *imports swelled to more than two hundred fifty tons a year*   Martin and Stiles, *Ivory Markets*, p. 11.

170 *"How many got away?"*   Wilson and Ayerst, *White Gold*, p. 149.

171 *government officials backed poaching in the national parks*   Iain Douglas-Hamilton, "Back from the Brink," *African Elephant and Rhino Newsletter*, no. 1 (January–June 1983).

171 *the country's entire elephant population . . . had been reduced by 90 percent*   Meredith, *Elephant Destiny*, p. 204.

171 *the ubiquitous Soviet-designed AK-47 assault rifle*   Arms imports to Africa increased from $500 million in 1970 to $4.5 billion in 1980; Jeremy Gavron, *King Leopold's Dream* (New York: Pantheon, 1993), p. 151.

171 *in countries like Angola*   In 1988 Angolan rebel leader Jonas Savimbi sent Secretary of Defense Frank Carlucci a full-sized model of an AK-47 carved from ivory and wood in appreciation for U.S. support of his movement. This appalling memento mori is now in the Smithsonian. For more detail on Savimbi's vast ivory poaching operations, see the author's *A Certain Curve of Horn* (New York: Atlantic Monthly Press, 2002), pp. 186–89.

172 *long-standing smuggling networks*   Peter T. Dalleo, "The Somali Role in Organized Poaching in Northeastern Kenya, c. 1909–1939," *International Journal of African Historical Studies* 12, no. 3 (1979), pp. 472–82.

172 *"poaching of elephants was a temptation to African men"*   Alpers, "The Ivory Trade," p. 362. The sharp rise in ivory prices, coupled with the decline in per capita GDP in Africa, made poaching even more attractive. See Tom Pilgram and David Western, "Inferring Hunting Patterns on African Elephants from Tusks in the International Ivory Trade," *Journal of Applied Ecology* (1986), p. 512.

172 *the government denied there were irregularities*   "Kenya Denies Scandal in Ivory; Deplores Reports on Kenyattas," *New York Times*, June 14, 1975.

172 *London's* Sunday Times *ran a three-part series*   *Sunday Times*, August 10, 17, 24, 1975. See Bonner, *At the Hand of Man* p. 51; Gavron, *King Leopold's Dream*, p. 158. Kenyatta, after receiving five thousand letters in 1972–73 expressing concern for Ahmed, a Marsabit bull carrying perfectly matched 150-pound tusks, issued a presidential decree that the elephant be guarded by soldiers. Ahmed died in 1974.

173 *"a blow to many small shopkeepers in Nairobi"*   Bonner, *At the Hand of Man*, pp. 51–52.

173 *"Two leading authorities . . . presented diametrically opposed views"*   Pilgram and Western, "Inferring Hunting Patterns," p. 503.

174 *an exhaustive report on the ivory trade*   Parker's 870-page 1979 report to the U.S. Fish and Wildlife Service, "The Ivory Trade," showed how much information on the status of the African elephant was contained in import/export statistics.

174 *elephants must be hidden in the central rain forests*   Western, "An African Odyssey," p. 60. See also Meredith, *Elephant Destiny*, p. 207.

175 *"The number of tusks . . . increased more than 100 percent"*   Pilgram and Western, "Inferring Hunting Patterns," p. 511.

175 *"A considerable portion of the ivory exported from Zanzibar . . . was stolen"*   Moore, *Ivory: Scourge*, p. 177.

176 *The most egregious example was that of Burundi*   Gavron, *King Leopold's Dream*, pp. 4–5.

176 *"the ivory capital of the moment"*   I. S. C. Parker and Esmond Bradley Martin, "Further Insight into the International Ivory Trade," *Oryx* 17, no. 4 (1983), p. 199.

176 *"all that ivory traders had to do to avoid controls"*   Meredith, *Elephant Destiny*, p. 213.

176 *"Such flow and counter-flow"*   Parker and Martin, "Further Insight," p. 194.

177 *a new low . . . 11.4 pounds*   Western, *Discover*, p. 62.

178 *"carvers will suffer a reduction in the raw material"*   T. Pilgram and D. Western, "Managing African Elephants for Ivory Production Through Ivory Trade Regulations," *Journal of Applied Ecology* 23 (1986), p. 515.

178 *"a worldwide campaign to reduce the demand for ivory"*   Cynthia Moss, *Elephant Memories* (Chicago and London: University of Chicago Press, 2000), pp. 298–300.

179 *"not one African country was in favor of a ban"*   Bonner, *At the Hand of Man*, p. 114.

179 *exposés featuring footage of poached ivory*   See Allan Thorton and Dave Currey's highly partisan *To Save an Elephant: The Undercover Investigation into the Illegal Ivory Trade* (London: Transworld Publishers, 1991). See also Bonner's cautions on their account; *At the Hand of Man*, p. 127.

180 *It also provided anti-poaching grants*   Anthony C. Beilenson, "United States Politics and Elephant Conservation," in Shoshani, *Elephants*, pp. 210–12. See also Bonner, *At the Hand of Man*, pp. 147–48.

181 *Douglas-Hamilton . . . described it as "idealistic, imaginative and moral"*   Bonner, *At the Hand of Man*, p. 149.

181 *sixty tons of firewood and a hundred and forty gallons of gasoline*   "World Notes Kenya," *Time*, July 31, 1989.

182 *"we were the rebels and therefore unpopular"*   Quoted in Kate B. Showers, "The Ivory Story, Africans and Africanists," *Issue: A Journal of Opinion* 22, no. 1 (Winter Spring, 1994), p. 44.

8. THE IVORY BAN

Esmond Bradley Martin's comprehensive ivory trade reports; Kumi Furuyashiki's *Ivory Tales: Policy and Discourse of Wildlife Conservation in Japan*, OCEES Research Paper no. 17 (December 1999); and I. J. Whyte, "Headaches and Heartaches—the Elephant Management Dilemma," in Schidtz and Willot (eds.), *Environmental Ethics* (New York: Oxford University Press), among other studies, supplemented press reports.

183 *my meeting with Karen van Rooyen*   September 28, 2005.

186 *"sporadic and infrequent" elephant losses* Richard Leakey, "A Wildlife Director's Perspective," in Shoshani, *Elephants*, p. 214.

186 *"The only way to . . . stop poaching is to destroy the ivory market"* Ibid., p. 215.

186 *"the failure of some states to utilize it constructively"* Edward Barbier, Joanne C. Burgess, Timothy M. Swanson, and David W. Pearce, *Elephants, Economics and Ivory* (London: Earthscan Publications, 1990), pp. 146–47.

187 *"in the value of its tusks"* "The Ivory Paradox," *Economist*, March 2, 1991, p. 16.

187 *"where enforcement of bans is imperfect"* Rasmus Heltberg, "Elephant Economics, Ivory Trade and Poaching," 1999, University of Copenhagen working paper; see www.ccon.ku.dk/derg/papers/ivory. Heltberg adds, "The conclusion is neither that markets for products from threatened natural resources should be liberalised indiscriminately, nor that trade bans should form the core of conservation efforts. Rather, it should be investigated how legal marketing channels can be set up and safeguarded."

187 *nine African states were holding at least one hundred tons* H. T. Dublin, T. Milliken, and R. F. W. Barnes, *Four Years after the CITES Ban: Illegal Killing of Elephants, Ivory Trade and Stockpiles*, IUCN/SSC African Elephant Specialist Group Report (1995).

188 *on an equal footing, which is almost equally offensive* While acknowledging that when it came to the issue of the ivory ban "there seemed to be no solution that respected all the realities," Katy Payne goes on to state that, instead of harvesting elephants for the benefit of people, "I would propose that both be allowed to live." Payne, *Silent Thunder*, pp. 205, 273.

188 *"cast as despoilers when presenting their own views"* Showers, "Ivory Story," p. 42.

189 *"the moral imperative for banning the ivory trade"* David Harland, "CITES '92 and Beyond," *Pachyderm*, no. 15 (1992), p. 19.

189 *"Make Elephant Habitat Viable Against Human Encroachment"* Ibid., p. 20.

190 *a freighter docked in Toyko Bay* Furuyashiki, *Ivory Tales*, p. 1.

190 *5,446 elephant tusks* Martin and Stiles, *Ivory Markets*, p. 9.

190 *its adherence was less than enthusiastic* In 1984 CITES adopted a resolution criticizing Japan for its poor implementation of the convention. Furuyashiki, *Ivory Tales*, p. 13n.

191 *to police their members better* Lucy Vigne and Esmond Bradley Martin, "Japanese Ivory Traders Co-operate," *Pachyderm* 4 (July–December 1984), p. 19.

191 *the members accounted for 98 percent of total Japanese ivory imports* The ivory trade associations in Tokyo and Osaka later formed the Japan Federation of Ivory Art and Craft Associations, or JIA. Furuyashiki, *Ivory Tales*, p. 15n.

191 *more stringent guidelines on ivory imports* Tom Milliken, "Recent Developments in the Japanese Ivory Trade and the Implementation of CITES in Japan," *Pachyderm* 5 (1985), pp. 15–16.

191 *its widely unpopular whaling policy* Japan's position on whaling is a subject beyond the scope of this book, but it should be noted that the cases that can be made for sustainable use of whales and elephants are quite different, as are the politics. For a concise update, see Chris Hogg, "The Forces That Drive Japanese Whaling," *BBC News*, June 15, 2006.

192 *"When Namibian President Sam Nujoma visited Tokyo"* Furuyashiki, *Ivory Tales,* pp. 16–17.

192 *retail sales of ivory would be recorded and checked* Martin and Stiles, *Ivory Markets,* p. 9.

193 *upwards of thirty thousand Japanese made their living from ivory* Much of the following description of the Japanese ivory industry is drawn from Martin's various reports, especially *Japanese Ivory Industry.*

193 *half the country's imports between them* Ted Gup, "Cover Stories," *Time,* October 16, 1989.

193 *kept under the floors of his house in Nagoya* Martin and Stiles, *Ivory Markets,* p. 18.

194 *once crafted a cane with an ivory dragon handle* Masatoshi [as told to Raymond Bushell], *The Art of Netsuke Carving* (Tokyo: Kodansha International, 1981), pp. 11–15.

194 *"I feel as though I were caressing one of my children"* Ibid., p. 50.

195 *produced in quantity for piano makers Yamaha and Kawai* According to Gup, at least two and a half tons of ivory were used for this purpose in 1988. See also Martin, *Japanese Ivory Industry,* p. 30.

195 *two inches long and half an inch wide* 1.2×6 cm to 1.5×6 cm; Martin and Stiles, *Ivory Markets,* p. 16.

196 *some still made entirely by hand* Ibid. In the pre-ban days, 80 percent of the *hanko* finished in the town of Rokugocho were of ivory; by the late 1990s the percentage of ivory *hanko* had declined to 30 percent.

196 *loopholes which could be exploited* Masayuki Sakamoto, "Is the Internal Control of Ivory Trade of Japan After 2004 Amendment in Accordance with All Requirements of Resolution Conf. 10.10 (Rev. CoP12)?" Japan Wildlife Conservation Society (JWCS), September 2004; copy in author's files.

197 *mixed in with a shipment of chopsticks* Tomo Nishihara, "What's Wrong with Selling Southern African Ivory to Japan?" *Wildlife Conservation* 106, no. 6 (November/December 2003), p. 17; Martin and Stiles, *Ivory Markets,* p. 12.

197 *"Japan should be, once again, designated as a trading partner"* CITES Secretariat, SC54 Doc. 26.1 (Rev. 1), pp. 8, 11.

198 *China was "the single most important influence on . . . illegal trade"* CITES Secretariat, Technical Mission Report, "Verification Mission Related to the Control of Internal Trade in Ivory in China," 7–11 March 2005, SC53 Doc. 20.1 Annex, p. 2.

198 *Chinese contract workers . . . returned home with illicit ivory* Meera Selva, "Chinese Demand for Ivory Threatens African Elephants," *Independent,* December 5, 2005.

198 *China clearly hoped to "eventually become a legal importer of ivory"* CITES Secretariat, Technical Mission Report, SC53 Doc. 20.1 Annex, p. 4.

199 *the country boasted seven billionaires* See William Mellor and Allen T. Cheng, "China's Uneasy Billionaires," *Bloomberg Markets* (July 2006), p. 35.

199 *an ornately carved ivory-cased mobile phone* *Guangzhou Daily,* October 16, 2006.

199 *Grace said, swiveling in his chair* December 4, 2004.

200 *unless it's a bona fide antique* Confusingly, the EU defines "antique" as at least fifty years old.

200 *exporters included France, Canada, and Japan*   Douglas F. Williamson, *Tackling the Ivories: The Status of the US Trade in Elephant and Hippo Ivory* (Washington, D.C.: TRAFFIC North America, September 2004), pp. 18–19.

200 *No raw ivory, including sport-hunted trophies, may be reexported*   Between 1995 and 2002, 1,328 African elephant trophies (i.e., potentially 2,656 tusks) were brought into the United States. Ibid., p. 2. Sport-hunted trophies may, in certain circumstances, be reexported for personal, noncommercial use.

202 *You can purchase museum-quality netsuke*   The United States is second only to China in the number of ivory items available at retail (Esmond Bradley Martin, pers. comm.).

203 *8,325 ivory items for sale in 776 retail outlets in London alone*   Esmond Martin and Dan Stiles, "Europe's Ivory Markets," *Swara* 28, no. 3 (July–September 2005), p. 54; also, Stiles and Martin, "Agony and Ivory," *BBC Wildlife* (November 2005), pp. 54–55.

203 *willing accomplices in the deception*   Cahal Milmo, "From Africa to UK High Streets, via China: Inside Lucrative World of Ivory Smuggling," *Independent*, November 27, 2004.

203 *"shipments of illegal ivory . . . were intercepted and seized from more than 80 countries"*   Williamson, *Tackling the Ivories*, p. 30.

203 *three researchers . . . studied the question in a 2004 paper*   Nigel Hunter, Esmond Martin, and Tom Milliken, "Determining the Number of Elephants Required to Supply Current Unregulated Ivory Markets in Africa and Asia," *Pachyderm*, no. 36 (January–June 2004), pp. 116–28.

203 *elephants are killed each year to supply Africa and Asia*   Perhaps forty to eighty Indian tuskers are poached each year to supply illegal trade there. Ibid., p. 126.

204 *The animal toll in the war-torn Congo*   S. Blake et al., "Forest Elephant Crisis in the Congo Basin," *PloS Biology* 5, no. 4, e111 (April 3, 2007).

204 *researchers looked into trace element analysis of tusks*   N. J. van der Merwe et al., "Source-area Determination of Elephant Ivory by Isotopic Analysis," *Nature* 346, 744–746 (August 23, 1990).

204 *striking differences in carbon isotope ratios*   Ruth Flanagan, "Tracing Illegal Ivory," *Earth* 4, no. 4 (August 1995), p. 12.

204 *a technique . . . to drill out core samples from tusks for analysis*   See Menno Schilthuizen, "Squeezing Jumbo Genes from Ivory," *Science Now*, December 2, 2003, p. 2.

205 *most likely originated from a narrow band of southern Africa*   Samuel K. Wasser et al., "Using DNA to Track the Origin of the Largest Ivory Seizure Since the 1989 Trade Ban," *PNAS* 104, no. 10 (March 6, 2007).

206 *hippo ivory . . . into the United States*   Williamson, *Tackling the Ivories*, pp. 40–41, 47–48.

206 *Congolese rebel groups . . . are responsible for the depredation*   Xan Rice, "Elite Rangers Take on Rebels to End the Slaughter of Congo's Hippos," *Guardian*, December 22, 2006.

206 *the remaining nonelephant trade in ivory*   Hornbill "ivory" isn't ivory at all; it's keratin, but it's still prohibited. And the ivory-billed woodpecker has no such thing; ivory, in this avian context, refers to the color of its beak. Warthog ivory is not regulated.

206 *mammoth ivory was going for $300 a pound*   Barry Newman, "Mammoths May Be Extinct, but They Save the Elephants," *Wall Street Journal*, July 16, 1991, p. 1. A decade later these rising prices raised the opposite set of concerns; see Guy Gugliotta, "Ban on Elephant Ivory Could Endanger Fossils," *Washington Post*, October 15, 2004, p. A03.

207 *A Yakut can make $25 to $50 a pound by turning in the tusks*   Steven Lee Myers et al., "Old Ways of Life Are Fading as the Arctic Thaws," *New York Times*, October 20, 2005; Ryann Connell, "Mammoth Merchants Make No Bones About Pulling Wool over Your Eyes." *Mainichi Daily News*, April 18, 2005.

207 *mammoth tusk from Sibera's Tamyr peninsula went for £6,000*   September 26, 2006; the tusk was forty inches in length on the outside curve.

207 *Hong Kong imported seventy-seven tons of it*   Ed Stoddard, "Ivory From Extinct Mammoths in Big Demand," *Reuters*, October 6, 2004.

207 *artificial ivory might be able to be grown in vitro*   C. S. Young et al., "Tissue Engineering of Complex Tooth Structures on Biodegradable Polymer Scaffolds," *Journal of Dental Research* 81 (October, 2002), pp. 695–700.

207 *"a satisfactory alternate for the jewels of the noble elephant"*   Moore, *Ivory: Scourge*, p. 225.

208 *"a deep fear of ivory deprivation"*   Donal Henahan, "No Tickling the Plastics," *New York Times*, April 26, 1981.

208 *Bösendorfer . . . sold 150 pianos with ivory keyboards a year in the United States*   Conniff, "Music in Our Parlors," p. 92

209 *"I'm relatively insensitive in that respect"*   Quoted in Malcolm W. Browne, "With Ivory in Short Supply, Pianists Tickle the Polymers," *New York Times*, May 25, 1993, p. C1.

266 *who paused to listen before the chisels were brought out*   Alexander Chancellor, "Key Largo" (The Talk of the Town), *The New Yorker*, February 22, 1993. The argument that confiscated wildlife materials should be available to museums for restoration of objects such as musical instruments—not simply ivory but such materials as crow quills for harpsichord plectra—is made by Laurence Libin, "Materials from Endangered Species in Musical Instruments," CIMCIM Publications, no. 3, 1994.

213 *Ian Whyte . . . is Kruger's elephant man*   April 12, 2006.

220 *Instances of noncompliance . . . would be enough to put a stop to the plan*   Amendments to Appendices I and II of the convention adopted by the COP at its twelfth meeting, Santiago, Chile, November 3–15, 2002, 3f.

9. ELEPHANT DREAMS, ELEPHANT REALITIES

Media reports on human-elephant conflict in the African, European, and North American press supplied much valuable material.

223 *The Saggy Baggy Elephant*   Kathryn and Byron Jackson, *The Saggy Baggy Elephant*   (New York: Golden Press, 1947). Gustaf Tenggren worked for Disney in the 1930s and for Little Golden Books in the 1940s and 1950s. He also illustrated the immortal *The Poky Little Puppy*.

223 *Parker . . . met me at the door*   April 15, 2006.

225 *a Kenya-based wildlife consultancy*   Wildlife Services Ltd.; Parker, *What I Tell You Three Times Is True: Conservation, Ivory, History and Politics* (Kinloss: Librario Publishing, 2004) p. 107. See also his *Ivory Crisis* (London: Chatto and Windus, 1983).

225 *Parker had it down to a science*   Current thinking on elephant culls is that shooting remains the most humane method. Trials with drugs such as scoline (succinyl-choline), which shuts down muscles, proved cruel to elephants; they would stop breathing but be fully conscious.

225 *"It doesn't matter to an elephant . . . it's death"*   Advocates of translocating elephants might want to think about its effect on survivors. "For the ones that are left behind," Ian Whyte pointed out to me, "what is the difference between a cull and a translocation? All this noise, and some of the elephants disappear. They have the trauma of herds being halved and families broken up."

226 *elephants would been fading out even without the demand*   Parker points out human population in Africa was increasing 2 to 3 percent annually for most of the twentieth century, roughly the rate at which elephants have lost range. "Human increase and elephant decrease are two poles of the same phenomenon." Parker, *What I Tell You,* pp. 365, 368, 371.

227 *"she herself went away like a cork"*   J. H. Williams, *Elephant Bill* (New York: Bantam Books, 1950), p. 56.

229 *"School Closed After Invasion by Elephants"*   *Daily Nation,* January 27, 2003.

229 *to bury their mangled bodies*   "Kenya Elephant Buries Its Victims," BBC News, June 18, 2004.

229 *Another elephant seemed to have stepped out of the past*   Rolf D. Baldus, "Tanzania: Game Scouts Shoot 100-Pound Tusker," *African Sporting Gazette,* May 8, 2006.

230 *a steady pileup of sad statistics*   By contrast, if a tourist gets trampled, that's often news with a global reach (e.g., "Elephant Kills British Man on Honeymoon, Say Officials," *International Herald Tribune,* October 2, 2006. One British woman, badly injured by an elephant while jogging at a Kenyan bush lodge, successfully sued the community ranch. "Our people have been killed by wild animals and we only get Sh30,000 per person as compensation," the local councillor pointed out. "How come we are now required to pay a huge amount of money to a tourist injured by an animal owned by the State?" Mwangi Ndirangu, "Ranchers Pained by Sh150M Bill for Elephant's Fury," *Nation* (Nairobi), July 5, 2007.

230 *Elephants . . . become increasingly boxed in and stressed*   See Charles Siebert, "An Elephant Crackup?" *New York Times,* October 8, 2006.

230 *Asia's dwindling population . . . struggles in its fragmented habitats*   See Tom Wright, "Pachyderm Patrols Fend Off Elephants Rioting in Sumatra," *Wall Street Journal,* December 6, 2007; and Tarquin Hall, *To the Elephant Graveyard* (New York: Grove Press, 2000).

231 *I was catching a flight to Laikipia*   April 18–21, 2006.

232 *Swelling populations of both elephants and humans*   "If the human population is growing at say 5% per annum, then after 10 years the rate of raiding will have increased to 1.6 times its former level. But if both elephant and human populations are growing at 5%, then after 10 years the rate will be 2.7 times its former level." R. F. W. Barnes, "Treating Crop-raiding Elephants with Aspirin," *Pachyderm,* no. 33 (July–December 2002).

233 *grieving relatives of someone killed by an elephant*   Nicholas Wadhams, "In Kenya, Elephants Are Hated," *San Francisco Chronicle*, January 18, 2007.

233 *over half the livestock died*   Marie-Louise Gumuchian, "Millions Still Face Hardship from East Africa Drought," Reuters, August 17, 2006.

234 *"We've had to put it up to protect lives and livelihoods"*   This plan is not without its critics, who regard it as "a ploy to separate white ranchers from peasants." See John Mbaria, "New Fence to Separate Haves from Have-nots," *East African* (www.nationmedia.com), August 28, 2006.

235 *"It's a classic case"*   See Amos Kareithi, "Stray Wildlife Could Cost Ranchers Farms," *East African Standard*, January 21, 2005. Elephant problems in Laikipia are nothing new; see Theodore Roosevelt's prescient observations in his *African Game Trails* (New York: Charles Scribner's Sons, 1925, reprint of 1910), Vol. I, pp. 295–97.

236 *"with the stroke of a pen"*   Iain and Oria Douglas-Hamilton, *Battle for the Elephants* (New York: Viking Penguin, 1992), p. 113.

237 *"The only ivory I ever sold . . . was for thirty-five shillings a pound"*   Other professional hunters made a bit more from the odd hundred-pounder. See Brian Herne, *White Hunters: The Golden Age of African Safaris* (New York: Henry Holt, 1999), pp. 188–90.

240 *local communities who had a stake in wildlife*   Zimbabwe's Communal Areas Management Programme for Indigenous Resources, or CAMPFIRE, pioneered empowering local people to make wildlife decisions, turning poachers into gamekeepers. Although used as a template for successful programs elsewhere in Africa, it has suffered at home in the chaos of the end days of the Mugabe regime. See Peter Godwin, "Wildlife Without Borders," *National Geographic* (September 2001), pp. 24–8, and Bonner, *At the Hand of Man*, pp. 272–78.

242 *elephants they would never dare tackle in daylight*   Damian Whitworth, "The Killing Fields," TimesOnline, October 4, 2006.

244 *what is left of its shrinking glaciers*   Charles J. Hanley, "On Africa's Great Peaks, Glaciers Are in Retreat," *Washington Post*, December 31, 2006.

244 *Martin invited Nigel Hunter . . . to join us for tea*   April 21, 2006.

EPILOGUE: 2007

Key CITES documents for the Fourteenth Conference of the Parties, June 3–15, 2007, are available on its Web site, www.cites.org.

251 *the foundation's position statement*   AWF Position Statement on Proposals on the Fourteenth Meeting of the Conference of Parites to CITES, June 2007, author's files.

251 *Sue Mainka, the head of the IUCN delegation*   Quoted in "CITES Trade Controls Should Not Increase Poverty," IUCN News Release, Gland, Switzerland, May 30, 2007.

251 *To them, any consumptive wildlife use is suspect*   Behind the idea that elephants should never be killed for their ivory is an even bigger idea, of course: that elephants shouldn't be killed for any reason.

252 *such stockpiles . . . should be put "permanently beyond use"*   Travers has indicated that "a permanent public education display" might be "culturally appropriate" in

some countries, presumably to promote an anti-ivory message. See Charlie Furniss, "On the Tusks of a Dilemma," *Geographical* (November 2006), p. 53.

252 *"Because believe you me, we need the money"* Quoted in Nicole Itano, "Old Ivory Ban Faces Fresh Opposition," *Christian Science Monitor*, November 12, 2002.

252 *crippling legitimate commerce would help stop illegal trade* The argument that as long as any trade in ivory is permitted there will always be a black market shadowing it loses some force when it's acknowledged that ivory isn't uniquely problematic in that regard. In fact, the list of desirable goods dogged by smuggling is practically endless: art, diamonds, drugs, liquor, tobacco, nuclear technology . . . Esmond Bradley Martin observes that anti-ivory trade campaigners invariably agree that perfect enforcement of the ivory trade is impossible, but when asked if they would be satisfied if ivory trade controls were 99 percent effective, "they never answer the question."

252 *The extensive database* The database is Etis, the Elephant Trade Information System.

253 *to gain an undue influence on the wildlife policies* See also Richard Black, "African Deal Cut on Ivory Trade," BBC News, June 14, 2007.

253 *Kenya, supported by Mali* Tom Milliken, TRAFFIC's director for eastern and southern Africa, pointed out that some of the countries backing a twenty-year moratorium were themselves guilty of failing to crack down on illegal ivory. "Mali, for example, has reported one seizure in eighteen years," he said, although it had been implicated in forty-two other incidents of criminal trading.

253 *"elephants are dramatically becoming depleted"* Quoted in "African States Call for a 20-year Ban on Ivory," AFP, April 24, 2007.

253 *Kipng'etich . . . told the* Standard *in Nairobi* Beatrice Obwocha and Winnie Chumo, "Birth Control for Elephants to Start," *East African Standard*, February 1, 2007.

253 *"We want communities to continue benefiting"* Quoted in "SADC Parks Authorities to Discuss Ivory Ban Trade," *BuaNews* (Tshwane), April 17, 2007.

254 *Susan Lieberman, WWF's Global Species Program director* "CITES Permits 60 Tons of Elephant Ivory to Be Sold," Environmental News Service, June 4, 2007.

254 *Travers wrote in disgust on his Born Free blog* Posted June 2, 2007, at http://www.bornfreeusa.org/blog/?cat=5.

254 *had lined up nearly two dozen African countries* Joe Ageyo, "Kenya Pushes for Total Ban on Ivory Trade," *Nation* (Nairobi), June 7, 2007.

255 *"illegal killing has been so low as to be insignificant"* Quoted in Richard Black, " 'Last Chance' for Elephant Deal," BBC News, June 13, 2007.

255 *"we do not want to be punished for the wildlife mismanagement in Kenya"* Quoted in John Mbaria, "Country May Be Losing Fight to Protect Its Rare Wildlife," *Nation* (Nairobi), June 10, 2007.

255 *"We really need a practical way out"* Arthur Max, "Countries Deadlock over Ivory Trade Ban," *Kansas City Star*, June 12, 2007.

256 *a "resting period" of nine years* However, countries that have elephant populations listed in Appendix I, such as Tanzania, would presumably be able to apply to CITES to downlist their populations to Appendix II during the "resting period." The decision (Amendment to Proposal COP14 Prop.4 and Related Draft Decisions) included additional provisions covering trade in hunting trophies, live animals, hides, hair, leather goods, and certain noncommercial carvings in Namibia (*ekipas*) and Zimbabwe.

256 *seizure of a shipment of nearly three tons of illegal ivory in Osaka*   There are three options under CITES to deal with seizures of illegal ivory: give it to research institutions, return it to the country of origin (if known), or incinerate it. But the prospect of destroying the huge amount of ivory intercepted by the Osaka Customhouse has dismayed the Japanese. "METI Reluctant to Incinerate 3 Tons of Seized Elephant Ivory," *Yomiuri Shimbun*, August 9, 2007. Nonetheless, it was destroyed in March, 2008.

256 *Iain Douglas-Hamilton said his group*   Quoted in "CITES Clears Way for One-off Ivory Sale, Extends Ban," Deutsche Presse-Agentur, June 14, 2007.

256 *Julius Kipng'etich, the KWS head, did an about-face*   Quoted in Alister Doyle, "Africa's Elephants Get a 9-year Ivory Export Break," Reuters, June 14, 2007. Kipng'etich wrote a muddled editorial about the implications of the decision on July 2, 2007, for the *East African Standard.*

257 *tighten enforcement and border checks for illegal shipments*   See Peter J. Stephenson, *WWF Species Action Plan: African Elephant 2007–2011* (WWF, Gland, Switzerland, 2007), p. 10.

257 *fifty tons of stockpiled ivory in Kruger alone*   South Africa also has additional ivory stockpiles outside Kruger; as a "pro-use country," it welcomed the sale. Leseho Sello, the environmental affairs, biodiversity, and heritage chief director, told a parlimentary committee, "We don't believe in preserving or conserving elephants just to watch them." South Africa would look for ways to benefit from elephants "in any manner possible for the development and upliftment of communities." "SA Ivory Sales Waits on Provinces," SAPA, August 14, 2007.

257 *"The Secretariat will closely supervise this sale"*   "Ivory sales get the go–ahead," CITES press release (Geneva), July 16, 2008." The CITES–supervised four-nation sale of just over 100 tons of tusks took place October 28 to November 6, 2008, at auctions held in each country, with Japanese and Chinese buyers in attendance. It netted over $15 million in total. Namibia realized $1.2 million from seven tons; Botswana, $7 million from 43.3 tons; Zimbabwe, $480,000 from 3.8 tons; South Africa, $6.7 million from 47 tons. Among many media reports, see "S. Africa holds huge ivory auction," *BBC News*, November 6, 2008.

ACKNOWLEDGMENTS

I owe thanks to a number of people for invaluable assistance and great generosity during the researching and writing of this book.

In Connecticut, Richard Moore kindly met with me, and granted permission to quote from the diary and other writings of his father, E. D. Moore; Robbi Storms, Ivoryton Library Association director, gave me access to unpublished ivory-related material and permission to reproduce several of the photographs in the association's collection; Brenda Milkofsky, senior curator of the Connecticut River Museum in Essex, also granted permission to reproduce photographs and documents in the museum's collection and to quote from correspondence in the Cheney-Downing Collection Archive. Edith DeForest of the Deep River Historical Society shared her recollections of her years at Pratt, Read; Frank Stopa, ex-foreman in the key division, answered questions about ivory cutting. Don Malcarne, Essex town historian, shared his deep knowledge of the history of the ivory industry in the Connecticut River Valley; Anne Farrow of the *Hartford Courant* opened her files on the ivory industry in the state and lent important texts. Lorraine Kerr Faison, former director, Kent Memorial Library, and the library's helpful staff, located a number of scarce texts, and Jason Wright of South Kent suggested several museum contacts. William Jenks of Falls Village supported my efforts early on, as did Jackie Markham and Allan Priaulx of Kent.

In New York, Clare Flemming, curator of research collections at the Explorers Club, let me prowl in the club's library and examine its four-tusked elephant skull; Ross MacPhee, curator, Division of Vertebrate Zoology at the American Museum of Natural History, was available for repeat interviews and shared a sizable chunk of his articles and papers;

Christopher Norris, the museum's director of collections and archives in the Division of Paleontology, explained ivory subfossils; Rory Callahan twice assisted with travel arrangements to Africa; James Mellon let me inspect Mohammed's splendid tusk and gave me copies of rare photographs.

In Washington, D.C., Edward Grace, senior special agent of the U.S. Fish and Wildlife Service, answered questions and supplied copies of pertinent regulations. Syd Butler of the American Zoo and Aquarium Association discussed elephants in captivity. Rick Parsons, director of wildlife conservation of the Safari Club International Foundation, shared the trophy hunters' perspective on ivory importation. At the African Wildlife Foundation, Patrick J. Bergin, CEO, and Craig Sholley, senior director of development, encouraged and supported my research from the beginning and helped me set up the Ivory Project to secure travel funds; David Shayt of the National Museum of American History at the Smithsonian Institution made available his extensive files on ivory, ivory manufacturing, and billiards; David Miller, armed forces historian at the Smithsonian, let me examine antique ivory-inlaid firearms, and the staff of the Archives Center at the National Museum of American History helped in searching through the center's vast corporate records. Virginia and Robert Hurt opened their home to me on my visits.

In the UK, Dorothee Dines of the Victoria and Albert Museum's press office and Diane Bilbey, secretary of sculpture in the museum's Department of Sculpture, Metalwork, Ceramics and Glass, answered inquiries; Claire Frankland of the Museum in Docklands helped gather critical documents on ivory importation in London; Daphne M. Hills, Zoology Department, Natural History Museum, supplied information on how the Kilimanjaro tusks entered the museum's collection; Simon Keynes in Cambridge and Randal Keynes in London were both marvelous hosts.

In South Africa, Jeremy and Liz Anderson in White River offered hospitality and much useful advice; their neighbors John and Jennifer Ilsley shared their experiences in the pre-ban ivory trade; Petri Viljoen discussed Chinese attitudes toward wildlife. In Cape Town, Holly T. Dublin, chair of the IUCN Species Survival Commission, gave me an invaluable overview of elephant policy in the African range states;

Cheryl-Samantha Owen discussed her research on Botswana trophy elephant quotas; Sarah Borchert, *Africa Geographic*'s editor, made several suggestions for further research, as did Brian and Merle Huntley, Terry Robinson, and John and Carol Hanks, also my hosts in Greyton. Rudi van Aarde of the University of Pretoria sent me his overview of the Kruger culling issue. In Kruger National Park, I was assisted by Karen van Rooyen, and Ian Whyte spent the better part of a day with me at the park's headquarters in Skukuza. In Pretoria, Jakkie Potgieter of Safer Africa discussed the proliferation of military weaponry in postcolonial sub-Saharan states and its effect on poaching.

In Kenya, Esmond Bradley Martin supplied copies of all his many ivory trade reports and answered numerous inquiries; Nigel Hunter offered an overview of CITES ivory policy; Leo Niskanen, program officer, IUCN African Elephant Specialist Group, explained human-elephant conflict; Ian Parker had a far-ranging talk with me on very short notice; Iain Douglas-Hamilton shared some of his latest research with me over the phone; Tony Dyer kindly assented to an on-the-spot interview; Anthony King, director of the Laikipia Wildlife Forum, and Nicholas Georgiadis, then director of the Mpala Research Center, discussed elephant policy in detail; Philip Muruthi of the AWF's Nairobi office answered my CITES queries.

Other researchers in different parts of the globe—Richard Estes, Abdul Sheriff, and Jared Hudson—answered my questions or assisted in other ways; Stuart Marks shared his findings and allowed me to quote from his unpublished work.

Several people who were already of great help—Don Malcarne, Esmond Bradley Martin, and David Shayt—allowed me to impose on them again, this time to look over portions of the text. Other sections and chapters were also read by Edward Alpers, Department of History, University of California, Los Angeles; Anthony Cutler, Department of Art History, Penn State University; Mark Elvin, Research School of Pacific and Asian Studies, Australian National University; Robert Harms, Department of History, Yale University; Charles Little, Curator in the Department of Medieval Art and the Cloisters, the Metropolitan Museum of Art; Enid Schildkrout, Chief Curator of the Museum for African Art; and Randall White, Department of Anthropology, New York University. These readers alerted me to various mangled facts and saved me from several scholarly stumbles. Whatever failings remain, however, are my responsibility.

My agent, Kim Witherspoon, and Alexis Hurley at InkWell Management, were marvelously patient, supportive, and encouraging during the five years I worked on this book. Morgan Entrekin, Grove/Atlantic's publisher, once again extended to me the time I needed to complete it. Joan Bingham, my editor, applied just the right carrot-and-stick mix of enthusiasm and critical questioning to spur me to another revision, and Alex Littlefield put his finger on several passages that needed another look. Eric Price offered important guidance on permissions; although I made every effort to contact holders of copyrighted materials, I was not always successful.

In addition, thanks are due several friends whose generosity at certain points was critical to the project: Anne Dodgson and the late Bill Dodgson; Mary Kay and Woody Flowers, who also put me up in their New York apartment on numerous occasions, as did Bridget Potter. Jonathan Alexander at the Institute of Fine Arts, New York University, put his art history library at my disposal, never once mentioning the two scarce texts I didn't return for three years, and put me in touch with several prominent ivory experts. I'm most grateful for all their support, and for that of the late Elizabeth Crow, who told me how much she was looking forward to reading the book. I like to think she wouldn't have been disappointed.

Finally, I'm grateful to my sister, Barbara Walker, and my brother, William Walker, for their long-standing encouragement of all my efforts. My greatest debts are to my son, Gavin Walker, for his careful reading of earlier drafts, incisive comments, and help in checking obscure Asian references, and to my wife, Elin McCoy, for taking time away from her own writing to give the manuscript a meticulous reading. There are few pages that haven't been improved by her suggestions.

ILLUSTRATION CREDITS

Kilimanjaro tusks: A.C. Gomes & Son, Zanzibar, 1898

Pleistocene, Egyptian figures: John Frederick Walker

Tusk diagram: Gary H. Marchant, modified after Ngure 1996, and the editor of *Pachyderm*

Symmachi panel: V&A Images/Victoria and Albert Museum

Ivory pyxis: Courtesy of the Hispanic Society of America, New York

Grandisson triptych: Maskell, 1905 / British Museum

Ming medallion: The Metropolitan Museum of Art, Purchase, Friends of Asian Arts Gifts, 1993 (1993.176)
Image © The Metropolitan Museum of Art

Benin pendant mask: The Metropolitan Museum of Art, The Michael C. Rockefeller Memorial Collection, Gift of Nelson A. Rockefeller, 1972 (1978.412.323)
Image © The Metropolitan Museum of Art

Seated Ganesha: The Metropolitan Museum of Art, Gift of Mr. and Mrs. J. J. Llejman, 1964 (64.102)
Image © The Metropolitan Museum of Art

The Death of Cleopatra: V&A Images/Victoria and Albert Museum

Piéces excentriques: *Recueil d'Ouvrages Curieux de Mathématique et de Mecanique, ou Description du Cabinet de Monsieur Grollier de Serviére, 1719*

Beauty Revealed:	The Metropolitan Museum of Art, Gift of Gloria Manney, 2006 (2006.235.74) Image © The Metropolitan Museum of Art
George Read and Co.:	Ivoryton Library Association
Julius Pratt:	Deep River Historical Society
Ivory goods catalogue:	Deep River Historical Society
Harvey and Ford:	National Museum of American History, Smithsonian Institution
Burroughes and Watts:	National Museum of American History, Smithsonian Institution
Tippu Tip:	Winterton Collection of East African photographs, Melville J. Herskovits Library of African Studies, Northwestern University
Ivory and slave routes:	E. D. Moore, "Ivory Poachers and Elephant Graveyards," *Asia*, October, 1931
Ivory hunter:	Ivoryton Library Association
Ivory hunter's caravan:	E. D. Moore, *Ivory: Scourge of Africa*, 1931,
Ivory scale:	E. D. Moore, *Ivory: Scourge of Africa*, 1931
E. D. Moore:	Courtesy of Richard Moore
Tusks in cart:	Connecticut River Museum
Eburnea:	National Museum of American History, Smithsonian Institution
Botswana Elephants:	John Frederick Walker
AK-47:	National Museum of American History, Smithsonian Institution
Accessories to Murder:	African Wildlife Foundation
Kruger ivory vault:	John Frederick Walker
Japanese craftsman:	Esmond Bradley Martin
Baby elephants:	John Frederick Walker
Kruger bull:	John Frederick Walker

Index